HIDDEN STO
STEPHEN LAWF

Personal reflections

Richard Stone

This book is dedicated to Stephen Lawrence, who in the words of his mother to the Stephen Lawrence Inquiry:

"Had he been given the chance to survive maybe would have been the one to bridge the gap between black and white, because he didn't distinguish between black or white. He saw people as people."

HIDDEN STORIES OF THE STEPHEN LAWRENCE INQUIRY

Personal reflections

Richard Stone

First published in Great Britain in 2015 by

Policy Press
University of Bristol
1-9 Old Park Hill
Bristol
BS2 8BB
UK
t: +44 (0)117 954 5940
pp-info@bristol.ac.uk
www.policypress.co.uk

North America office:
Policy Press
c/o The University of Chicago Press
1427 East 60th Street
Chicago, IL 60637, USA
t: +1 773 702 7700
f: +1 773 702 9756
sales@press.uchicago.edu
www.press.uchicago.edu

© The Policy Press 2015

British Library Cataloguing in Publication Data A catalogue record for this book is available from the British Library.

Library of Congress Cataloging-in-Publication Data A catalog record for this book has been requested.

ISBN 978 1 4473 0847 8 paperback

The right of Richard Stone to be identified as author of this work has been asserted by him in accordance with the Copyright, Designs and Patents Act 1988.

All rights reserved: no part of this publication may be reproduced, stored in a retrieval system, or transmitted in any form or by any means, electronic, mechanical, photocopying, recording, or otherwise without the prior permission of Policy Press.

The statements and opinions contained within this publication are solely those of the author and not of the University of Bristol or Policy Press. The University of Bristol and Policy Press disclaim responsibility for any injury to persons or property resulting from any material published in this publication.

Policy Press works to counter discrimination on grounds of gender, race, disability, age and sexuality.

Policy Press uses environmentally responsible print partners.

Cover design by www.thecoverfactory.co.uk
Front cover: photograph kindly supplied by www.istock.com
Printed and bound in Great Britain by CMP, Poole

Woodland
CARBON
www.woodlandcarbon.co.uk
CMP (UK) LTD
Printed in Carbon Captured paper

Contents

A note on the typography

The following typographical styles have been used for displayed/ block quotations.

Quotations from the Stephen Lawrence Inquiry Report:

> Stephen Lawrence had been with his friend Duwayne Brooks during the afternoon of 22 April. They were on their way home when they came at around 22:30 to the bus stop in Well Hall Road with which we are all now so familiar.

Extracts from transcripts of the Inquiry:

> THE CHAIRMAN: Please, please, be quiet. I know how difficult it is for you but let me see what is being said – let me hear what is being said.

Paraphrased accounts:

> *"It's a crime isn't it? Wasting police time? 'Cos that's what they're doing. Instead of winding us up they should be off following up crimes. Why don't they get prosecuted for wasting police time?"*

Transcripts of the Inquiry (Appendix C):

P-324
< 1>   MR COOK: I think it is the clarity of the message is
< 2>   important. It needs to be a little less equivocal.

Quotations from all other sources:

> Violent scenes erupted as the five principal suspects in the Stephen Lawrence killing left the inquiry into his murder.

About the author

Dr Richard Stone was a panel member of the Stephen Lawrence Inquiry into racism in policing (1997–99) as Adviser to the Judge, Sir William Macpherson. At the time he was Chair of the Jewish Council for Racial Equality.

His *Independent review of the Stephen Lawrence Inquiry 10 years on* (http://richardstonesli.wordpress.com) was launched by the Secretaries of State for the departments of Justice, Home Office, and Communities and Local Government in February 2009.

For 20 years Dr Stone was senior partner of a general medical practice in London. For 14 years he worked with British Muslims as chair of the Runnymede Islamophobia Commission, and in 2004 he founded Alif-Aleph UK (British Muslims and British Jews). In 2010 he was awarded the OBE for public and voluntary service.

He is an Honorary Fellow of the Cambridge Centre for Muslim-Jewish Relations and an Honorary Research Fellow in the Department of Criminology at the University of Westminster.

In 2009 Richard Stone closed his grant-making Stone Ashdown Trust (formerly the Lord Ashdown Charitable Settlement) following a structured 'spend down' strategy over a five-year period.

Acknowledgements

I make no apology for thanking above all others, my Ruth. She is my mentor-in-chief and my sparky much-loved wife of 42 years. Our three children and two sons-in-law, have been immensely supportive and also given me wise counsel. I have benefited enormously from the support and advice given generously to me by Doreen Lawrence. I thank her for the photo of her son Stephen with which this book opens. We have, I think, both enjoyed our occasional lunches together in town. I have been immensely fortunate to have gained emotional as well as modest financial support from Juliet Prager at the Joseph Rowntree Charitable Trust. Behind her has been the overall director of the Trust, Steve Pittam. He and I were colleagues in Notting Hill in the 1980s, and we struggled with issues of equality in funding in the 1990s at the Association of Charitable Foundations. Juliet and Steve moved on from the Trust in December 2012.

In the delicate field of race relations I have never led a project without a close multicultural group of trusted advisers, some of whom have mentored me on more than one project over the years. This time Nathalie Stewart and Yvette Williams have kept me rooted in the black experience. In addition my dynamic, thoughtful team has been Urmee Khan, Nadine Dinall, Maqsood Ahmad, Nadia Habashi, Veenal Raval and David Muir. Each of those brought invaluable expertise and understanding, without which I could easily have fallen into traps for the unwary. I will miss them all when this is over.

I am grateful to The Policy Press for supporting me to publish my book. They have enabled me to tell my personal story from my unique position within the Inquiry. I have not been an easy author for The Policy Press, but Karen Bowler, my editor, valiantly reordered my first thoughts into eight short and well ordered chapters. Kathryn King and Alison Shaw have kept my wilder fantasies at bay. This may not have been a simple task. I am grateful to them all.

Preface

Publication of this book takes place within weeks of the 20th anniversary of the death of Stephen Lawrence on 22 April 1993. Alas, today there is still too much of the negativity that was felt 20 years ago by the Lawrence family and other black families towards the police. The black experience in the UK is now shared by many British Muslims. I have found anger and disappointment to be even greater now than it was then, which are justified by the lack of progress in achieving equality of treatment and equality of opportunity in policing.

Stephen would have been 38 now. Would he have become the established architect that he wanted to be? Perhaps with the help of an organisation like the Stephen Lawrence Trust he might have got there. The Trust was set up in his memory, and is in crisis now after three major central government grants have not been renewed. Even with outside help I fear the obstacles for Stephen may have been too many.

And what would Stephen have made of the legal action that his younger brother has felt it necessary to take against the Metropolitan Police this year for what he feels were 25 unwarranted stops and searches?[1]

It is now 14 years since the Stephen Lawrence Inquiry produced 70 recommendations,[2] yet racism is still evident in our policing. The Report recommended wide-ranging changes in police practice and processes, including openness and accountability, and in reporting, recording, investigation and prosecution of racist crimes.

The Inquiry found the Metropolitan Police guilty of professional incompetence and a failure of leadership by senior officers;[3] the previous recommendations of the 1981 Scarman Report[4] into the race riots in London, had been apparently ignored.

Damningly, the Inquiry found and defined a culture of institutional racism within the force.

With such a catalogue of carefully constructed exhortations for so many years – Scarman was published over 30 years ago – I feel justified in shouting from the roof tops "A plague on all your houses!" Enough of definitions. Enough of thick volumes of reports and plans for the future. Enough of promises. Enough, too, of process. Positive outcomes are what are needed, preferably verified by quantitative and qualitative data.

There has been so much written, so much discussion, so much analysis, so much training. No police officer, no doctor (my profession), nor anyone older than about 20 for that matter, can justify not knowing what 'institutional racism' is or how to tackle it. The time has come for leaders of institutions, heads of businesses and activists to take sustained action and tell everyone just to stop doing it. The hopes of commissioners to be the instruments of transformational change will be wiped away if the roots of racist attitudes within the institution are not addressed.

To think that disparities in stop and search for black people have rocketed from 3–5 times in 1999, to 8–10 times in 2009, to 28 times in 2012![5] That can only mean that the brakes demanded by the Stephen Lawrence Inquiry are now completely off.

Involvement in this case has joined me with white, as well as black, police officers who see ourselves as critical friends of police services. After 15 years it all seems eminently sensible and perfectly plain to me. There still exists a deep streak of racist attitudes and behaviour among some police officers. It has to be dealt with from the top, with sustained leadership and total commitment to address the attitudes and practices of the police, and that is what this book is about.

Introduction

Until January 2012 the murder of Stephen Lawrence in 1993 remained one of the most high profile unsolved cases of recent years. The investigation into Stephen Lawrence's death was, from the very beginning, marred by accusations of poor police work and racism in the Metropolitan Police.[1] After two investigations and two internal reviews into what had gone wrong, there were still no convictions for the murder and a great deal of discontent within the black and minority ethnic communities in London and across the UK.

In 1997, a public inquiry into the investigation of the murder was launched; an inquiry that would take 15 months and would cover thousands of pages of submissions. The conclusions of the Inquiry were unequivocal in their condemnation for the poor policing that occurred and in the conclusion that this was as a result of institutional racism from within the police force.[2] The Inquiry made 70 recommendations intended to improve policing and eliminate racism from public institutions.[3] This book looks back at the Inquiry from my perspective as one of three appointed Advisers to the Chair Sir William Macpherson, and thus from a privileged position I witnessed the Inquiry unfold. It also looks at how the police have responded to those recommendations. It commends police services for successful implementation of some of the recommendations; sadly, too many of them have been undermined and destined to fail. Racism continues to be a problem within the British police forces and until strong leaders are in place across the force who are committed to addressing the issue, it is likely to continue to be so.

Why write about the Stephen Lawrence Inquiry now?

After several years of being high profile in the media, from the time of Stephen Lawrence's murder in 1993 and during the Inquiry in 1997–99, the Stephen Lawrence case and the Inquiry largely disappeared from public consciousness. February 2009 saw the 10th anniversary of the Stephen Lawrence Inquiry, and a new revival of interest. Three Secretaries of State – for Justice, Home Office, and Communities and Local Government – held a joint conference to mark the anniversary. Joint activities of three government departments at such high levels are incredibly rare. It is significant that the Justice Secretary in 2009 was Jack Straw who, as Home Secretary in 1997 had set up the Stephen Lawrence Inquiry in the first place. He has frequently been reported as saying that the Stephen Lawrence Inquiry has been his most significant political achievement.[4]

At the anniversary conference, Jack Straw (Justice), Jacqui Smith (Home Office) and Hazel Blears (Communities and Local Government) launched two reviews of the Inquiry carried out by the Runnymede Trust[5] and by me.[6] Speaking at the conference, the Metropolitan Police Commissioner, Sir Paul Stephenson, told the audience that "all the recommendations of Stephen Lawrence Inquiry have been implemented". He added:

> The label of 'institutionally racist' no longer applies after 10 years of race reform.... Pockets of 'stupidity and bigotry' remain in the police 16 years after the racist murder of Stephen Lawrence.
>
> Stephen's legacy is that equal treatment for all, whether within or outside the force, has become a yardstick for success.... We must move on from an obsession with race. Diversity is no longer an end in its own right. I do not want the Met to be distracted by the debate about institutional racism. That label no longer drives or motivates change as it once so clearly and dramatically did.
>
> What matters to the people of London is that we continue to change. It is actions, not definitions, that solve problems. The racist murder of Stephen Lawrence was a transformational moment, not just for the Met, not just of the service but for society. We have changed but I do not hide the fact that there is much more to be done.[7]

My report and the Runnymede report strongly disagreed with both of his statements. Both reports found that there had been a welcome improvement in professionalism in all areas of policing, *except* in those that had negative impacts on people from black and minority ethnic backgrounds. The tide of change built up by the Stephen Lawrence Inquiry had by then not just slowed, but turned backwards, as tides do. Although the Commissioner had been sent advance copies of both reports, from his totally positive take on policing 10 years on, I believe that he had either not read them or chosen to disagree with them. His remarks were not welcomed by the National Black Police Association members present at the conference.[8] Even worse for me, was to hear Jack Straw following the lead of the Commissioner, attempting to dump the label of institutional racism for which the Inquiry had fought so hard (see Chapters Four and Six).

Less than a year later, Sir Paul Stephenson left the Metropolitan Police in something of a hurry, resigning amid speculation about a connection to the News International phone hacking scandal.[9] In 2011 he was replaced as Commissioner by Bernard Hogan-Howe whose policing career was previously outside London except for a three-year spell as Assistant Commissioner for Human Resources. For those hostile to previous police attitudes his arrival does feel like fresh air flowing through Scotland Yard.[10] When asked about allegations that the Metropolitan Police was still institutionally racist, Hogan-Howe said "I hope we are not but it is a bit like asking someone if they are a nice person. Are we the best people to ask?"[11] That is in itself, a major step forward for an organisation that has been primarily self-policing for so long. Let us hope that Commissioner Hogan-Howe will continue to provide the strong positive leadership required for overcoming the deep-seated and poorly addressed issues of racism inside the Metropolitan Police Service (see Chapter Seven).

The issues raised by the Stephen Lawrence Inquiry continue to be relevant for policing. Hogan-Howe has said that the police force is "hugely different from where we were" at the time of Stephen Lawrence's death. However, he described stop and search as still "a real challenge" for the force and recognised concern at figures which show more than 90% fail to lead to arrest.[12] A radical overhaul of controversial stop and searches in London was announced in

January 2012 which hopefully will now reduce the racial disparities in stop and search, given the very slow progress since the Inquiry's recommendations 14 years ago (see Chapter Seven).[13]

The Metropolitan Police Service considers itself to be the most respected force in Britain, if not in the world. Yet this was, and regrettably still is, not the view of Stephen Lawrence's parents.[14]

In October 2010, two of the original five prime suspects were arrested: Gary Dobson and David Norris. Dobson had been acquitted of the murder in 1996 and until 2003 was immune from further prosecution for the same offence. Perhaps to Dobson's chagrin, the Criminal Justice Act of 2003 implemented recommendation 38 of the Stephen Lawrence Inquiry: that the ancient protection of double jeopardy could be removed in very exceptional circumstances, such as the development of new DNA techniques (see Chapter Six). The Inquiry gained a small kudos from the successful implementation of its recommendation 38 on double jeopardy, and I believe that the public recognised that Gary Dobson could not have been charged had it not been for the Inquiry's recommendation. The successful trial of Dobson and Norris in 2012 and their convictions for the murder of Stephen Lawrence has also revived interest in the Stephen Lawrence Inquiry's agenda.

But, by the time that the conviction and sentences were handed down on Gary Dobson and David Norris in January 2012, Neville and Doreen Lawrence had endured 19 years in which:

- two separate police investigations of the murder failed to find any significant evidence;
- an official trial was discontinued by the Crown Prosecution Service;
- a second trial brought privately by Mr and Mrs Lawrence also failed due to the lack of evidence;
- a harrowing inquest failed to get the 'prime suspects' to answer any questions, replying even to "Is your name David Norris?" with "I claim privilege";
- a Police Complaints Authority (PCA) inquiry made significant criticisms of the police, but denied any contribution of racism;

- the exhausting one-and-a-half year Stephen Lawrence judicial inquiry, which was more robust than that of the PCA, continued to face challenges and obstacles;
- their hopes that the recommendations of the Inquiry would significantly reduce racist outcomes of police activity have been dashed;[15]
- they have been, and are still, liable to meet those suspected of the murder of their son in their neighbourhood; the gang who murdered Stephen Lawrence were five men; only two of them are now in prison.

The hidden stories

There is a convention whereby people inside an inquiry do not tell people outside about anything that was said or is being done. This is important; while an inquiry is under way its members must be able to speak freely with one another knowing that their discussions will not be leaked to anybody outside. During the Inquiry I kept my lines of communication open to a number of key black individuals and organisations, since I saw that as part of my 'community' role on the panel (see Chapter Two), but I had no difficulty in doing this while maintaining complete silence on internal matters of the Inquiry.

Once the Inquiry was over I kept to the convention of silence for many years; the final text of the Report was the definitive view of the Inquiry, and that was that. But it has become increasingly obvious to me that my silence has been counter-productive when it comes to pushing the agenda set by the recommendations of the Inquiry itself.

A few years ago it dawned on me that, once the internal discussions had been translated into the text of the final report, the process of how we reached our conclusions could be helpful for people who want clarification, especially about contentious issues discussed in the Inquiry, such as the definition of institutional racism. The 'hidden stories' of the Stephen Lawrence Inquiry presented in this book are therefore mainly about what happened inside the Inquiry, by means of information that has hitherto been unavailable and inaccessible (see Chapter Five). Some stories are about external events that had an impact on the Inquiry while it was operating, or events in the following years that relate to the conclusions and recommendations of the Inquiry Report.[16] Various oddities have been revealed when examining these stories; many show how the Inquiry's conclusions and recommendations, in my opinion, have been undermined in both subtle and more overt ways.

The stories focus on those areas where my experience of sitting on the panel as one of the three Advisers to the Judge offers insights that cannot be gained from other sources. I have also obtained a copy of the transcripts and scoured the documents held at The National Archives at Kew. Reading the transcripts is a fairly new pleasure, since they only became officially available in 2005 – six years after the end of the Inquiry. I wish I could have also consulted, during the years since the end of the Inquiry in 1999, the notes I took at the time of the discussions held within the Inquiry, as well as the memos I sent to and received from the Chair. I expected within months to be able to access the archive where my notes, as well as the correspondence files, were stored by the Home Office. Only in 2012 (after this book was started) was I given access to the correspondence, yet my own notes were still not to be seen. There are other papers of the Inquiry that are still not available today, 13 years since the Inquiry took place. These delays are in themselves one of the more bizarre of the oddities surrounding the Stephen Lawrence case and Inquiry; this is explored in Chapter Five

When I set out on the journey of exploring the uncomfortable stories and conspiracy theories of the Stephen Lawrence Inquiry I became anxious about the direction in which some of the facts appeared to be taking me. These doubts have been dispelled by confirmation of my conclusions when more evidence came my way. For example, my suspicions that there was something more sinister behind the attempt to cancel the Inquiry's visits to Birmingham in 1998 (see Chapter Three), was a view backed up by other sources.

First, letters in the correspondence files which only saw the light of day in 2011, 12 years after the end of the Inquiry, the most dramatic of which was a letter from a Birmingham Councillor that confirmed that the Secretary to the Inquiry had not made the rigorous search for venues in Birmingham that was claimed.[17]

Second, meeting community activists in Birmingham, who went even further than I had done in suggesting dark and suspicious plots around the Inquiry and, perhaps more importantly, how this undermined the recommendations of the Inquiry with the black and minority ethnic communities there.[18] Recently, the Hillsborough Inquiry late in 2012 has revealed a cover-up within the police, the Home Office and local policing[19] which suggests that my conclusions about the smoke and mirrors within the Stephen Lawrence Inquiry need not be as tentative as I have made them.

The most obvious hidden story of the Stephen Lawrence Inquiry is the story of the hidden archive (Chapter Five). The Hutton Inquiry of 2003 was into the death of David Kelly, the weapons expert who killed himself after his identity was revealed at the Parliamentary Inquiry into the Second Gulf War. Within four months of the end of that Inquiry the transcripts, the correspondence files and all the rest of the archive were made available to the public on a special website created for the purpose.

At the end of the Stephen Lawrence Inquiry, four years earlier in 1999, I was told that the transcripts and the rest of the archive would be released within four to five months on the Home Office website. Five years later nothing at all had been released. I consider that to be a significant oddity that no one else appears to have noticed, let alone commented on.

Throughout the writing of this book a common thread appeared, in that the stories almost all pointed to ways in which the authority of the Inquiry was undermined. That common thread was odd in itself. I was surprised to find that I was not just writing about curious hidden stories; a pattern was emerging of denial. One can understand that powerful people may use everything in their power to deflect threats to it. This book describes manoeuvres that I believe were used to undermine the changes that the Inquiry demonstrated were necessary. The oddities with which I began turned into an analysis of power and problems of which I had been only vaguely aware during the Inquiry.

Denial is perhaps inevitable if people with power are given reasons why they must give up some of that power. Curbing racism, particularly institutional racism, is very much about limiting the discretion of those who have more power to disadvantage people with less power.

When the Stephen Lawrence Inquiry recommended that police officers should record the reason for every stop and search they perform (recommendation 61) there was widespread criticism and undermining of the very idea (Chapter Six). The recommendation aimed to do just what the officers sensed it was meant to do: curb their discretion to stop anyone. The recommendation would lead to a reduction in their power that very few could contemplate. Without strong leadership support within the police (Chapters Four, Six and Seven), it was inevitable that the vast majority of officers would find ways to circumvent and undermine the recommendation. It appeared that recommendation 61 was doomed, but if it died, down with it would go the whole authority of the Inquiry as an instrument of improving professional policing. There are few measurable outcomes in policing, and stop and search is one. This is why it is so important in being able to assess progress.

ONE

Why there was an inquiry

The retelling of the Stephen Lawrence case may be thought unnecessary by those who watched and read about the case in 1993. Readers may also remember the media response to the public hearings of the Stephen Lawrence Inquiry in 1998. The intensity of coverage was similar to that for the Leveson Inquiry[1] in 2012 with day after day of unbelievable revelations filling TV and newspaper reports (for a summary of key events see page 161).

For most teenagers and young adults today the Stephen Lawrence story must feel as old as black and white movies. They may have been bored or fascinated by the more recent trial and conviction in 2011–12, but they will have no memory of the saga of the Lawrence family; they were only small children during the Inquiry and probably not yet born when Stephen was stabbed to death in 1993. Unsurprisingly most young people who come into contact with police officers on the streets today, have little idea of the significance of the Stephen Lawrence case.

What actually happened on the night of 22 April 1993?

There is no better telling of the story than the summary of it by Sir William Macpherson, the Judge in the Stephen Lawrence Inquiry. It was written in 1998, five years after the murder.[2]

The murder of Stephen Lawrence

1.1 Descriptions of the murder of Stephen Lawrence have been given in thousands of newspapers and television programmes since his horrific death on 22 April 1993. The whole incident which led to his murder probably lasted no more than 15–20 seconds. [...]

1.2 Stephen Lawrence had been with his friend Duwayne Brooks during the afternoon of 22 April. They were on their way home when they came at around 22:30 to the bus stop in Well Hall Road with which we are all now so familiar. Stephen went to see if a bus was coming, and reached a position almost in the centre of the mouth of Dickson Road. Mr Brooks was part of the way between Dickson Road and the roundabout when he saw the group of five or six white youths who were responsible for Stephen's death on the opposite side of the road.

1.3 Mr Brooks called out to ask if Stephen saw the bus coming. One of the youths must have heard something said, since he called out *"What, what nigger?"* With that the group came quickly across the road and literally engulfed Stephen. During this time one or more of the group stabbed Stephen twice. One witness thought that Mr Brooks was also attacked in the actual physical assault, but it appears from his own evidence that he was a little distance away from the group when the killing actually took place. He then turned and ran and called out to Stephen to run and to follow him.

1.4 Three eye witnesses were at the bus stop. Joseph Shepherd knew Stephen. He boarded a bus which came to the stop probably as Stephen fell. He went straight to Mr & Mrs Lawrence's house and told them of the attack. Alexandra Marie also boarded the bus. She was seen later, and gave all the help she could. Royston Westbrook also boarded the bus. It was he who believed that Mr Brooks had also been physically attacked. None of these witnesses was able later to identify any of the suspects. All of them said that the attack was sudden and short.

1.5 The group of white murderers then disappeared down Dickson Road. We refer to them as a group of murderers because that is exactly what they were; young men bent on violence of this sort rarely act on their own. They are cowards and need the support of at least a small group in order to bolster their actions. There is little doubt that all of them would have been held to be responsible for the murder had they been in court together with viable evidence against them. This murder has the hallmarks of a joint enterprise.

1.6 Mr Brooks ran across the road in the direction of Shooters Hill, and he was followed by his friend Stephen Lawrence, who managed somehow to get to his feet and to run over 100 yards to the point where he fell. That place is now marked with a granite memorial stone set into the pavement.

1.7 Stephen had been stabbed to a depth of about five inches on both sides of the front of his body to the chest and arm. Both stab wounds severed axillary arteries, and blood must literally have been pumping out of and into his body as he ran up the road to join his friend. In the words of Dr Shepherd, the pathologist, *"It is surprising that he managed to get 130 yards with all the injuries he had, but also the fact that the deep penetrating wound of the right side caused the upper lobe to partially collapse his lung. It is therefore a testimony to Stephen's physical fitness that he was able to run the distance he did before collapsing"*.

1.8 No great quantities of blood marked the scene of the attack or the track taken by Stephen, because he wore five layers of clothing. But when he fell he was bleeding freely, and nearly all of the witnesses who saw him lying there speak of a substantial quantity of blood. There are variations in their description of the amount and location of the blood. The probability is that the blood came out in front of his body as he lay by chance in the position described, which appeared to many witnesses to be the *"recovery"* position. His head looked to the left into the roadway and his left arm was up.

1.9 The medical evidence indicates that Stephen was dead before he was removed by the ambulance men some time later. The amount of blood which had been lost would have made it probable that Stephen died where he fell on the pavement, and probably within a short time of his fall.

1.10 What followed has ultimately led to this public Inquiry. Little did those around Stephen, or the police officers, or indeed the public, expect that five years on this Inquiry would deal with every detail of what occurred from the moment of Stephen's death until the hearings at Hannibal House, where this Inquiry has taken place.

1.11 Stephen Lawrence's murder was simply and solely and unequivocally motivated by racism. It was the deepest tragedy for his family. It was an affront to society, and especially to the local black community in Greenwich.

1.12 Nobody has been convicted of this awful crime. That also is an affront both to the Lawrence family and the community at large.

For the first two weeks after Stephen's murder it was seen as just another in a series of murders of black boys in South-East London. Rohit Duggal and Rolan Adams both died in racist incidents within the previous year, and now Stephen Lawrence. None of the murders were given much publicity beyond the local newspapers. All but one of the victims was black and it was widely believed within the community that the arrival of a British National Party office in neighbouring Bromley was connected in some way with the spate of stabbings.[3]

Black communities across London were angry that the police did not appear to be taking these cases seriously.[4] Lee Jasper, then director of the leading black community charity The 1990 Trust, summed up the black experience vividly as "blacks are under-policed as victims of crime, and over-policed when going about their law-abiding business".[5] On 4 May 1993 Stephen's parents, Neville and Doreen Lawrence held a press conference to complain that not enough was being done by the police to catch Stephen's killers. Doreen Lawrence made her feelings clear when she stated that "If a black person had committed a murder they would have arrested him by now. But because it's a black and they're white it's almost as if they're condoning what these people are doing."[6]

Then everything changed. On 6 May, 13 days after the killing, Neville and Doreen Lawrence were seen on TV and in newspapers with Nelson Mandela at their side. Mr Mandela compared the murder of Stephen Lawrence with the experience of black people under apartheid: "I know what it means to parents to lose a child under such tragic circumstances. Such brutality is all too commonplace in South Africa, where black lives are cheap." He added, "Their tragedy is our tragedy."[7] It was deeply shocking for

British people to hear Mr Mandela draw parallels with modern Britain and apartheid South Africa. His message was clear: black lives here are as cheap as black lives in his own country had been when a racist government had been in charge.

The day after the Mandela meeting, detectives went in and arrested the five 'prime suspects' whose names had been handed in to them again and again during the previous two weeks.[8] The Stephen Lawrence Inquiry found that no more evidence was available to the police on that day than there had been two days after the murder.[9] According to the rules on arrest at the time (in the 1984 Police and Criminal Evidence Act) the police had sufficient information to arrest within two days of the murder. It is very likely that, had there been a quick and thorough investigation, they would have found evidence which could have convicted the 'prime suspects' soon after the murder, rather than 19 years later. We will never know what evidence there was in their homes on the days immediately after the murder, but the suspects were seen three days after the murder taking large full black bin liners away from one of their homes.[10]

How significant was the intervention of Nelson Mandela? A judicial inquiry must avoid statements which could be used by its critics to undermine its authority, so a bald statement that Nelson Mandela's words were the stimulus for the arrests, could well have led to criticism of him for interfering in the internal affairs of the United Kingdom. It could also have undermined the authority of the Inquiry which could be criticised for suggesting a link for which there was only circumstantial evidence. The Inquiry's Report only mentions the name of Nelson Mandela in quoting a "suggestion" put to the Senior Investigating Officer (SIO) by Mike Mansfield QC on behalf of the Lawrence family:

> that the ultimate decision to make the arrests which took place on 7 May, was simply made on the spur of the moment because Mr Weeden [the SIO] and his team had become concerned about extraneous pressure, in particular the visit of Nelson Mandela to the Lawrence family and a planned demonstration in relation to racist murders and activity which was to take place on 8 May.[11]

Needless to say, this suggestion was denied by Mr Weeden.[12]

What was so wrong with the investigation of Stephen Lawrence's murder?

Mr and Mrs Lawrence were handed anonymous notes right from the day after the murder giving the same five names as the killers of their son. They passed these on at once but the police appeared to be doing nothing with this information.[13] The Lawrences kept asking their family liaison officers (FLOs) when arrests would be made.[14] Within a few days of their son's murder Mr and Mrs Lawrence sensed already that the police were not trying hard enough to find the killers.[15] They were assured by junior and senior officers that everything that could be done was being done, and that there were more officers on this murder investigation than on any other in London, all working long hours on the case. These assurances were repeated time and again over the following two years. Never once in the first year did the SIO in charge of the murder investigation meet with Mr and Mrs Lawrence.[16]

The family liaison was a complete failure with "inappropriate behaviour and patronising attitudes" towards the Lawrence family.[17] Yet police officers blamed Mr and Mrs Lawrence for the failure of family liaison in the case. The Lawrences had appointed a solicitor to deal with the FLOs, something that had never happened before. The solicitor and, through him, the Lawrences were accused of "bombarding the Incident room by letter, fax and telephone..."[18] asking for information. This was reported to be so bad that it was interfering with the progress of the investigation.[19] (The Inquiry explored this 'bombardment', which turned out to be no more than three letters, a fax and some telephone calls.)

The Inquiry found that mistake was piled on mistake; decisions which should have been made were not made, or if they were it was the wrong decision; notes of meetings apparently held to discuss major decisions did not exist. If they were taken they had disappeared, or they were never taken[20] ... or perhaps the meeting was never held.

By July 1993 the Crown Prosecution Service announced that they did not intend to prosecute two of the five, due to lack of evidence.[21]

At the end of the year, Deputy Assistant Commissioner (DAC) David Osland ordered a review of the failed murder investigation to be led by Detective Chief Superintendent John Barker. This review sadly turned out to be "flawed and indefensible".[22] Most spectacular of the flaws was that Mr Barker failed even to mention an informer who was given a pseudonym of 'James Grant'. Grant was a 'skinhead' who walked into the police station less than 24 hours after the murder. He gave information on Neil and Jamie Acourt and their gang; he accurately described them, where they lived, that they kept knives and other weapons, and the names of other local people they had stabbed. Instead of being called upstairs by the Deputy SIO, his address was taken and he was sent home. He was visited by Detective Sergeant Davidson the following day, who says he gave more or less the same information again. Whether or not he gave that information or whether or not Davidson visited Grant we cannot be sure; no notes were taken of the visit. What we do know is that almost nothing was done to follow up the information.[23]

Yet even I, who am no detective, was drawn to ask Tom Cook, our former detective on the panel of the Inquiry, if Grant could have been one of the gang and could even have been there at the murder. Tom Cook agreed. It may be that conversation which influenced this statement in the Inquiry Report:

> It is apparent to us that he himself [the Deputy SIO] ought to have followed up such a vital potential witness, whose information raised the suspicion that James Grant himself might have been involved in the murder ... or with witnesses who might have given vital information about the murderers.[24]

The Inquiry concluded that this was:

> a most important aspect of the case ripe for investigation by the Review team. Yet Mr Barker's Review makes no reference to James Grant whatsoever, so that anybody reading the Review would think that Mr Barker had never heard of him. [...] James Grant's information was fundamental to this investigation and lack of any mention of it in the report is extraordinary.[25]

The Inquiry was told that, ordinarily, this sort of review would be wholly the responsibility of the commissioning officer, in this case, DAC Osland. However, the then Commissioner of the Metropolitan Police, Sir Paul Condon, involved himself in a number of ways. I am most fascinated by one detail which was not included in the Report of the Inquiry, which shows the extent of his involvement. The copy of the review that we were shown had on the top right corner of its cover the initials 'PC' in red ink, with a neat tick alongside them. We were told that Sir Paul Condon used red ink for notes and PC were of course his initials; this was his standard mark on documents that he had seen and signed off. So it does seem that the Commissioner saw and signed off a review that had missed a glaringly obvious episode of abysmal failure on the part of his own police force.

What happened next?

With the delays and lack of follow up in the investigation, the only real evidence that the police had was what Duwayne Brooks, Stephen's friend, saw on the night. This was a glimpse of a man whose details he tried to describe to the police on several occasions. When asked to give details to a forensic artist, he described clothing and hairstyle in good detail, but could not describe anything about the attacker's face. Duwayne Brooks had been deeply traumatised from seeing his friend stabbed and die in front of him; he had narrowly escaped the same fate as well. As he recovered from the stress, his memory clarified what he saw. He was obviously desperate to help the police and gave his evidence many times.[26] From a legal point of view, the minor changes in his versions may have clarified what he saw, but they also made him vulnerable to cross-examination by the barristers defending the suspects. Witnesses who change their story can all too easily be torn apart as unreliable. As a result of the dreadful mistakes made by the detectives in this investigation, there was no hard evidence to back up Duwayne Brooks' witness statement. By April 1994, charges against the remaining three members of the gang were dropped by the Crown Prosecution Service (CPS) because of a lack of evidence. They all walked away as free men.

Shortly after, Mr and Mrs Lawrence decided to bring a private prosecution, this time led not by the CPS but by their own legal team: Mike Mansfield QC and his barristers, with Imran Khan the family's solicitor. Inevitably, being faced with the same lack of evidence, the prosecution collapsed and the defendants were handed down verdicts of not guilty.[27]

Accusations of racism in the police

Mike Mansfield QC represented Mr and Mrs Lawrence at every stage of the investigations; this included at the inquest, at the private prosecution brought by the Lawrences, as well as at the Inquiry. In his opening address to the Inquiry he summed up the view of Mrs Lawrence thus:

> The gist of what she said to the inquest last year, on behalf of both herself and Neville Lawrence, was that she and her family and many of the members of her community, both the black and white, community, felt that the system, the judicial system, starting with the prosecution investigation, right the way through to what happened at the Old Bailey, had let them down. They felt that there were serious deficiencies at all stages.[28]

Later, in commenting on the key role of family liaison by the police, Doreen Lawrence summed up her criticism thus:

> Their attitude towards the family as a whole was patronising. [...] The whole thing, how they were talking: I don't know, I can't say that, if it was a black police officer, it would have been better. I mean, how many black police officers do you know anyway? How many black police officers do you see within the force? So I don't know who they would use for a family like ours. Perhaps it would have been different. That is something that we will never know. [...]
>
> Once the information started coming in [we wondered] "Why has no-one been arrested?" It started dawning on me that, if

it had been the other way around that night, somebody would have been arrested, regardless of whether they had done it or not.[29]

I think that what Mrs Lawrence meant by "the other way around" was that if Stephen had been white and the alleged killers black, somebody would have been arrested once the information started coming in regardless of whether or not they were guilty. In the end it was the unanimous view of the Judge Sir William Macpherson and of all three of us, his Advisers, that Mr and Mrs Lawrence's suspicions and fears about the police were vindicated.[30]

TWO

The Inquiry and how I came to be an Adviser on the panel

The Stephen Lawrence Inquiry was set up in July of 1997, three months after the general election which brought in the New Labour government. The new Home Secretary, Jack Straw MP had met with Stephen Lawrence's parents in the previous year. Having heard their story he promised them that, if Labour were elected and if he was appointed Home Secretary (as he anticipated he might be), he would give them a judicial inquiry into what went wrong with the police investigation.

The terms of reference of the Inquiry were:

> To inquire into the matters arising from the death of Stephen Lawrence on 22 April 1993 to date, in order particularly to identify the lessons to be learned for the investigation and prosecution of racially motivated crimes.[1]

The Inquiry was in two parts. Part One (March–September, 1998) was a 'quasi-judicial' hearing which sought to find the facts of the investigation into the murder of Stephen Lawrence. Part Two of the Inquiry (September–November, 1998) was very different. The Inquiry's Report describes Part Two as follows:

> Part 2 of the Inquiry was aimed at the second part of our Terms of Reference. We sought to gather information and opinions in order to help us to make recommendations as to the "investigation and prosecution of racially motivated crimes".[2]

Where the Inquiry was held

After a long search for adequate premises for the Inquiry in or near Eltham where Stephen Lawrence had been murdered, the Inquiry's Secretary had to accept that he would have to look further afield. We finally settled into the third and fourth floors of Hannibal House, an empty NHS tower block which rises out of the shopping centre in the middle of the Elephant and Castle one-way road system in Central London. The shopping centre was painted pink, taken generally to suggest it was a pink elephant. I always felt Hannibal House to be more of a white elephant, a seedy and run-down elephant of a half-empty 1960s building of concrete and glass inelegance. But, to commemorate its colour, the cover of the Report of the Stephen Lawrence Inquiry was an identical shade of pink.

The chamber used by the Inquiry for public hearings had space for only 150 chairs for members for the public. More than half of the public each day were regulars who turned up day after day. With only 20 to 50 new faces at each of the 59 days, probably no more than about 2,000 people actually attended. Most people therefore have little idea of how the Inquiry operated, or of what actually happened. Most of what they do know will have come from the television and newspaper coverage at the time. I therefore feel a degree of obligation to tell, from my position at the centre of the Inquiry, just how difficult issues were dealt with.

Who was involved in the Inquiry?

The Chair

The Judge appointed to oversee the Inquiry was Sir William Macpherson of Cluny, recently retired from the High Court. From what I observed from close to, I can only say that my admiration for Sir William grew and grew through the course of the Inquiry. A mark of the man is that on several occasions in public he has said his name should not be on the Inquiry or the Report (it is usual for an inquiry to be named after the chair), but that the name to be remembered should be that of Stephen Lawrence.

Unfortunately, Sir William Macpherson's appointment was not without controversy. No sooner had the public hearings started on Monday 16 March 1998, they had to be adjourned. Mr and Mrs Lawrence had demanded an urgent meeting with the Home Secretary to discuss concerns about Sir William, which stemmed from an article in the previous day's *Observer* newspaper.[3] The article reported that in the past he had been insensitive in handling race issues. The most ominous of four examples given in the *Observer* story was that seven years previously, on an appeal from an employment tribunal, Sir William had dismissed the case half way through. The article claimed that the motivation for the dismissal was racist and that he had dismissed the case early so that he could take his wife to the Ascot Races.

The article also highlighted with apparent authority that there were complaints by the Lawrence family that their legal team had been denied access to significant documents in the possession of the Inquiry. On the Monday morning Mike Mansfield QC, lawyer for Mr and Mrs Lawrence, opened with a statement that denied this allegation:

> the problem that we have faced is not a denial of documents – and here I make it clear on behalf of the family that any suggestion that we have been denied anything is false; we have been denied nothing.[4]

I knew this to be true myself. The Inquiry had been asked for documents that were not immediately available, in particular from the Police Complaints Authority's (PCA) Inquiry a year before and I was present when Sir William struggled with the chair and director of the PCA to convince them to make complete disclosure of all material they had. This took quite some time so there were indeed delays in delivering the information required by the Lawrence team, I believed that everything requested by the Lawrence family's team had been delivered. However, the damage had been done. Mike Mansfield and Mr and Mrs Lawrence themselves had made personal phone calls to Home Secretary Jack Straw telling of their distress that he had appointed an inappropriate Judge to lead the Inquiry into the investigation of their son's murder and to request a new chair.[5] They informed the Home Secretary that they were withdrawing their co-operation.[6]

An adjournment was agreed on the Monday morning. On Monday evening Jack Straw phoned me at home (it transpired later that he phoned the other two Advisers as well on that evening). He told me of the difficulties he faced in deciding how to proceed when the Lawrences were so unhappy about the Inquiry and asked for my opinion on the Judge's credibility. I had not yet been able to speak with Sir William about the accusations and was not able to confer with my fellow Advisers, so I felt quite vulnerable to be asked such a critical question. I told him that I had heard or seen nothing suggesting that Sir William was weak on racism. I confirmed that the stories in the *Observer* were entirely new to me and that I planned to explore them tactfully with Sir William in person when we met the next day. I was at least able to tell the Home Secretary that I was surprised at any suggestion that Sir William had been dragging his feet on answering requests for documents. Far from denying access to documents, he had fought doggedly for three months with the PCA and with the Metropolitan Police for access to every page of the PCA investigation that had been conducted in 1996 into the failings of the Stephen Lawrence murder investigations, for example. He also insisted that the Metropolitan Police hand over the personal files of a number of police officers connected with the investigation.[7]

The following day, Tuesday, was Budget Day. It is customary for the whole Cabinet to be present on the floor of the House of Commons to support the Chancellor of the Exchequer, especially as this Budget was the first presented by the New Labour government since its election the previous May. One Cabinet member absented himself that afternoon: Home Secretary Jack Straw left the Commons chamber to give two hours of his time to talking with Mr and Mrs Lawrence. Jack Straw had been given unanimous backing for Sir William Macpherson from his three Advisers,[8] all of whom had recommended that Sir William should be judged on what was to happen in the Inquiry, not on old stories about old cases. I believe the Home Secretary told the Lawrences that the Inquiry could be set back six months if another judge had to be found. Even then the

Inquiry could have been fatally damaged if led by a judge who would be seen as a second choice, and who would find it difficult to go over all the ground the Inquiry had covered in the previous six months.

Fortunately for everybody the Lawrences gave their consent (albeit warily) to back the Inquiry still with Sir William at its head.[9] Everyone knew, though, that the Lawrences and their lawyers would be watching carefully every word and every action not only of Sir William but also of every one of the key individuals in the Inquiry team, including myself.

On the following day I felt I had to ask Sir William for his version of the *Observer* story. He told me that when he was due to hear the employment tribunal appeal mentioned in the article, his clerk came to him at eleven in the morning to announce that the parties had settled the case out of court. Sir William then asked his clerk if there was any other business for him that day and was told that there was none, so he decided to take his wife to the races. His version of the story had a ring of truth about it and he would be highly unlikely to have made up a story which could be so easily verified if I asked to see the court records.

The Inquiry resumed the following Tuesday. I reckon that the week's adjournment cost the Home Office about £100,000. There would be other adjournments later on which would shake the credibility of the Inquiry (see Chapter Three).

The Advisers

The 1964 Police Act established the current system for judicial inquiries into policing. There have only been two as yet: the Scarman Inquiry into the Brixton riots of 1981[10] and the Stephen Lawrence Inquiry (1997–99). For the Inquiry into the Brixton riots Lord Scarman acted alone with a small team of civil servants. Photographs at the time show him walking into pubs and along the streets of Brixton, accompanied only by the Secretary to the Inquiry.[11] In session, he sat alone.

With the Stephen Lawrence Inquiry Home Office officials and ministers felt it necessary to give the Judge three 'Advisers'. No reasons were given for the significant difference to this Inquiry, nor

—

were any guidelines drawn up on how the advice was to be given. There were no terms of reference for the Advisers, but we swiftly developed close and effective working relationships with the Judge.

The Advisers were:

- Tom Cook, former Deputy Chief Constable in the West Yorkshire Police. He had been a senior detective so his opinions on what should and should not have happened, as well as what can and cannot be done by police were invaluable.
- The Right Reverend Dr John Sentamu, then Bishop for Stepney (now Archbishop of York). He was in a strong position because he was not only a Bishop of the Church of England, but before fleeing from Uganda he had been a barrister and a judge there.
- Dr Richard Stone, then Chair of the Jewish Council for Racial Equality (my role is discussed in more detail below).

The Secretary

We also had a Secretary to the Inquiry, about which I explain a little here because the background is relevant to Chapter Three.

The title of Secretary to an inquiry is a relic of times past. The origin of the word is from the Latin *secretus*, a secret. In mediaeval times *secretarius* was used to describe a 'confidential clerk'.

In modern dictionaries three definitions are listed: (a) a person employed to handle correspondence, to keep files, and to do clerical work; (b) an officer who keeps records, takes minutes of the meetings, and answers correspondence, as for a company; (c) an official who presides over a government department, as in Secretary of State.[12]

The modern use of the word 'secretary' is almost always definition (a). It describes in most people's minds someone who does routine administrative tasks, takes dictation and does typing and may also keep the manager's diary and so on. Definition (b) accurately describes a more senior and responsible role which is dropping fast out of common use, but is retained for government inquiries.

Stephen Wells was the official Secretary to the Stephen Lawrence Inquiry. His job description was decisively (b): he was responsible for managing the organisation and administration of the Inquiry, answerable directly and solely to the Judge. The administrative work was the job of the Assistant Secretary Alison Foulds. Her role was mainly within the more common understanding of 'secretary'.

In the Inquiry into the policing of the Brixton riots of 1986, Lord Scarman's Secretary was the only senior member of staff. He organised all the hearings and was the only person to accompany the Judge on his walkabouts of the streets − a very important role.

Subsequently, I was a panel member of another government inquiry: three years after the end of the Stephen Lawrence Inquiry I was appointed by the NHS to the Independent Inquiry into the Death of David Bennett.[13] For both inquiries it was taken for granted that the government department would appoint one of its civil servants to be seconded as the official secretary. This is considered as a 'donation in kind'. It is particularly helpful for the chairs of inquiries to have support from the start to deal with a number of preliminary jobs. Were they to start off without a seconded secretary, it would add time to the inquiry to make an appointment of an independent secretary. But as we will see later, a seconded secretary could potentially be caught between two masters (see Chapter Three).

My role as Adviser to the Inquiry

Introducing his Advisers to the public for the first time Sir William Macpherson gave his own brief description of the role he expected from each Adviser.[14] He introduced my role as to "advise me primarily upon community and racial aspects of this Inquiry". After his introductions he invited each Adviser in turn to make an informal statement for the record and for the public present. My statement came last because on this occasion we spoke in alphabetical order.

These introductions came a week after the Inquiry had been rescued by Jack Straw, following questions over the appropriateness of the Judge. In their introductions, Tom Cook and John Sentamu were specific and clear in their backing for Sir William Macpherson, but I sensed it might be seen as verging on the sycophantic and therefore insincere, to single him out for a third time. On the spur of the moment I felt it better to make sure I was heard to give my backing for him, but as one of the team, all of whom I praised.

Here is the text of my introduction, much of which can be seen to be off the cuff.

I am Richard Stone and as you probably know I spent 20 years as a general practitioner in the Notting Hill and Bayswater parts of London. I suppose it is important to say that inevitably in the Notting Hill community as a local family doctor I did find myself very much involved in my local community which, of course, in that area is the Caribbean community of Notting Hill and the Notting Hill Carnival and the areas around there. At the same time it is also important to recognise that as a local GP I inevitably worked very closely also with the local police, particularly in my case in the areas of child protection.

What I wanted to just say this morning, rather like Tom has done, is make a bit of a personal statement, remind people that nine days ago there was a moving and passionate vigil for Stephen Lawrence at the spot where he died. I was privileged to be allowed by my new friend Bishop John here to read there the ancient kaddish prayer which the Jewish people have for over 2,000 years chanted as a memorial for the dead. It was a moving and passionate occasion. For me it was probably the nearest I will ever come to knowing Stephen. From what I have heard about him and from what I have read I think he is someone whose company I would have enjoyed.

Now I and the other 20 or more in this Inquiry team have to do what we can to find out all that is possible to find out about how he died. We also have to use every ounce of our passion, our intellects, our instincts to sort out the injustice that no one has been found responsible for that dreadful murder.

In my 20 years as a National Health Service GP I learned from my patients something which has been confirmed by almost all surveys of patients. People do try alternative therapies and the main reason they give is that they want more time and they want to feel they have been listened to. Listening is so important and it is listening which this Inquiry is about to do for 6, 8 or 10 weeks. In addition to our listening I do hope the people from all communities will every day fill the 185 seats we have provided here for the public. One of my mentors, Rabbi Hugo Gryn, used to say that one of his main hopes in life was to have wall to wall congregations. It will help us to focus our minds if we have wall to wall public presence with us during all of the weeks of the Inquiry.

In addition to listening there has to be the capacity of the listener to change his or her mind. I have been spending an average of two days a week for the last seven months in the company of the 15 or so key members of this Inquiry. What has impressed me most is the steely determination of every one of those people, the secretaries, the lawyers, the civil servants, the other two advisers, Bishop John and my other new friend, Tom Cook and our Judge, Sir William Macpherson himself. All of these people have that determination to get to the core of the issues raised by this racist murder of Stephen Lawrence. Every single one of these people I have found has a remarkable capacity to listen. Everyone not only gives the time to listen, but I have also noticed a rare willingness amongst all of them to change their attitudes. That gives a reasonable hope even to a wary person like me that we will find out most of what we all want to know about the murder and about the investigations of it. I do not think we can ever know one hundred percent but I am confident that the Lawrence family and all of those other people who have serious concerns about this case will feel that all that can be done to bring a sense of justice will have been done. Of course more may be revealed in years to come but there will be nothing of real importance left to seek out, all of the major issues at the centre of the case will have been dealt with once and for all.

That I think is what is needed to bring peace and to move forward any necessary changes in the judicial process that will make Britain a better place for us all to live in.[15]

After Sir William had weathered the *Observer* storm there was a new warmth between him and his Advisers. He knew that we had each in our own way supported him to the Home Secretary. His Advisers valued him and all of us had stuck our necks out to support him when under fire. We were not just loyal; we were also dependable. From then on it appeared to me that the Advisers were on a slightly more equal basis with the Judge. Ultimately, any responsibility for mistakes would still be borne by him alone, but the four of us worked together and I believe we were equally committed to the findings of the Inquiry.

How I came to be on the panel of an inquiry into racism in the police

When I discuss the Stephen Lawrence Inquiry I am frequently asked "How did you get to be appointed to the Stephen Lawrence Inquiry?" Behind the question is a puzzled "How odd! You're not a lawyer, you're a doctor. You're not black. Why you?" I could feel offended at being asked, but I understand the question. Being a former NHS general practitioner and Chair of the Jewish Council for Racial Equality does not fully explain why I was appointed to a judicial inquiry into professionalism in policing and institutional racism, so I will explain a little more about my background.

After two years of National Service in the Royal Navy, I read for a law degree (in jurisprudence) at Oxford University. This academic degree was intended to prepare me for a career in cinema and television management. After five years with Granada Television (my mother's family business), I decided that I would after all be better off following in my father's footsteps as an NHS general practitioner. Starting medical studies 10 years late and with no sciences it took until 1972, when I was 35 years old, to join as a partner in a general practice. My base for the 20 years thereafter was in Notting Hill and Paddington, Central London. We had a mix of patients living in grand Bayswater houses, in Paddington council estates, and on the streets of Notting Hill. I soon learned that 80% of what I had been taught in medical school was not relevant to what my patients brought to me, no matter what their background.

As a doctor I was in a position of relative power and could (and did for a while) spend more time with patients from a similar background to myself. In the area of West London in which I was a GP there were also a number of Bangladeshi homeless families placed in the warren of cheap hotels around Paddington station, by housing officers from boroughs in the East End of London, which had shrinking stocks of council housing. Those hotels were the most health-damaging environments I had seen in Britain. The families there had a multiplicity of problems – medical, social, housing, financial – which they brought along to the surgery, as well as asking me how to get a child into a school "so she can finish her exams next month". They needed more of my time than the allocated 10 minutes per patient. Most white middle-class patients could manage on less than 10, but I was unwittingly giving them more time than they needed, and the Bangladeshi families a lot less than they needed. When a Bangladeshi father of five told me off for rushing him through, I was shocked. I decided I had to reverse the ratio. I worked hard to find ways to give to these disadvantaged families the time appropriate to their needs. I then slept better at night, knowing I had been thoroughly professional with the Bangladeshis as much as I had with white middle-class patients. In the words of Sir William Macpherson a decade later, my change of priorities led to "appropriate and professional" behaviour with Bangladeshi patients as well as with white British patients.

On the Notting Hill side of the practice I was welcomed into Caribbean communities whose teenage sons seemed to be in constant conflict with the police and I worked hard to help them. About 3am one Saturday night the phone rang:

> "Dr Stone. Mangrove Frank here."

Frank Crichlow was a local black community leader who owned the Mangrove restaurant in All Saints Road, Notting Hill. This short road was the frontline of the anti-racist struggle in the 1960s, 1970s and 1980s. Frank actively put himself up to make peace between police officers and the black community.

> "One of our lads been swept up by the police, Dr Stone. Handcuffed behind his back and ..."

> "I know, thrown face down in the police van, with wrists handcuffed behind his back."

> "How d'you know that, Dr Stone?"

> "Because it was the same story last month, and the other times before that."

"Well, when they took him out into Notting Hill police station, Dr Stone, he was covered in blood and bruises. His family's real worried. Can you go in, please, to make sure he's all right?"

How could I say no? This time, though, I pleaded:

"Frank, when I've been out in the middle of the night I'm not so good the next day. I'm on call this weekend, Frank, and you called me out last night as well. Do me a favour. Call one of the other doctors in your rota this time?"

There was a long pause, then:

"But Dr Stone, you are the rota."

I was shocked. I had no idea that I was the only doctor who went into police stations at the request of relatives to examine people allegedly beaten by police. I did turn out that night, but later I contacted all the local GPs I knew. Every one of them had a reason for not making up a rota. They had a new baby in the family. Or there was a new partner to train up. One was off on a sabbatical. Another was studying for a further degree. I remained the sole member of the rota for another 15 years.

Mangrove and Notting Hill were only part of the community activities that I became involved in as a local GP. It was a great help to have a grant-making family charitable settlement from which I could make donations to charities, an increasing number of which over the years were black-led or supported anti-racist community action. I also founded and sometimes funded projects to respond to the needs of homeless families.

By 1990 we had built up the single-handed practice that I had joined in 1972 into a powerhouse of five doctors and a nurse practitioner, with managerial and reception staff of seven full and part timers. However, the strain of 10 years of cuts to health and social services was beginning to tell. Virginia Bottomley was then Secretary of State for Health and her department ordained that GPs must prevent heart attacks. My wife suggested I take her advice. I left medical practice at the age of 54½ and never had that heart attack.

The following five years were spent building closer relationships with people from black and minority ethnic communities, working on other voluntary sector activities including prevention of illness and health promotion, and positive Muslim-Jewish relations. By the 1990s I had explained to Mangrove Frank that all of his activities were charitable. One outcome was that I became vice-chair of the Mangrove Trust that we established together. There was a similar set-up with other activists, most notably with Pepe Francis whose steelpan training of young people from a variety of backgrounds was similarly consolidated into the 'Ebony Steelband Trust for the abled and disabled'. In the final years of the 1980s the 'black workers group' of members of the National Council for Voluntary Organisations discussed setting up as a separate charity along the lines of Mangrove. This created the national 'umbrella' charity for the black voluntary sector, The 1990 Trust. Outside working with and for black-led charities, I became trustee and vice-chair of the Runnymede Trust, and a Council member of Liberty. I have also enjoyed being the founding chair of the Stephen Spender Memorial Trust, and founder of Alif-Aleph UK (British Muslims and British Jews).

In the lead-up to the general election in 1997 Alun Michael, Labour MP for Cardiff South and Penarth, had taken on all shadow ministerial roles relating to the voluntary sector. I attended one of his manifesto roadshows in London. About 120 people squeezed into a room in Westminster Hall. I estimated that half of the audience were black and a quarter Asian. Alun Michael sat on the platform with his son who was then his researcher. Two white women were also on the platform. All four of the panel were competent and well briefed. Nonetheless the high proportion of people from black and Asian backgrounds in the audience contrasted starkly with the all-white panel. I waited for someone to remark on this, but nobody did. So in the final few minutes I made a brief and perhaps somewhat tart comment, for which I was thanked by a number of colleagues on the way out. When I asked why they hadn't commented themselves they replied "It's difficult when you're black yourself." I know about that. When there's a whiff of anti-Semitism it is difficult for me as a Jew to say it; much better if non-Jewish colleagues smell it too and speak up for us.

The upshot was that I set up three meetings in which Alun Michael could engage with some of the dynamic, mainly younger, black (and a few Asian and Muslim) colleagues with whom I had been working.

When Labour took over the government in 1997, a number of these became constructive special advisers in relevant government departments. After the election Alun Michael was appointed Minister of State in the Home Office, number two to Jack Straw MP the incoming Home Secretary. When Jack Straw was looking for a third panel member to advise Sir William Macpherson in the Stephen Lawrence Inquiry, unbeknown to me, Alun Michael put forward my name. By now he was aware of the significant degree of trust in me that existed in many black communities. He was also aware of my academic law degree. Jack Straw agreed to my appointment.

The appropriateness of the qualifications of Sir William, Tom Cook and John Sentamu were obvious, but knowledge of my law degree and of my 20-year track record in the anti-racist struggle would have been known only to the Judge and the Home Office ministers. To the outside world I had little apparent qualification or experience to explain my role on the Inquiry's panel.

It also is worth recognising here that the title used for me by the Inquiry was not what the officials offered at the beginning: "I take it, Dr Stone, that for the record we describe you as 'a former doctor in Notting Hill Gate'?" Well, no actually. I didn't want to be a former anything. Also, Notting Hill *Gate* is an underground station on the old Watling Street Roman Road. The street credibility that he was perhaps seeking for the Inquiry with this suggested title was that I was known among anti-racists as an activist in the Notting Hill frontline of the struggle. Nearby Notting Hill Gate in that context was a very different scene from the Hill.

As distinct from the job from which I had retired five years before, what I actually was at the time of the Inquiry was the recently elected Chair of the Jewish Council for Racial Equality (JCORE). That was the title I chose and it is the title used in the preface to the Report of the Stephen Lawrence Inquiry. Oddly, whenever the Inquiry was being introduced to a new audience, sometimes I was described as the Chair of JCORE and sometimes as a "former doctor in Notting Hill"; sometimes I was both. (At least they remembered to omit the 'Gate'!) I grant that the title I chose draws attention to my Jewish identity (which comes up in Chapters Three and Four), but it does so in a way that attaches the Jewish part to Racial Equality. The history of Jewish participation in the anti-fascist struggle is something of which to be proud.

The special responsibility of white men in addressing racism

A criticism of the Inquiry heard soon after publication of the Report was that it wrongly assumed racism was practised only by white people against black people.[16] I do not deny that racism exists in other combinations of victim and perpetrator. Of course racism by black people towards white people exists, but in no way could that be said to be the sharp end of racism in Britain. The view that racism is a 'black issue' for black people to sort out is equally dangerous. Change has to come from outside those communities. It seems to me that there is only a limited amount that black and minority ethnic people can do to reduce racism towards them. They can bemoan prejudice against them and lobby the authorities to do something about it, but the people who perpetrate this discrimination are outside the communities affected. Real change can only come from the perpetrators, not from the victims.

The more power a perpetrator has, the more capacity that person has to increase or reduce the disadvantage of the weaker (or minority) group. The leaders of the largest institutions have the greatest potential for positive leadership and the greatest opportunities for change.

No one can ignore the fact that our leaders are mainly men; and mainly white men at that.[17] Middle-class middle-aged white men, like me. I may not perceive myself as powerful, but black Britons, British Muslims and women from almost any background may see me and people who look like me as more powerful in their world. Therefore we have a special responsibility to change our "processes, attitudes and behaviour"[18] to deliver services, to employ people, to engage with others in all aspects of life, in ways that no longer disadvantage people from minority backgrounds. When women fought for the vote after the First World War, their tactics of throwing themselves under horses and chaining themselves to railings raised the temperature of the suffragette campaign. However, the actual change had to come from a sufficient number of men in parliament being prepared to vote to amend the law.

So I do not see it as a problem that I, a white man, was on the Inquiry. It is surely very appropriate that I was there. If only black people argue against racism, their arguments can be more easily dismissed, as my experience at Alun Michael's roadshow demonstrates. It becomes more difficult for those who can effect change to ignore arguments when those from privileged white backgrounds also argue that discrimination against black and minority ethnic people must stop.

Within the Stephen Lawrence Inquiry, as long as the experience of racism was present in the Inquiry at the highest level, then I was comfortable with being there. John Sentamu brought relevant skills and experience to his position, one aspect of which was the experience of being black in Britain. I could bring an understanding of racism by proxy, but without John on the panel as well, my position would have been untenable. Tackling racism is a challenge that I relish. I hope that I will be able to continue for many years to use all my intellect, my emotions and my experience to reduce overt and institutional racism.

THREE

Cancellations and reinstatements

In the introduction I suggested that things happened during the Inquiry that had the potential to undermine its credibility and authority within, and outside, the black and minority ethnic communities. This chapter highlights two such incidents. The first was the cancellation and reinstatement of an overflow room for the public when the five suspects were due before the Inquiry. The second was the cancellation and reinstatement of the Inquiry's visit to Birmingham, home to the second largest black community in Britain.

The suspects face the Inquiry

Monday 29 June 1998: the 50th day of the Inquiry's public hearings. This was the day for which Doreen and Neville Lawrence, many black Britons and British anti-racists had been waiting. The five 'prime suspects' of the murder of Stephen Lawrence, notorious after having their photos splashed across the front page of the *Daily Mail* under the headline 'Murderers!' five years previously,[1] were now due to face the Stephen Lawrence Inquiry.

There was nothing in the terms of reference for the Inquiry (see the Introduction) nor was there any guidance about the degree of openness of the Inquiry to the scrutiny of the public or the media. During the preliminary discussions the Judge and his three Advisers agreed that every effort had to be made to ensure that the public would find it easy to be present during the proceedings and feel welcomed. This was a major part of the responsibility of the Secretary to the Inquiry. Also, the main hearings in Part One were 'quasi-judicial'. This was to ensure that those summoned would be required to appear before the Inquiry to be questioned; if they refused to come they would be guilty of contempt of court and could end up in prison.

All witnesses were given all the protection to which they would be entitled if their statements were being heard in a court of law. They could be represented by barristers if they so wished and, when appropriate, their lawyers would be funded by the Inquiry. The Inquiry also sent out what are known as 'Salmon' letters (as recommended by Lord Salmon after his Inquiry into public ethics in 1976) to all witnesses, which notified them in advance of the main topics about which they would be questioned.

Most witnesses were police officers who had taken part in the failed investigations of the murder. The five 'prime suspects' would also be called and would have to answer questions, unlike at the earlier inquest and private prosecution when they had almost always exercised their right to silence. An example of how difficult it was to get any of the five to say anything meaningful at the inquest is given in the Inquiry's Report:

> David Norris refused to answer any questions. "Are you called Mr Norris", asked Mr Mansfield, in some exasperation. "I'm claiming privilege", said Mr Norris, to general ironic laughter.[2]

Cancellation of the overflow room

The Inquiry anticipated that hundreds more people than usual would arrive at the Inquiry on these two days to witness Mike Mansfield QC in action questioning the five men on behalf of Mr and Mrs Lawrence. The routine presence of seven legal teams had resulted in some of the space originally planned for the public being allocated to the lawyers. We would need more than the 150 chairs usually supplied in the chamber, even with extra chairs and a limited number of people standing round the walls, it was clear that an overflow room would be needed. In the weeks before, plans had been proceeding well for an overflow room for 300 more visitors, connected to the chamber by video and sound links. At the very last moment, the Secretary, Stephen Wells, was informed by police that the planned overflow room breached health and safety regulations and could not be used. This was an alarming situation and the Secretary felt obliged to cancel the overflow room.

The first health and safety issue was the heavy cabling which was needed for the audiovisual links. By amazing coincidence I had experience of managing just such cables from my time working at Granada TV in Manchester. Many were the times I had taped heavy video cables down the sides of 1960s buildings almost identical to Hannibal House. They fitted snugly into the hollows of the vertical supporting girders between the swing opening windows, so I knew that the cables could be used quite simply and in ways that would fulfil the criteria of the health and safety regulations. No one could have ever forecast that a past life in charge of outside broadcast equipment might turn out to be relevant to challenging police advice, but this inside knowledge led me to believe that the police advice might not have been as solid as it seemed. Having helped out with the cabling, it was one health and safety problem solved; one to go.

The second issue was that there was only one entry into the proposed overflow room with no separate exit. If there was a fire people could be trapped inside. As a member of the panel concerned with community issues I was keen to ensure that the overflow room was made available. I asked to see the proposed space, and on the Friday before the Monday morning hearing Stephen Wells agreed to take me. It was true that there was only one entry and exit, but the space was in fact a large empty cavern with only three walls. The entry and exit were indeed one, but the length of a London bendy bus! There was more than ample room to get everyone out in an emergency. I suggested to Stephen Wells that we might have been misled by police officers using the health and safety issues to keep out the anticipated large numbers of black people who were about to descend on the Inquiry. He disagreed and said it would "have to go higher".[3] I was concerned that we were heading towards an irrevocable split, which could damage the work of the Inquiry. It was time to get out and go home. As I left I urged Stephen to do all he could to get the room up and running, but I feared it was a lost cause.

Three days later, on Monday 29 June, people crowded into the streets around the Elephant and Castle to get into Hannibal House where the Inquiry was based. They came from all backgrounds: from

South-East London where Stephen Lawrence had been murdered; from the rest of London; from Birmingham; from Manchester; from all over Britain. This was the chance for communities and the public far and wide to see for themselves what these men looked like, and what sort of character showed on their faces. Yet the Inquiry was seen not to have arranged adequate accommodation for all those people who had come to be present when the sparks began to fly.

The suspects were escorted in turn to the witness seat in front of the Judge and the panel of the Inquiry. They would be questioned principally by the formidable Mike Mansfield QC, representing the Lawrence family, while Ed Lawson, QC for the Inquiry, also tried within the limits of allowable questions to get helpful answers from them, as did Ian Macdonald, QC for Duwayne Brooks.[4] On their left the suspects would see 10 teams of barristers, swollen to 12 by their own lawyers. The witness chair was face on to Mr and Mrs Lawrence only 20 feet away. Twenty feet behind the Lawrences were 185 chairs set out for the public. As expected, all 185 seats were full, with as many as 50 more people standing round the walls.

All five suspects had already been questioned on two occasions – at the inquest and during the private prosecution brought by the Lawrences – and both times they had exercised their right to silence. At the Inquiry they had no right to silence so would have to talk. The price of no right to silence was, rightly in law, that there were severe restrictions on the questions allowed. This was an inquiry into "matters arising from the death of Stephen Lawrence" but it had no legal power to stray into anything that could be perceived as investigating the crime itself. Still, we believed that if anyone could expose the suspects it was Mike Mansfield QC.

The first hour was an anti-climax. The Judge had to negotiate with barristers acting for the five, to finalise what questions the witnesses could and could not be asked. Their lawyers had already taken the Inquiry to the High Court to have this clarified. The ruling confirmed that this was not a Court of Law, but an inquiry into policing, therefore questions about their involvement in the murder were forbidden, as were questions about almost any topic of significance.[5]

Perhaps the best example of the limits placed on Mr Mansfield can be found in his questioning of Luke Knight, the last of the five to be questioned. It demonstrates the huge gap between what we wanted to be asked and what was able to be asked in law. The barrister representing Luke Knight is Mr Williams.

MR MANSFIELD: Michelle Casserly. Do you know her?

MR KNIGHT: She is an ex-girlfriend of mine.

MR MANSFIELD: Any reason why she would have it in for you, particularly?

MR KNIGHT: I was a bit of a bastard to her.

MR MANSFIELD: You were. You see, I want to ask you whether you can help. You, amongst others, were named in her diary as having –

MR WILLIAMS: Sir, again I rise. I try not to rise too often, but Mr Mansfield, I fear, is trespassing again within the territory that the High Court ruled only 2 weeks ago.

THE CHAIRMAN: Is this a policing question?

MR MANSFIELD: It is in the sense that Michelle Casserly is part of the Casserly family whose diary was taken.

MR WILLIAMS: It was made quite clear in the High Court by His Lordship that issues that are only incidental to issues you are concerned with –

THE CHAIRMAN: We know, Mr Mansfield, about the entry. Of course, that is part of the evidence. If you have a question, tell me what you want to ask and I will rule whether it can be asked or not.

MR MANSFIELD: May I just put it under this category. I was not going to ask more than this. It relates to the nature of the information that the police had and actions that were taken. This diary was recovered –

THE CHAIRMAN: Ask a question, do not answer for the moment and I will rule whether you can have an answer, because you have had a long time now.

MR MANSFIELD: Yes, I appreciate that and I am grateful. The question is this: did you say anything to any of your friends in the week or two that followed, in particular the days that followed the murder, that might suggest you knew who was involved?

MR KNIGHT: Knew who was involved in what?

MR WILLIAMS: Again, sorry –

THE CHAIRMAN: I am afraid not, Mr Mansfield. The exploration of this has been gone into with the police officers. I do not think you should trespass into this. Thank you very much.[6]

The first of the five to be called was Jamie Acourt. After an hour of the preliminary wrangling between the barristers he swaggered in. He had been 16 years old at the time of the murder and now appeared to me to be a cocky and arrogant 22-year-old. He was dressed in a sharp two-piece dark grey suit with a white open-neck shirt. He lolled in his chair fielding questions from Mr Mansfield far more competently than most of the 60 police officers who had occupied the witness chair before him.[7] He presented himself to be more intelligent than I expect many had anticipated. He appeared to have been well briefed on what not to say, and what he could say without incriminating himself.

We had all seen Mr Mansfield QC reduce tough police officers to jelly with penetrating questions which had exposed their unprofessional, sloppy policing of the murder.[8] It was clear that the public wanted the suspects exposed for what they were widely believed to be: vicious racist murderers. But on this day Mr Mansfield was uncharacteristically floundering. Almost every question he wanted to ask was forbidden. All he could do was hope that in answering questions such as, "In 1993 you lived in Kidbrooke did you not?" or "This knife: was it yours?", the witness might let slip some jewel of information that would tie him to the murder.

The Metropolitan Police had earlier secretly recorded a film of four of the five, which was full of violent and racist abuse. Jamie Acourt was not in the film because he had been in prison at the time for a different minor offence, but he had been shown the film earlier. Mr Mansfield attempted to goad him into an unguarded remark by repeating what his brother said on tape and asking him to comment:

MR MANSFIELD: Neil Acourt says, whilst picking up a knife from a window ledge in the room and sticking it into the arm of a chair he says: "You rubber lipped cunt. I reckon that every nigger should be chopped up, mate, and they should be left with nothing but fucking stumps." Now, Jamie, you have forgotten that?

MR ACOURT: Yes, I have, yeah.

MR MANSFIELD: Now I have reminded you of that passage, and there are plenty more, in that vein, do you understand?

MR ACOURT: Yes.

MR MANSFIELD: Right. Shocked, are you? An honest reply, please?

MR ACOURT: I ain't shocked. It is nothing to do with me, is it? I ain't shocked.

MR MANSFIELD: You are not shocked. It is to do with you, this is your brother, and I suggest you should think twice. I am only going to ask it once again to give you one final opportunity on

—
41

this topic: do you now, looking at this passage and all the others in this tape of a similar ilk, are you now honestly shocked by the views expressed by your brother?

MR ACOURT: I have no comment on my brother – it's up to –

MR MANSFIELD: You have no comment on your brother. Alright. Have you ever heard him say these things on other occasions?

MR ACOURT: No.

MR MANSFIELD: Never?

MR ACOURT: No.

MR MANSFIELD: No other occasions?

MR ACOURT: No.[9]

The suspects face the public

After nearly an infuriating hour of questioning it was clear that Jamie Acourt was winning the war of nerves. Members of the public expressed their frustration with grunts, sniggers and occasional cries of "rubbish!", but the tension was broken by a commotion in the corridor leading to the chamber. A moment later the door burst open and in marched six members of the Nation of Islam.[10]

Suresh Grover, who was managing the Lawrence family campaign at that time, worked with other black leaders on that day to organise an orderly rotation for people excluded from the hearings to take it in turns to come into the Inquiry. It is when the police decided to block a group of Nation of Islam members from taking their turn that Leo Muhammad, the Nation of Islam's UK leader, pushed his way past security and marched in.[11]

The Inquiry and the public seemed frozen in shock. Police and stewards reacted swiftly, but not before Leo Muhammad was nose to nose with Jamie Acourt. At this point, Leo Muhammad faltered. My guess is that his plan was to get into the hearing and that was all that he wanted. He could not have foreseen that he would so quickly end up so close to one of the widely hated Acourt brothers. For the first time that day Acourt's face showed fear. He froze, as did everyone else in the room. (I doubt if he knew that the Nation of Islam turns young black men away from violence, so an assault by Leo Muhammad was very unlikely.) Within moments, however, Acourt relaxed back into an insolent slouch, probably sensing he was protected by the Inquiry's police and security. He then gave an obscene two-finger wave to the Nation's members. Sir William Macpherson called loudly for an adjournment. By now Leo Muhammad and his followers had moved back away from the witness chair, looking puzzled and at a loss about what to do next. Police and volunteer stewards supplied by the Lawrence family campaign waded in to remove the invaders from the room; Jamie Acourt was spirited out the back.

Reports of that day highlight the tensions that were running high outside as well as inside the Inquiry chamber. One BBC report gives a flavour of it:

> Questioning of the five men who were charged but not convicted of the murder of the black teenager Stephen Lawrence, had begun. But [people] confronted policemen, shouting "You are stopping the public from coming into the inquiry. You are disrespecting black people."
>
> [...] Inside the chamber, which was almost full to its 250 capacity, there was strong support for the Lawrence family. About 20 stewards from the Stephen Lawrence Family Campaign sat between the witness stand and the public gallery which contained 30 of Nation of Islam members....[12]

> Outside the chamber there was a volatile demonstration by more than 100 people who were unhappy about being

excluded from the hearing. Scuffles broke out in which police released CS gas. Two people were arrested.[13]

Inside the Inquiry Sir William Macpherson and Mr and Mrs Lawrence called for calm:

(Disturbance in the Chamber)

(The witness withdrew)

(The disturbance continued)

THE CHAIRMAN: Ladies and gentlemen, I will have to suspend the Inquiry until order is restored.

MRS LAWRENCE: Hello everybody, this is Doreen Lawrence speaking. I am going to ask you this on behalf of myself and my family. At no time within my life or my son's life have we ever interrupted anything whatsoever. The whole idea of having these boys here is for them to answer questions into what happened on the night of my son's death. With people behaving in this manner –

MEMBER OF THE PUBLIC: (inaudible) on our side, sister

MRS LAWRENCE: Well, I am sorry to hear that. Since the time of our son's murder the police attitude to us that and our family and people in the black community has been disgraceful. Now, all I wish to say is, for the safety of everybody, please could you keep calm. I am sorry for what's happening. The police are going to have their own tribunal to answer to eventually because they have been out of order, so just, please, in order for us to continue, I am going to ask everybody, please. Thank you. (Applause)

THE CHAIRMAN: We will stop for a short time, but I hope we will be able to resume soon.

(Adjournment)[14]

After about 20 minutes an attempt was made to resume and Mr Lawrence reopened the hearing with a characteristically dignified short statement:

> Everybody, thanks very much for coming this morning. As I said downstairs earlier on, this is about Stephen and everybody knows we have waited five years for this. I would like to ask people not to cause any more interruption while these proceedings are going on and if anybody feel that they cannot comply with this Inquiry I will then ask them to leave and make their protests somewhere else. Thank you very much.[15]

This was followed by discussion between the Judge and the Inquiry's own barrister, Ed Lawson QC, on how best to retrieve the timetable of the hearings. I suspect that in an ordinary court of law this discussion would have been held in private, so it is to the credit of Sir William Macpherson in this 'quasi-legal' judicial Inquiry that he recognised that the public should hear him and his barrister sorting out an embarrassing and awkward point in the proceedings.

Mr Conway, the barrister representing Jamie Acourt pleaded concern for his client's position having been "rushed at ... and assaulted",[16] and asked for the possibility of Jamie Acourt being interviewed by video link from somewhere away from the public. This led to the first major eruption by the public in 50 days of hearings, sufficient for Sir William Macpherson to have to ask the public for quiet so that the hearing could continue:

> THE CHAIRMAN: Please, please, be quiet. I know how difficult it is for you but let me see what is being said – let me hear what is being said.[17]

Mr Kendal, who represented another of the suspects, also asked for protection for his client. While Mr Conway was almost too polite, Mr Kendal was, in my opinion, too aggressive and was in danger of straying beyond his brief in a scattergun attack:

> Further, if the shouts of, 'They were spraying CS gas,' are correct, one wonders what, if any, the effect of the x-ray machines at the entrance to this building have on security.[18]

The transcripts show that the public responded pretty effectively by reducing his speech to "(inaudible due to interruption in the Chamber)".[19]

Both Mr Conway and Mr Kendal used the invasion of the Inquiry to attempt to have their clients questioned away from the hostile public. Mr Kendal stated that

> [My client] wants to give his evidence, but he would like to think that he could do it without fear of violence to himself or the others in the room.[20]

Sir William Macpherson responded to this vigorously:

> THE CHAIRMAN: Yes; thank you. I have taken advice and, in any event, would on my own initiative have made the same decision as I now make. There is [no] question at all of an audio or visual link. Those cases in which such a system is used are nearly always for young children and cases of that kind in criminal courts. So that is rejected. Secondly, the only reason for which we might contemplate hearing this evidence in private would be if all parties involved and represented, and everybody involved and represented agreed that that should be so because it would be impossible to hear the evidence otherwise. At the moment that certainly is not the case, so that that application is rejected.
>
> I noticed this morning, and I was very careful to observe what was happening, that those who were present in the Chamber behaved themselves with absolute decorum until the proceedings were broken and marred, I hope not irreparably, by the invasion of this Chamber by a group of people who I hope may be identified and identifiable. We propose to continue with the hearings at 2 o'clock. We hope there will be an audio

link by that time, but, if not, we will proceed with the hearing in any event. The information that I have from the senior police officer who is in charge is that, provided this corridor here is kept free, security of this Chamber and of those in it and of the witnesses can be guaranteed because those who are here, as I say, behaved this morning perfectly well and will do so again this afternoon, I am absolutely certain. So we will proceed at 2 o'clock.[21]

In praising the public as Sir William did in the above quote he was, as ever, courteous and respectful and insisted on continuing the hearing in public. He reiterated this with thanks to the public present and a commitment to the public hearing in a statement at the end of the same day:

... this morning's events were distressing to many people and very unfortunate. I hope that all who have been here this afternoon and who have listened to the evidence, which has been given calmly and almost in silence from the point of view of the members of the public that you will all realise that that is the right way for an Inquiry to proceed; violence and shouting and demonstration does not help us to reach the truth. [...] We will do our best to see that as many as possible of you can hear what is said and see what is said and the evidence of these young men will be completed tomorrow.[22]

The questioning of Jamie Acourt resumed with 300 or so extra members of the public able to hear him and see him by sound and video link in an overflow room beneath the Inquiry rooms as originally planned. Although, with the lack of helpful responses offered by the young men, some of those in the overflow room may have felt attending hardly worth the effort. Neil Acourt followed his brother Jamie. Evading the questions appeared to be a game to him – in 68 days of public hearings I cannot remember a single other witness who laughed at a question put to them. It did not take long to finish the questioning of Neil Acourt, so there was still enough time left that afternoon to call David Norris to the witness chair.

Questioning this witness, Mike Mansfield at one point broke off in mid-question claiming that David Norris's mother was indicating to her son what answers he should give.[23] Norris repeatedly said he could not remember details of meetings when he visited his father, Clifford Norris, who was in prison at the time.[24] Frustration with the mindless stonewalling of David Norris showed when Ian MacDonald QC, on behalf of Duwayne Brooks, asked David Norris: "Still got this general amnesia?" to which Norris replied: "It's not amnesia at all. I just simply can't remember."[25] His response was, not unsurprisingly, met with by now familiar mocking laughter from the public.

At the end of this first day of interviewing the suspects, the following statement from Mr and Mrs Lawrence was read out in front of the main entrance to the Inquiry:

> Today has been a very stressful day. We have heard first-hand from three of the suspects, but we feel they have been coached and are lying. They keep saying they can't remember and show no remorse whatsoever. It is clear that they are racist and violent. For us the struggle continues until we get justice.[26]

On the second day of interviewing the suspects Sir William asked his Advisers and the Secretary in private what they thought of acceding to a request for the five suspects to leave at the end of the day down the back staircase away from the public seething outside. I do not believe that we were being vindictive when we all agreed they should leave the Inquiry via the front entrance, not at the back.[27] The five men had clearly not come to help the Inquiry. On the contrary, they had made every effort not to remember anything of any significance and had openly shown arrogant disdain for the Inquiry and the public. Before they left, the five released a joint written statement, as the Lawrences had done the day before, denying any involvement in the murder of Stephen Lawrence and arguing that the case had been twisted and sensationalised by the media:

> In 1993 we were all arrested for the murder of Steven [sic] Lawrence, which we all vehemently deny. We do sympathise with Mr and Mrs Lawrence and the tragic loss of their son. We

understand their quest to discover what happened to their son and why no one has been convicted of his murder.

We have no knowledge of this murder, we were not involved, we did not kill Steven [sic] Lawrence.

It has been said that we have built a wall of silence around ourselves. The truth is that we have not publicly sought to argue this case through the media. Others have used the media – this case has been twisted and sensationalised. We have been powerless to have our side put across or our account given, without fear of our words being manipulated or distorted for the media's sensationalism.

We have had to defend ourselves against the prosecution by the state, an investigation which continued for almost two years, including police surveylance [sic] and bugging our homes and subsequent private prosecution.

Throughout all these proceedings there has never been a case against us which stands up to any form of scrutiny. The case was thrown out by a magistrate against two of us. At the Old Bailey, the family's private prosecution had to accept there was no case – they offered no evidence and three of us were found not guilty. Five years have now past [sic] and we are still being forced to prove our innocence, despite being acquitted. We continue to be portrayed as guilty men.

Our lives have been changed forever – we will fight these accusations until we are satisfied that our names have been cleared. It is time for us to say "enough is enough – we are innocent". We think it is time the public heard this from ourselves.[28]

In my opinion the public – black and white alike – wanted to see these men at close quarters and they themselves also had a right to be heard. As the five suspects left through the front entrance they would have protection by police officers from being physically attacked, but we agreed that they should not otherwise be helped to avoid the consequences of their behaviour. The result was well reported in the media:

> Violent scenes erupted as the five principal suspects in the Stephen Lawrence killing left the inquiry into his murder.
>
> The young white men were pelted with missiles thrown from the angry crowd of 200 who had been waiting outside the inquiry in Hannibal House in Elephant and Castle, south London. Protesters hurled abuse, shouting "murderers" and "racists" as the men walked swiftly down a ramp.
>
> As they did so fighting broke out between protesters and the men as they were attacked from either side of the ramp.
>
> Hot coffee and bottles were thrown and one of the five, David Norris, traded punches and insults with demonstrators.
>
> The men were bundled into a white van by police officers who protected the bottom of the ramp. The van sped away preceded by a police car. Police made no attempt to smuggle the men out of a back door in the building, instead opting to control the crowd.[29]

> Outside the inquiry, the five were shameless. They spat at photographers and blew kisses to the crowd. At one point they became involved in a fist fight with members of the public, who pelted them with eggs.[30]

Damage done to the Inquiry

It is my opinion that our failure to have an overflow room ready in time for the start of this day of the hearings damaged trust and confidence in the Inquiry, particularly from the very communities for whom the Inquiry was established. It is hard to imagine a more obvious example of insensitivity to community needs, especially when an acceptable overflow room was capable of being brought into action in just a few hours.

I hold no satisfaction in being proved right about the need for an overflow room; it was my failure to make it happen when I realised it was necessary. If I had shared my concerns with my fellow panel members, all three of us together could have reported the problem to Sir William, and a united demand from the panel could have changed the outcome. In my defence I can only say that time was not on my side. By the time I had reached the impasse with Stephen Wells it must have been 4pm on the Friday before the questioning was due to start on the Monday. The idea of getting agreement to overrule the Secretary this late in the day, let alone organising the room on a Saturday or Sunday, all seemed impossible.

It was a pity that there had been no terms of reference or job description for me as an Adviser. Similarly I cannot find any for the Secretary. Neither I nor Mr Wells had procedures on how we should deal with disagreement and conflict. In the end, I chose to back down, hopefully before lasting damage was done to our working relationship. However, the damage to the authority of the Inquiry was considerable and criticism of the Inquiry was implicit in much of the press coverage at the time.[31]

I do not know why the Secretary accepted the decision taken by the police not to approve the overflow room. I had done my best to explain to him that it was a decision which would expose both of us as well as the Inquiry to criticism from black communities. I had argued that it was possible that the police involved were manipulating the health and safety argument to avoid the need to deal with a public likely to be hostile to the police; that I was as vulnerable as he to that manipulation and that we needed to work together to sort out what was best for the Inquiry. It did not occur to me at the time to question what he meant by "having to go higher" in response to my complaints on the issue. The subject never came up in discussions with the Judge, so I have to assume that it was with his senior at the Home Office that he took it up. But what was it about this incident that needed to go higher within the Home Office? If it was about my position on the Inquiry and the only fall out was damage to my reputation within the civil service, I can live with that easily enough. However, to make a decision for the benefit of the Inquiry contrary to the recommendations of the police (who are also indirectly employed by the Home Office), without guidance from senior Home Office colleagues would have been very difficult for Stephen Wells to do. I recognise that any secretary to an inquiry who is there by virtue of secondment from his civil service job may therefore be put in an impossible position of conflict of interest.

The cancelled visit to Birmingham

Some months later Stephen Wells and I had our second serious disagreement, this time over a proposal to cancel the Inquiry's visit to Birmingham, to meet the large black community there. It seems to me that the significance of this visit may not have been made clear to the Judge by his Secretary. Whatever Mr Wells gave as a reason, it must have been in terms of urgency or insignificance that the Judge did not turn to his Advisers before agreeing to cancel. This time it was not just one Adviser who disagreed with the proposal, but two: John Sentamu as well as me. On this occasion the proposal was overruled before the event, not during it. It was a decision of the Inquiry to discuss our recommendations with black communities outside South-East London.[32] We would have looked foolish and not been thorough enough in our collection of public evidence if we did not include Birmingham in our visits.

I have puzzled over why it was even considered that we drop the Birmingham visit given the significance of this black community. Why did the topic not come to the Advisers before a decision was made? For the next few years the only remotely valid reason I could think of for the cancellation was that maybe Mr Wells decided that pressure from the Home Office to deliver our Report before the Christmas vacation was of greater importance than a day of hearings in Birmingham.

In the end, the Report was completed in early 1999 rather than late 1998. I cannot say whether or not the delay undermined the Report in any way; I am not privy to conversations about this that may have taken place within Whitehall. I have not heard anyone complaining from a community perspective. What I do know is that the visit to Birmingham could not be ignored.

The problems with the visit to Birmingham began with a press release which gave venues and dates for Part Two hearings of the Inquiry and announced visits to East London, to West London and to Manchester, Bradford and Bristol.[33] Muhammad Idrish of the Asian Resource Centre in Handsworth, Birmingham, responded to this press release with a firecracker:

> We were given to understand that the second part of your Inquiry will travel round the country [...] I am disappointed that you do not plan to visit Birmingham.
> [...]
> Black populations of Birmingham have suffered from acts of Racism [in the] same way as Black people in other part of the country but it has got its own unique characteristics. Never forget that [the] notorious Enoch Powell River of Blood speech was made in Birmingham – its ghost still haunts us.
> We demand that your Inquiry comes to Birmingham and listens to us.[34]

The reply Muhammad Idrish initially received was discouraging, stating that the visit to Birmingham had been difficult to arrange because of "diary availability of the Inquiry team ... [particularly] at a time when there are many Jewish festivals for [Dr Stone] to attend" and because of a lack of suitable venues.[35]

Even now, 14 years later, I feel uncomfortable reading this letter. The Secretary has written to a total stranger, with an obviously Muslim name, about the need "to be sensitive to Dr Richard Stone's [...] position as a senior member of the Jewish faith". I can see no need to single out any of the Advisers in this correspondence; the reasons for our unavailability would be irrelevant to Mr Idrish. He continues "you, I am sure, would wish us to be sensitive to the community and faith-based commitments of the Inquiry team". The main issue, according to the letter sent to Mr Idrish was the problem in finding a venue in a week when all appropriate venues were apparently booked up, but there is no suggestion that venues could be sought for another week.

It so happened that Muhammad Idrish and I have a mutual respect for each other's religious background. His immediate response to hearing of the cancellation was to telephone me. It appears that the Bishop of Birmingham phoned my colleague on the Inquiry, Bishop John Sentamu, at more or less the same time that Mr Idrish telephoned me. The result was that Sir William Macpherson was immediately badgered by two of his Advisers about the cancellation.

Councillor Roy Benjamin, Chair of Equalities in Birmingham City Council, had also written to the Inquiry team and received a response in similar vein to that sent to Mr Idrish, apologising for not being able to visit to Birmingham. A letter of reply from Councillor Benjamin, found only in 2012 in the correspondence files made available in November 2011, throws an unflattering light on the process used by the Inquiry's Secretariat to find a venue in Birmingham.

> I am writing to request that you reconsider your decision to not hold a full inquiry session in Birmingham as part of your second stage hearings schedule.
>
> I have sought to gather together the rather unfortunate series of events which seem to have culminated in an impression being created that somehow there was no suitable venue available in Birmingham. Having this year hosted the European Home and Justice Ministers conference; G8; Eurovision and the International Lions Convention – not to mention a host of other large events, it seems somewhat inconceivable that the Inquiry was unable to find space in Britain's second city.
>
> The process used by your office for approaching Birmingham was, I have to say, somewhat perfunctory. According to my information only the Birmingham Convention and Visitors Bureau (BCVB) was contacted, furthermore according to staff at BCVB the first contact was only made on July 27th and in addition no indication was given which enabled the staff to distinguish your request from any other run of the mill enquiry. Given

> the terms of reference for your Part Two Hearings and
> given local Government's pivotal role in seeking to tackle
> racially motivated crime. I am surprised that no letter
> or contact was made with the City Council via either
> the Chief Executive or the leader of the council. I can
> assure you that had a single connection been made then
> this situation could have been avoided. Nevertheless, I
> do hope you will reconsider your decision. Birmingham
> is the regional focus for the Midlands. Over 20% of all
> black and minority people live in this region. [...][36]

In this letter Councillor Benjamin is angry enough to have gone to
considerable trouble to substantiate his criticisms. He concludes with
"I can assure you that [...] this situation could have been avoided".
These remarks strongly contradict the assurance made by Mr Wells
to Mr Idrish that "Staff here were at great pains to attempt to secure
a suitable venue in Birmingham."[37]

Shortly after, a venue was found and the visit to Birmingham
reinstated:

> I am pleased now to be able to write to say that Sir
> William found it possible to extend his period of
> consultation, and we now expect to hold a meeting in
> public [...] in the National Indoor Arena on Friday, 13
> November. [...][38]

It was very damaging for our reputation in the community. I spoke
with Muhammad Idrish 14 years after the visit to Birmingham, as
well as with Maxie Hayles, who was mentioned in one of Stephen
Wells's letters. Maxie Hayles was well-known as the Director of
a key anti-racist voluntary organisation, the Birmingham Racial
Attacks Monitoring Unit (BRAMU). He, like Muhammad Idrish,
has worked for many years in the same job; still fighting the forces
of discrimination (although, sadly, grants for BRAMU dried up in
2012 and it officially closed in September). I asked both of them if
they thought the decision to cancel the planned visit to Birmingham
had affected the authority of the Inquiry. They both said that it had.

Muhammad Idrish felt that the Secretary "may have misled him and others over the lack of venues"[39] and that it took six months after the cancellation then reinstatement, for local activists to get over their resentment at the Inquiry.

Summing up the effects of the two cancellations

What do these two incidents say about the Inquiry and how it was undermined? In the first, after all the drama, an overflow room took only about two hours to set up. There were hundreds of people, members of the public who had every right to view the proceedings, who were kept out. Many had come from distant parts of the country, as well as from areas across London miles away from the Inquiry venue. Media attention directed on the Inquiry at this crucial time was focused on the external tussles between public and the police, rather than on the young men being questioned and their responses.

The debacle around the visit to Birmingham is another example of the small ways in which the authority of the Inquiry was undermined with the communities. The reinstatement of the visit only partly redeemed its reputation and its authority; it had been a major gaffe. If the final conclusions of the Inquiry had not been so powerful it may not have survived the anger of the black and Asian communities in Birmingham. The lack of effort apparently made to find an appropriate venue and the speed with which the problem was later resolved echo the cancellation and reinstatement of the overflow room in Part One. The reasons for the cancellation were questionable; this is the problem with secondments and the possible conflicts of interests that then arise. One community leader went so far as to suggest that the Birmingham cancellation was influenced by the city council/West Midlands Police. There is no evidence to support this, but this is what can happen when there is a lack of transparency and independence.

Both incidents were distinctly unhelpful to the reputation of the Inquiry. The cancellation in Birmingham if it had gone ahead, and coupled with cancellation of the overflow room had that not been reinstated, would surely have attracted negative publicity. Imagine in the final months of the Inquiry headlines such as: 'Stephen Lawrence

Inquiry yet again insults Black communities!'; 'Judge again refuses to answer Black community needs.' The overturning of these two misguided decisions surely justifies the Home Office decision to attach three Advisers to the panel of the Stephen Lawrence Inquiry and raises questions about how a seconded Secretary can remain independent. This is a topic to which I will return in the final chapter.

FOUR

The Commissioner takes the stand

Part One of the Stephen Lawrence Inquiry exposed incompetent policing at every level, from the bottom of the hierarchy of the Metropolitan Police to the very top.[1] These findings were reported widely in the media throughout the Inquiry so by June 1998, towards the end of Part One, there was mounting pressure for apologies from senior representatives of the police force.[2] Surely the Metropolitan Police Commissioner at the time, Sir Paul Condon, would come to the Inquiry to express the vast apologies required to wipe away six years of inefficiencies and false reassurances at every level? Sadly, it was the Assistant Commissioner (AC) Ian Johnston, who appeared in Part One of the Inquiry with the brief to make the apologies.[3]

AC Johnston had been Deputy Assistant Commissioner at the time of Stephen's death. On 17 June 1998, day 45 of the 57 in Part One, he was due to be a witness to clarify his own role in the murder investigation. First thing on that morning he asked if he could make a statement. As a public apology, this statement would logically have been made after all the witnesses had been questioned, which would make the appropriate time for it at the end of Part One, rather than in the middle of it. Making the apology too early brought the quasi-judicial proceedings of Part One to a juddering halt at a time of high tension.

AC Johnston apologised to the Lawrences. He apologised to them again. He apologised on behalf the Commissioner. He apologised on behalf of the whole Metropolitan Police. He apologised for his own earlier refusal to apologise. I felt embarrassed for this quiet, well respected senior officer as he read such a cringeworthy statement.

> Mr Lawrence, I wanted to say to you that I am truly sorry that we have let you down. It has been a tragedy for you: you have lost a son, and not seen his killers brought to justice. It has

---

been a tragedy for the Metropolitan Police, who have lost the confidence of a significant section of the community for the way we have handled the case. I can understand and explain some of what went wrong. I cannot and do not seek to justify it. [...] I am very, very sorry and very, very sad that we have let you down. Looking back now, I can see clearly that we could have and we should have done better. I deeply regret that we have not put his killers away. On behalf of myself, the Commissioner – who specifically asked me to associate himself with these words – and the whole of the Metropolitan Police, I again offer my sincere and deep apologies to you. I do hope that one day you will be able to forgive us. Finally, I would like to add my own personal apologies for supporting the earlier investigation in ways in which it has now been shown that I was wrong. I hope the reasons for my support will be understood, and I hope that, eventually, you will forgive me for that, as well, Mr Lawrence.[4]

It was a pity that Mrs Lawrence was not there to hear this apology. Since there had been no forewarning of the statement she would not have known to change whatever diary commitment took her elsewhere that day.

AC Johnston could have been forgiven for expecting to be able to move on now to questions about his role in the murder investigation; Ed Lawson, QC on behalf of the Inquiry, customarily only questioned witnesses to clarify facts which needed to be put on the record. He would then hand over to the barristers representing the Lawrence family and Duwayne Brooks, whose questions would dig deeper. On this day, Mr Lawson felt it necessary to ask a preliminary question about racism in the police:

... arising out of what you have just said – as you have, if I may say so, properly acknowledged with hindsight that you, collectively, could and should have done better?

A. Yes.

> Q. And mistakes were undoubtedly made, as I think you acknowledge?
>
> A. Yes, sir.
>
> Q. I think I should ask you to address two issues that go beyond incompetence and the making of mistakes. You know it has long been suggested by the Lawrence family and by others that the investigation was tainted by racism?
>
> A. Yes, sir.
>
> Q. What, if any, views do you wish to express about that?[5]

Reading the transcripts 13 years later, I am reminded of how AC Johnston's body language, as well as the verbal language he used, appeared to change dramatically at this point. From hesitant and almost grovelling during the statement, his back straightened; now he was no longer reading out a statement of 'his master's voice', but using his intelligence and experience to struggle with a tricky question.

> A. If the Lawrences feel that, that is very, very important; and it is for us to demonstrate that that is not the case. It is my firm belief that that is not the case. It is quite right that their concerns about it should be thoroughly and properly explored; and I can understand some of the analysis that leads them to that conclusion. [...] I do hope that colleagues who have been here have left some impression of their views around this issue and the extent to which they were influenced or not by racist attitudes.[6]

AC Johnston had been put in an impossible position: torn between loyalty to his officers, but confronted with the need for the whole police service to acknowledge they had failed a decent black British family. Only the Commissioner had the authority to stray beyond the carefully crafted wording of the statement, but I suspect that the Metropolitan Police's chief officers had not planned for any follow-up questions on the statement. I think AC Johnston had genuine feelings for the plight of Mr and Mrs Lawrence, but I sensed that he could not say what he really felt.

The questioning continued in this vein (with some responses more coherent than others), until an important point was revealed:

> Q. Do you recognise, on behalf of the Metropolitan Police – and I ask you these questions because you are, after all, the senior serving officer who I understand we are to hear from – do you recognise that because of, if you like, the sheer volume of mistakes (which I think, by and large, now are conceded) that the police service has opened itself to the suggestion that if it was not overtly affected by race, there may have been some subliminal or some subconscious effect of race?[7]

It was highly unusual for Mr Lawson to 'go for' a witness in this manner; more aggressive lines of questioning were usually left to the other legal teams. Sadly, Ed Lawson died in 2009, so I can only surmise why he broke with usual practice. What is clear from the question above is that Mr Lawson takes it for granted that the Assistant Commissioner was going to be the most senior officer to appear at Part One of the Inquiry.

When Sir William Macpherson had choices, particularly in delicate matters to do with community sensitivities, he brought them first to his Advisers before making a decision. I have no memory of any prior discussions about the Commissioner not appearing in Part One of the Inquiry (as he would be expected to do), nor, as far as I can tell from the limited correspondence files available at the time of writing, there are no copies of letters to or from the Commissioner about this.[8] The lack of discussion and Mr Lawson's words suggest to me that the non-appearance in Part One by the Commissioner had been presented as a *fait accompli* to Sir William. If this were so then I assume that Sir William would inform Mr Lawson that questions we had wanted to put to the Commissioner now would need to be presented to his Assistant Commissioner. It is possible (and speculation on my part) that Mr Lawson realised that Mr Mansfield and Mr Macdonald (Counsel for the Lawrences and for

Duwayne Brooks) were not aware that this was their only chance to raise issues which they would have been expecting to present to the Commissioner himself. By going, quite startlingly, outside his brief and into their territory, was he sending them a signal that this was the highest ranking officer that they would be able to question under oath? Unless Mr Lawson was unable to pass on such information, indirect signals were not really necessary – Mr Mansfield and Mr Macdonald sat only a few feet away from Mr Lawson; they were able to whisper to one another during the Inquiry proceedings and send one another notes. Perhaps there was some other reason why Mr Lawson felt moved to go for Mr Johnston.

In the correspondence files made available at The National Archives in March 2012, I found a small extra nugget from this saga: a personal note to Sir William Macpherson from Ed Lawson. It is perhaps almost too personal to include here, but it is in the public domain along with the other correspondence and documentation of the Inquiry. My recollection of Ed Lawson was of his absolute commitment that no information should be hidden which tells the truth; an obituary noted him also to be "renowned for his ability to inject humour or venom into proceedings as required".[9]

On reflection I decided to include his note in the book. The hand-written memo in Ed's writing reads: "Bill. Re Johnson's proposed 'opening statement'. See the attached. Please try to read it (a) with a straight face, & (b) without throwing-up! EL" Then a note is added in Bill's writing: "Seen & heard! WM. 2.7.98."[10]

It was bad enough to see AC Johnston floundering during Ed Lawson's questioning, but it was also pretty obvious to me he was floundering because he was not the Commissioner. As I listened to the Assistant Commissioner squirm, I felt growing anger towards the Commissioner for his failure to make an apology to the Lawrences and to the public in person. Despite assertions made openly that the Commissioner was at the Inquiry's disposal, I felt we had been fobbed off with his Assistant Commissioner. The Lawrences made a statement later that day calling Sir Paul Condon to answer in person questions to the Inquiry and calling for his resignation.[11] When he did appear in Part Two of the Inquiry, the Commissioner faced a hostile reception from the start. I believe that this began with his undermining the sincerity of the Metropolitan Police's apologies by sending his Assistant Commissioner to make them.

Sir Paul Condon faces the Inquiry

So, the Commissioner of the Metropolitan Police Service, Sir Paul Condon (now Lord Condon), chose to come before the Inquiry only during Part Two. In Part Two the Inquiry was no longer quasi-judicial; witnesses were not bound by oath and none of the rules about questioning and cross-questioning applied. At that stage, Sir Paul could not be pressed on any difficult issues. Even so, the day when the Commissioner presented to the Inquiry, on the third day of Part Two, it felt like a long-awaited climax to the proceedings.

The panel had hoped to hear the presentation of the Metropolitan Police before hearing from any other police organisations. This was largely because we had been told by the Commissioner that much had already been done to address the concerns that had been raised during the hearings in Part One of the Inquiry, including in AC Johnston's statement to the Inquiry discussed above. The panel thought it would therefore be helpful to know what the Metropolitan Police Service had already done and what it had plans to do, before being presented with suggestions for recommendations from other organisations and individuals. Unfortunately, this presented us with some organisational problems. The Inquiry's diary was tight and commitments of the Metropolitan Police officers due to appear before the Inquiry meant that dates needed to be changed. One potential date for questioning coincided with a Jewish High Holy Day: Yom Kippur, the Jewish Day of Atonement.

Yom Kippur meant that I would be in synagogue all day. Sir William suggested that I need not be there and that the Inquiry team could manage one day without me, but I felt that meeting the Metropolitan Police Commissioner at last was far too important for me to miss. That clinched it; schedules were rearranged and presentations from the Metropolitan Police Service were postponed into the following week.

Yom Kippur also had a significant impact on the way I questioned the Commissioner the following day. Yom Kippur is a day of communal acceptance of our sins and the possibility of repentance. As the 25-hour fast draws to its close with approaching dusk, much is made of the doors of repentance swinging shut, but the doors are still open until the first star of evening signals the end of the day. Echoes of Yom Kippur can be heard in my pleas to Sir Paul Condon to acknowledge institutional racism (see below in this chapter).

On the day of the hearing, 1 October 1998, day 3 of Part 2, Sir Paul Condon was accompanied by Assistant Commissioner (AC) Dennis O'Connor and Deputy Assistant Commissioner (DAC) John Grieve, who was then head of the new Racial and Violent Crime Taskforce. Unfortunately, these two officers did not get much of a look in, with the Commissioner being questioned throughout the morning.

The Commissioner did, at last, apologise personally in his opening statement to the Inquiry, over three months since the profuse apologies from AC Johnston:

> I believe, Chairman, that it is right and just as Commissioner that I should be here today, that I should experience the anger and frustration felt by many in the community about the tragic death of Stephen. Most of all it is my duty to be here to recognise the courage and dignity of Mr & Mrs Lawrence. I deeply regret that we have not brought Stephen's racist murderers to justice. I would like to personally apologise again today to Mr & Mrs Lawrence for our failures. Also, I do not forget Duwayne Brooks and his needs and the sense that he should have been given more support.[12]

A cynic might think that no apology the Commissioner made at this stage could have been acceptable. If it was too short whatever he said would be seen as too little and too late; if his apology was more profuse, it would be too much, and much too late. I suspect the public had become sick of apologies, having heard so many of them weeks before. Suffice to say that I remember a fair bit of tutting and sniffing directed at Sir Paul Condon from the public seats, although not enough (as yet) to warrant even a mild reprimand from Sir William Macpherson.

The Commissioner then pressed on with telling the Inquiry about the raft of improvements that had already been achieved in addressing the incompetence shown by his officers during the (by then) two investigations of the murder, and during the review of those two failed investigations by Detective Chief Superintendent John Barker. He was also keen to tell us about the plans he had for changing police culture to bring it into line with the agenda of the Stephen Lawrence Inquiry. After about 20 minutes of the Commissioner's catalogue of improvements in policing with regards to racism, improvements that he had implemented in recent months, Sir Paul started to recount a more personal story:

> [When] I joined the Met by accident on the first day, (pause) –[13]

That "(pause)" reported in the transcript, was Sir Paul looking round to find out where the heckling was coming from, but he was not to be deflected from telling his story. The story is a familiar one from people caught offending someone from a minority community; we Jews call it the 'some of my best friends are Jewish' story.

> literally by accident in becoming a police officer; literally by accident in terms of it was the first day that a colleague from an ethnic minority background joined the Met. So I have seen the development from just one colleague, one courageous colleague through to today. When I came back as Commissioner I had the privilege to meet again with that colleague on many occasions and I had the privilege of celebrating his career at his retirement party last year.[14]

The hubbub from the public was beginning to swamp the Commissioner's story. We, and many of the public, knew Sir Paul Condon's "courageous colleague". He had come frequently to the Inquiry, quietly sitting in the public area. His name was David Michael, a black Metropolitan Police officer who had brought a successful action against his employers for racist discrimination in the 1990s,[15] and who had indeed needed to be 'courageous' to take on the police establishment as he did. People were entitled to ask how Sir Paul had made such an ill-advised choice as an example to demonstrate his anti-racist credentials: a black officer and a white officer start out on the force together; the white one ends up as Commissioner, and the black one as a Chief Inspector with a nasty employment tribunal under his belt.

The mention of David Michael was made by way of introduction to statistics on the recruitment of minority ethnic staff:

> The number of colleagues from a minority ethnic community has increased by 50% during my Commissionership and is now at 865 that represents about 3.3% of the strength of the Met. At point of recruitment it varies from 6% to 8% year to year. So we are growing in terms of the number of colleagues from minority ethnic background, but I am impatient. It is not fast enough. It is not rapid enough.[16]

Police data collecting is fairly accurate;[17] the problem with it is the selection of data and spin added to it by senior officers. Here, the increase by 50% of minority ethnic 'colleagues' highlighted above makes no distinction between black 'staff' and black police constables. In my review of racism in the police 10 years after the Inquiry,[18] recruitment figures for black and minority police were quoted to be 7% – a significant increase from just 2% in 1998/99, which was therefore "well within the target" set 10 years before. In 2008/09 figures included the new police community support officers (PCSOs), but 10 years earlier this rank had not yet been invented. This was therefore not like for like data. Comparing data for constables alone, the increase in recruits was just 2.5%. A more recent Home Office report separates out figures for PCSOs, and gives the figure for black and minority ethnic officers in England and Wales as still only 4.8%. The largest proportion of minority ethnic officers is in the Metropolitan Police (9.6%) but with black and minority ethnic officers very underrepresented at senior ranks (across England and Wales only 3.3% at chief inspector or above).[19]

The charge of institutional racism

The Inquiry, in the pursuit to "gather information and opinions" as set out in the terms of reference, wanted to hear what the Commissioner had to tell us about positive changes and future plans. The Inquiry was, however, equally determined to hear from the Commissioner an acknowledgement that institutional racism existed within the police service. A large part of the morning was devoted to pressing for that acknowledgement by each of the panel members in turn, each of us choosing a different approach. It quickly became clear to us that this acknowledgement was a step too far for the Commissioner; he would not yield to any pressure to acknowledge institutional racism. He acknowledged most of the aspects of institutional racism, but appeared to be unable to take the final step to accepting that it existed within the Metropolitan Police:

> I accept that a central concern of this Inquiry is around racism in the Met and I will return to that in a few moments. I acknowledge that society and the police service, in particular, have not done enough to combat racist crime and harassment. The skills and resources that have been applied successfully to many other areas have not routinely been brought to bear on the issues of combating racial crime and I think there is clearly scope for far more to be done and it will be done and it must be done.

> This Inquiry, sir, has expressed concern about the disproportionate application of police powers to some minority ethnic groups and particularly stop and search. Race or stereotypes clearly have an opportunity to be played out in the exercise of that discretion and I will say more about that in a while.

> The academic analysis which you have had revealed to you, and there is far more, reveals the *complexity* of the issues of disproportionality and the limitations of seeking simplistic interpretation of the data. This is a *complex* issue and I know is

—

> central to many of your thoughts. My plea is that a superficial analysis that does not ignore the *complexity* of this situation will not actually take us forward.[20] [italics added]

Sir Paul seems to have been tangled up in a web of *complexities*. Perhaps he was getting tired, but the entanglement has affected his otherwise clear use of English. He has produced a double negative of complexities which leaves him proposing the solution that all members of the Inquiry panel were pressing him to accept.

Acknowledging 'institutional racism' is not a complex issue. The Commissioner accepts every premise of the concept and has instituted programmes that address it. Several of his colleagues have acknowledged it. All he has to do is acknowledge it too. By refusing to take this logical final step he must weave complexities to justify his position.

His refusal establishes a framework for failure to make the necessary changes. Faced with such a stated degree of "complexity" it was perhaps inevitable that the disparities in stop and search, and in the employment of black and minority ethnic officers still continue to be an unresolved issue in our police forces.[21] When Sir Paul Condon finally addressed the issue of institutional racism (perhaps surprisingly, it was he who raised the issue first when we had prepared to have to challenge him on the subject), it was, inevitably, prefixed with a couple of "complexities":

> Chairman, if I could mention the *complexities* of your task – if I may give an opinion on some of those *complexities*. Chairman, you and the members of the team have repeatedly pointed out the significance of words and phrases. You have raised important issues in your efforts, to use your words sir, "to grapple" with the concept of "institutional racism" as applied to the police service. Lord Scarman [...] concluded, "the direction and policies of the Met are not racist". I maintain this is still true to that definition. I have serious reservations – not for me or for the Met – I have serious reservations for the future of these important issues if the expression "institutional racism"

is used in a particular way. I am not in denial. I am not seeking weasel words.[22] [italics added]

Methinks the Commissioner doth protest too much.

I am not denying the challenge or the need for reform, but if … this Inquiry labels my service as "institutionally racist" (pause) then the average police officer, the average member of the public will assume the normal meaning of those words. They will assume a finding of conscious, willful, or deliberate action or an action to the detriment of ethnic minority Londoners. They will assume the majority of good men and women who come into policing to serve their fellow men go home to their families; go to their churches; go to their voluntary groups; go about their daily lives with racism in their minds and in their endeavour. I actually think that use of those two words in a way that would take on a new meaning to most people in society would actually undermine many of the endeavors to identify and respond to the issues of racism which challenge all institutions and particularly the police because of their privileged and powerful position. [...]

I am not hiding behind definition. I cannot wait for the world to settle on words or definitions.[23]

Pressing the Commissioner to acknowledge institutional racism

When Sir William Macpherson finally negotiated his way to the most crucial questions of the day about institutional racism, the Commissioner continued to be in denial. The exchanges on this point are so important that the transcript is given in full in Appendix C; the most significant points are included in this chapter:

> THE CHAIRMAN: ... do you accept or do you not accept that unconscious or covert racism was evident and at large in any area of the Stephen Lawrence Inquiry?

> SIR CONDON: I have been the most vigorous critic of the police service on many aspects. If I believed with my knowledge now all that I know of this case that racism or corruption by any normal use of those terms impacted this case in any way I would not have hesitated to say so, sir, or to say so today. I honestly sincerely believe that by any ordinary use of those words, those issues did not influence this tragic case. [24]

Sir William tries a different tack:

> Do you accept that in the police force, using another expression which I hope is clear, that there is apparent, not everywhere, but there is apparent in the police force a collective failure through the attitudes and approach of police officers, particularly at the lower level, and discrimination, conscious or unconscious, which amounts to a general malaise in certain quarters in the force.

> SIR CONDON: I will answer that specifically, but in relation to this case, in relation to this tragic case I have acknowledged insensitivities, clumsiness, lack of awareness, lack of consideration which should have been dealt with better. My anxiety again with this notion of some mysterious collective will that somehow people don't – intelligent, well-meaning people don't actually know what they are doing, I think again is a difficult definition to acknowledge. [25]

At the end of this answer Sir Paul attempts to draw in Assistant Commissioner O'Connor to assist, but Sir William brushes this aside:

> THE CHAIRMAN: Let me if I may give you two examples which may figure in our report. The first really comes from the evidence of Mrs Lawrence herself, who [...] said more than

> once "they were patronising", "they patronised me because I
> was black", and that was collective. It wasn't just one officer.
> It was the approach. That was a collective failure. The second
> example is this: Half a dozen officers in terms before us refused
> to accept that this was purely a racially motivated or a racist
> crime. [...] Nobody picked them up and nobody questioned
> that plainly wrong approach. So that is a collective failure. You
> accept that those features may amount to institutional racism?

> SIR CONDON: [...] by them describing those challenges and
> those issues as institutional racism I think you then extrapolate
> to all police officers at all times this notion that they are
> walking around just waiting to do something that is going to
> be labelled "institutional racism" because of some collective
> failure.[26]

The Commissioner does not yield an inch to the Judge, but worse,
in my opinion, his words demonstrate that he truly has not listened
and does not understand the issues:

> I am not defending what [the officers] said or how they behaved
> but I think when in such a challenging environment I think
> many of them took comfort in what they thought was safe
> territory. Safe territory is, say: I treat everyone the same, I
> am colour blind. I do not know what was in the mind [...] of
> the assailants...[27]

Only the previous week HM Inspectorate of Constabulary (HMIC)
had stated that it was no longer enough to treat people equally, we
have to treat them according to their needs.[28] This outright rejection
of the tired old "colour blind" dogma would soon be repeated by the
Inspectorate directly to the Inquiry, to cheers from the public present.
Not only had Sir Paul Condon apparently not listened to Mr and
Mrs Lawrence, he had not listened to his colleagues over at HMIC.

It was then the turn of the Advisers to question the Commissioner;
first up was Tom Cook who immediately requested a return to
the question of institutional racism. He read some highly relevant

paragraphs from the black charity The 1990 Trust, before taking up where Sir William Macpherson had left off:

> I recognise your difficulty with the label of institutional racism and your reluctance to accept it at any price, as it were, that has been quite evident here today. [...] But I do wonder whether the Metropolitan Police Service is over-defensive on this and related issues. I quote some of your words this morning, you said: "The police service can amplify social disadvantage" a nice sounding phrase, I am not entirely sure what it means but it seems to be a substitution for words such as "stereotyping" and "racism". [...]

> I accept [...] one could legitimately deny institutional racism if it is defined solely in terms of deliberate racist policies. No one, as I am aware, makes that suggestion. The Black Police Association certainly did not make that suggestion. ACPO in their presentation indicated equally a wish not to get hung up on abstract definitions but totally accepted the concept of institutional racism. ...[29]

As noted in Chapter One, Tom Cook was a former detective and a former Deputy Chief Constable. At the time of the Inquiry both he and Sir Paul Condon were members of the Association of Chief Police Officers (ACPO). In mentioning the Black Police Association alongside the highly respected ACPO was to treat the organisation with a new respect. This was also picked up by the media and by the Home Office, and suddenly the Black Police Association were no longer a minor player, a marginalised group in the anti-racist camp, they had moved into the big time.[30]

After going over the significance of disproportionality in stop and search, Tom Cook pushes the Commissioner to yield just a bit:

> [...] And if institutional racism or even if the word "institutional" were dropped and racism in the police service was described in those terms in that context, would you then accept that

the police service is racist and the Metropolitan Police Service with it? [...]

SIR CONDON: [...] So I acknowledge and I have said today, I thought I had said today, there is racism in the police service. [...] I am acknowledging now racism in the service, all of the things that you have described. If, in describing that in ways of unconscious or collective, I am not denying any of that, that does not stop me offering you the challenges of applying particularly to those issues.

MR COOK: [...] Would you accept the premise that "unconscious racism" by individual officers is widespread and leads to discrimination in the police service?

SIR CONDON: Not as you put it. If you say "widespread".[31]

For a moment I thought Tom Cook had done it, but it was not to be. The public left us in no doubt about their opinion on these comments and needed to be calmed by Sir William.[32] Sir Paul appeared to be rattled by this and, after repeating a number of times that he was not in denial, I could see John Sentamu was getting restless. I sensed from his body language that he was itching to try a different tactic to get the Commissioner to acknowledge institutional racism and I was beginning to wonder whether there would be any time for me to question to the Commissioner at all.

I confess I was unsure if I would be able to contain myself when questioning Sir Paul, in the face of his constant denial of institutional racism and his repeated protestations about hearing the anger and frustration felt by Mr and Mrs Lawrence. Yet I would not have forgiven myself if I had been alone in not attempting to puncture the Commissioner's empty rhetoric. Maybe John Sentamu had thought of an ingenious plan to force Sir Paul into a corner from which he could not escape without acknowledging institutional racism existed in the Met?

I want to put to you what Mr Paul Wilson said in evidence, a member of the Black Police Association. He said: "[...] we consider that institutional racism plays a significant part in the way the police perceive the black community and treat the black community. [...] The term 'institutional racism' should be understood to mean the way the institution or the organisation may systematically or repeatedly treat or tend to treat people differentially because of their race." In fact we are not talking about individuals within the service who may be unconscious as to the nature of what they are doing ... it isn't about there are people who smoke, but that because some people smoke there is a lot of smoke in the room. ...it seems to me you seem to acknowledge there is racism but actually don't seem to think it has got this pervasive effect cumulatively on the black community.

SIR CONDON: No, I would never say that, Bishop. I hope you are [sic] heard me in your presence many times not say that. To use your analogy, just one instance of racism by a police officer – if it is the smoke analogy – can contaminate the whole room. [...] You and I debated these issues on many occasions and hopefully you will give me credit for my acknowledgment of racism and how pernicious it can be within the police service.

BISHOP SENTAMU: You have read "Winning The Race", the special report. Again there was something there, in the summary it says: "There was continuing evidence during the inspection of inappropriate language and behaviour by police officers, but even more worrying was the lack of intervention by sergeants and inspectors". You acknowledge this is true of the Met as well?

SIR CONDON: Yes I do, absolutely.

BISHOP SENTAMU: That is what probably some people are referring to as "institutional racism".

SIR CONDON: If that is the term you wish to apply, fine. I mean, I am not challenging your right to do it. As I say, nor could I and should I. But for me the real challenge is how we move forward. I am not in denial. I have said to you. I have explained to

MR COOK: You have heard me say—

DR STONE: You have told us ten times. Please don't tell us again you are not in denial.[33]

I have curled up in embarrassment ever since that day when I remember how I so rudely interrupted John Sentamu at this point. Only when I read the transcript in 2012 did I realise that Tom Cook was doing the same. It appears that we all three had reached the limits of our patience at the same point. John Sentamu eventually asked the Commissioner:

... how are you going to change the attitudes and practices and what is your strategy? I haven't quite yet heard that. Maybe then I wouldn't be hung up about phrases.[34]

The question was passed over to DAC O'Connor who, in response, handed out summaries of the Metropolitan Police's plan for addressing racism and provided a full overview of its contents. We can reflect now that perhaps, however fine this anti-racist plan appeared to be in 1998, it did not produce the outcomes that it was intended to achieve.[35]

After AC O'Connor's outline of plans, it was my turn to question the Commissioner. We came to this hearing with a list of about 14 questions to put to the Commissioner and his team. The answers given to these questions would hopefully help us to formulate our practical recommendations for the police to reduce the likelihood of repeating the disasters exposed during Part One of the Inquiry. It proved quite difficult to get around to asking those questions. Hours had gone by and only one question had been addressed: institutional racism. What was I to do? Should I select the most urgent question from the list? Perhaps I should plough on with 'institutional racism'? Surely it would have been better to move on to something new, but my conscience would not allow me to do that. I decided that if Sir Paul left the chamber without acknowledging 'institutional racism', then all the other questions became largely irrelevant. I moved aside my list of questions and my notes and braced myself to ad lib as best I could:

> DR STONE: I have had a note from the judge asking if we could move on to another topic [but] because I feel we are working and working and working at this topic and trying to get our minds to meet in ways that are actually rather difficult. I just cannot quite let it go and I want to ask one more question, please, [...]
>
> [I]t seems to me, Sir Paul, that a lot of what you are doing is already addressing these issues. You have addressed an enormous amount of the issues that are at the heart of institutional racism and actually dealt with them. [...] You said that the sense of racism is corrosive of relations with the black communities. I think all of us on this panel have come to recognising increasingly during these months that in fact the sense of racism is corrosive of the relationships with the police with all communities, white and black, and I think it is important to recognise that this is the heart of good policing, good health service deliveries whatever, it is absolutely vital that we recognise it is not just an issue of trying to win around the black communities.
>
> SIR CONDON: May I respond very briefly, I think it is important.
>
> THE CHAIRMAN: Just hang on, Dr Stone will come to the question.[36]

That remark would have raised a laugh if the topic was not so serious.

DR STONE: [...] It seems to me that the one really powerful argument you are presenting to us, for not today acknowledging there is institutional racism in the police, is that you say the public would not understand and that relationships with the police would be damaged if you were to acknowledge there was institutional racism. [...] I actually think that to say that the public do not understand institutional racism is patronising of the public. [...]

[...] What I am, therefore, trying to get towards now is that you are nearly there. If you can acknowledge the list of things that you have touched on ... you are actually in each of those instances you have given us accepting that institutional racism exists within the police. [...] It seems to me, Sir Paul, that the door is open. [...] If you and we are to go forward together, as I think we must do, we [must] build a new trust.... If we are to go forward I say to you now: just say yes, I acknowledge institutional racism in the police and then in a way the whole thing is over and we can go forward together. That is my question, could you do that today? [...]

THE CHAIRMAN: You have given the challenge, or the question, Sir Paul what is the answer?

SIR CONDON: The answer is that it would be very easy to please the panel, to please this audience, to walk out of this room so that very superficial media coverage says, yes, they have said certain things....[37]

Despite my opening the door of repentance as wide as I could, the opportunity was not taken. There is little point in including the following 20 lines of the Commissioner's response here; we had heard it all before.[38]

Tom Cook led most of the remaining discussion, which was very much in his area of expertise to do with issues such as ways of reorganising policing, freedom of information, independent police authorities, and making the police subject to all the powers of the Commission for Racial Equality. John Sentamu and I also contributed with questions about building trust and confidence in the police and the issue of using volunteers to help teach police officers race awareness programmes.[39]

These issues, however, were an anti-climax after the difficult exchanges about 'institutional racism' that preceded them. I believe our failure to get an acknowledgment of institutional racism out of Sir Paul Condon was one of the defining moments of the Inquiry. Had the Commissioner come to the Inquiry and acknowledged that institutional racism existed in his Metropolitan Police force, he could have changed the future of policing of black and minority ethnic groups in many positive ways.

Still in denial

The Commissioner must have been as appalled as the public by the media coverage of the public hearings, but perhaps for different reasons. The Metropolitan Police consider themselves the best in Britain. They also present themselves as the best in the world, an accolade which is justified by the way in which they are called upon to sort out problems in police forces in other countries. It must have seemed inconceivable to the Commissioner that this proud force was being subjected to, in my opinion, such devastating public humiliation. He rightly recognised that what was going on in the Inquiry was having a seriously damaging effect on the morale of his officers, but it seemed to me that he was *not* justified in stating in public that "the Inquiry was damaging police morale".[40] In an interview a year after the end of the Inquiry, Sir William Macpherson, with characteristic straight talk, stamped on that suggestion:

> Sir Paul Condon said that Crime had risen "as officers, fearful of being branded racist, disengaged from stop-and-search procedures. Street crime alone was up by 30 per cent. A dozen officers were so traumatised after Macpherson's inquiry that they could 'no longer function as human beings'". The whole business, he decreed, had been "a tragedy" for the police service.

Did Macpherson accept that his Inquiry wrecked careers and lives? "I am very surprised he [Condon] said that. What happened was a tragedy for the Lawrence family. I don't believe it was a tragedy for the officers.... It was a very strange attitude for him to adopt. Undoubtedly, some officers were given a pretty rough time. They deserved it.... I simply do not believe that their experience was so damaging that they should be suffering from it a year afterwards."

[...] Then there is the charge that street crime rose because cowed officers steered clear of suspects. "That's not a condemnation of the report. That's a condemnation of officers and leadership in the police. If that was allowed to happen, it was quite contrary to what the report said: that stop and search was a valuable tool." Was Condon simply trying to deflect blame for the Met's defects? "I am afraid that is my conclusion. That is what happened. If – and it's a big if – the report was responsible for a cut in stop and search, that's a matter for the police. I cannot see how the rise in crime could conceivably be attributed to the report."[41]

The final nail in the institutional racism agenda came a decade or so after the Stephen Lawrence Inquiry. Trevor Phillips, Chair of the Equalities and Human Rights Commission (EHRC), led the way by announcing in 2009 that the blanket accusation of institutional racism was "no longer appropriate":[42]

Today most people would argue that despite the controversy, on balance the positive changes provoked by Macpherson have outweighed the cost of the political turmoil. But does this mean that I believe that the Met, or any force for that matter, should be pilloried with the single blanket accusation of being institutionally racist? I don't think so. That would imply that nothing has changed.[43]

This followed an earlier, highly criticised, announcement from Phillips that "multiculturalism has failed".[44] These statements, from the most senior black race relations expert in the country, provided powerful ammunition to the bruised battalions of government officials and police officers who resented the impact of the institutional racism agenda. Both slogans were simplified in public discourse to a belief that institutional racism is no longer relevant and "multiculturalism is dead".[45] Phillips' comments have been criticised in media and academic circles[46] and in my own discussions with activists in the black communities the lead given by Trevor Phillips is met with considerable venom.

Leadership backwards not forwards

At the end of that gruelling morning failing to drag Sir Paul Condon an extra step to acknowledging 'institutional racism', I felt him to be an irritatingly weak leader. Watching and listening to the police and to minority communities around the country since the Inquiry, I have increasingly come to believe that Sir Paul, as the head of the Metropolitan Police, actually showed powerful leadership. However, we tend to think of leadership always as taking things forwards. Think of the statue of King Richard the Lionheart outside the Houses of Parliament, twice life-size, sitting in full armour on his horse with his sword raised leading forever forwards. Now, 14 years after the Stephen Lawrence Inquiry, I believe that Sir Paul Condon demonstrated strong leadership. It appears to me as leadership backwards not forwards – almost seeking a return to a form of policing from the past (see Chapter Seven).

FIVE

Searching for the files of the Stephen Lawrence Inquiry

The Stephen Lawrence Inquiry ended with the publication of the Report[1] in February 1999. The transcripts, which are the most important parts of the archive, were made available in the autumn of 2005 six years later.

Similar archive material of the Hutton Inquiry in 2003 was available within four months. Lord Hutton's subject matter was the death of David Kelly, an officially anonymous expert in weapons of mass destruction in Iraq. This was narrower in its scope than the Lawrence Inquiry, and it lasted for six months compared to the Stephen Lawrence Inquiry's 20 months.[2] Nonetheless, the contrast is stark: four months to publication of all the material of Hutton; six years for some but still not all of Lawrence.

There are four parts of the Stephen Lawrence Inquiry archive:

- *The Report and its volume of appendices*: These have been on sale from the day of the launch (in February 1999) in hard copy from The Stationery Office, and online.[3]
- *The submissions:* These are the responses to requests made by the Inquiry for suggestions from the public which would help to formulate its recommendations. They came from academics, community groups and police representative bodies. Forty-one boxes appeared at The National Archives in the summer of 2005.
- *The transcripts:* Records of the public hearings, which turned up at The National Archives unannounced in 2006, soon after two parliamentary questions.
- *The correspondence files:* Correspondence and other notes and papers in the dozen or so filing cabinets dotted around the offices of the lawyers, the officials, the Secretary, the Judge, and of us the three Advisers. Most of these arrived at The National Archives in

---

November 2011, two weeks after a parliamentary question asking when they would be made available to the public. These have been redacted, but were in a right old jumble. The remaining papers are still (at the time of writing in January 2013) locked away in the Home Office's long-term storage, including all my personal notes and correspondence.

It is important to know that, with the hand over of the report of a government inquiry to the commissioning Secretary of State, the inquiry is over. It is disbanded and ceases to exist. Everything to do with the inquiry becomes the property of the government department. So, at the end of the Stephen Lawrence Inquiry in January 1999, all of us who were part of the Inquiry team were asked to hand into the Home Office all materials to do with the Inquiry. This included computer disks of transcripts, our own notes and drafts of the text of the Report. The Home Office also took away the correspondence files and filing cabinets, as well as hundreds of submissions from the public.

At the time, I told Home Office officials of my concern that I was already being asked by individuals and groups to pass to them documents and texts for academic research and personal analysis. I was assured that handing over everything to the Home Office was routine. All of the Inquiry material would be available after redaction "within a matter of months" in an orderly way on the Home Office website. Between 1999 and 2002 I telephoned the responsible Home Office officials several times about the transcripts (which I felt to be the most urgent part of the archive), each time I was told "In a few months everything will be available. You must understand Dr Stone, that the transcripts will have to be 'redacted' and that can take several months." ('Redaction' means blacking out the names of individuals who may be negatively affected; names and/or addresses of witnesses, for example, who might be vulnerable to threats or violence from the perpetrators, or police officers who might later face further action.) On one occasion I was also told that there were a large number of more urgent files to be prepared. That speaks volumes to me about the official commitment to the agenda set by the Stephen Lawrence Inquiry.

My understanding about redaction is that it should only apply to the transcripts of Part One of the Inquiry and to some of the correspondence and internal notes. Part One of the Inquiry was the 'quasi-judicial' part when detectives and others involved in the investigation of the murder were questioned. Names of witnesses were mentioned, but those who may have needed protection from the alleged perpetrators were given code names or pseudonyms. None of them were questioned in public by the Inquiry. Some witnesses of the crime were interviewed and their true names given, but not their addresses. I could see very little in the transcripts that actually needed to be redacted and, in my assessment, the job could have been completed in a matter of weeks, not months, and in no way should it have taken more than five years.

Most unfortunately some addresses *were* accidentally published by the Inquiry. They were in a list which was published as an appendix, in a separate volume published alongside the Report.[4] This was a horrendous error. These addresses should have been redacted but somehow they were not. The volume of appendices was stopped, and as many as possible recalled; the volume was republished a few days later, with the unredacted appendices removed. There are probably now no more than a dozen copies of the complete appendices out there, plus 25 or so copies distributed to members of the Inquiry team.

There is nothing in Part Two of the Inquiry that I can think of that would need to be redacted. Redaction is irrelevant to the mass of submissions to the Inquiry that come from the public. Of the hundreds of submissions, there are some that I have wanted to read in detail after the Inquiry ended. I was able to contact the authors of those I remembered and asked for copies, but was not even able to refer to my own notes. One of the authors I contacted made it plain that she thought me badly disorganised not to be able to find my own copy (and I'm not sure she entirely believed my story about delays due to redaction and so on).

I am aware that unofficially the transcripts of the Stephen Lawrence Inquiry appeared on the Black Information Link website[5] in 2001, so some of the material was available shortly after the Inquiry ended. This website was an offshoot of the black-led charity The 1990 Trust, which had sent in useful submissions to the Stephen Lawrence

Inquiry. In 2000 the director of The 1990 Trust, Karen Chouhan, with the charity's chair, Lee Jasper, authored a tough independent review of the Stephen Lawrence Inquiry from a black perspective.[6] Sadly, funding for The 1990 Trust was significantly reduced after the change of London Mayor in 2008; a casualty of this was the 'blink' website, which was taken offline and with it the Stephen Lawrence transcript.

In an attempt to get access to these materials I arranged for two written parliamentary questions in October 2004 and January 2005,[7,8] both asking for the same information: a date for publication of the transcripts. They were submitted by Peter Bottomley MP (Conservative) and Karen Buck MP (Labour). The answers were becoming irritatingly familiar. Like the answers to my telephone calls to the Home Office, the reply was that the transcripts would become available within a few months, after redaction was complete. Later in 2005, I was informed by the Home Office that the transcripts of Parts One and Two were available on the Home Office website. I sought for them in vain on the Home Office website, so telephoned The National Archives at Kew to see if they were there, but was referred back to the Home Office. A few months later, on one of my routine phone calls to The National Archives, I was told that "recently added" were 43 boxes of the Stephen Lawrence Inquiry. Two of these, I was told were marked confidential, the titles of the other 41 boxes indicated they were probably the submissions from the public to the Inquiry. There was no sign of the transcripts or of the correspondence.

In the spring of 2006 the transcripts did arrive, once again without any notification or publicity, and with no notice sent to the MPs who initiated the parliamentary questions, or to others who had expressed concern about them. Welcome though this was, still missing were the contents of the filing cabinets which contained all the correspondence files.

On 29 November 2011, Luciana Berger MP set down yet another written parliamentary question "To ask the Secretary of State for the Home Department when she expects the correspondence files of the Stephen Lawrence Inquiry to be made publicly available." The written reply from Home Office Minister Nick Herbert was:

> Most of the Home Office papers relating to the Stephen
> Lawrence inquiry have been released and are already
> available to the public.... The historic review programme
> of the remaining Home Office files for the Stephen
> Lawrence inquiry is currently being developed. Given
> the high profile of these papers, they will be included
> for review and transferred to TNA as a priority as soon
> as possible.[9]

On a routine visit to The National Archives in February 2012, my
researcher noticed a new category had been added to the submissions
and the transcripts, which turned out to be a large collection of
boxes of correspondence files. The date of accession to The National
Archives was 30 November 2011 – exactly two weeks after the
parliamentary question asking when the files would be made available.
My researcher tells me the files are in a chaotic state, totally unsorted
and with empty envelopes scattered among the letters. Redaction
has obviously been done but otherwise the transfer from the Home
Office to The National Archives appears to have been a rushed job.
I suspect that this is only part of the correspondence files as it appears
that my own notes are not included.

Sad to say, I find the way that archive documents are provided
at The National Archives is crude and unhelpful. The building is
elegant and modern; registering to access the archive is as tedious
as opening a bank account, which is probably also necessary. Once
through the gate to the readers' access area it is relatively simple to
get the transcripts up on a screen, but should the reader wish to take
the research further, there is no index to guide the reader to particular
days or pages. There is no search capacity to search by name of witness
or to find discussion of a particular issue. Even if only one page is
needed, help must be sought from a member of the well informed
staff and 20 minutes later the reader is handed a sheaf of papers to
examine at one of the many desks available. In the unlikely event of
finding the right day and the right page (there are around 30 pages
of transcripts for each day), don't expect to be able to get a useful
copy to take away. There is no way to copy into a digital format; one
must take the pages to a photographic machine. The reader opens

up the sheaf of papers and has to bend it open at the required page. This is then placed under the lens of the camera. The image to take home is a photograph of the top page of a bent-back bundle; some of the text will be out of focus due to the bending of the pages. It is of course, also not digital, so almost impossible to use for research or writing. Cut and paste? Forget it! Fortunately I have been able to access a set of the original floppy disks. The transcripts are now accessible without charge on my own blog site[10] with an index for ease of access to the material.

Do these delays and difficulties of access matter much? My opinion is yes, if only because they feed conspiracy theories. Withholding the material suggests the suppression of something embarrassing or incriminating, which inevitably leads people to ask who might be embarrassed by, or who could be incriminated by, that material.

The "smell of corruption"

During internal discussions of the Stephen Lawrence Inquiry panel we concluded that the "collective failure"[11] of officers from the bottom to the very top of the Metropolitan Police Service could not be typical of all murder investigations in London. There must have been some other factors at work. We considered the possibility of two significant factors that might have contributed to the failure: racism and/or corruption and collusion. There was ample evidence of institutional racism, which convinced us that this had contributed significantly to the string of failures by officers.[12] Mike Mansfield QC, lawyer for the Lawrence family, presented a number of circumstantial suggestions of corruption,[13] although nothing that could be considered as hard evidence. The panel also turned every stone we could find that might reveal corruption, including gaining access to the personal files of a number of officers, especially of those who had been subject to disciplinary hearings in relation to informal contacts with known criminals; all to no avail. As Tom Cook, my colleague on the panel, put it to us "People involved in corruption don't leave a convenient paper trail for subsequent Inquiries. They don't take minutes of their meetings, and they don't file papers which can be discovered by officials at a later date."[14] If there was any evidence recorded in files, the chances are that those files would turn out to be missing or hidden somewhere.

Sir William Macpherson made a carefully worded statement about corruption in his report: "We were not presented with evidence to persuade us that collusion and corruption infected the investigation of the murder."[15] It may be interesting to note that the opening words of that statement are less definite than those in the initial draft, which had read "There is no evidence that collusion and corruption infected… ."[16] We, however, felt there had been a 'smell of corruption' around the investigation, although clearly there was no proven evidence of this.

Mark Daly is a BBC reporter who in 2003 went undercover as a police officer recruit in Manchester and delivered a stinging exposure of police racism in a BBC *Panorama* programme called 'The secret policeman.'[17] As a result of that film the Commission for Racial Equality launched a formal inquiry into racism in our police forces which made 125 recommendations for change.[18] In a second programme 'The boys who killed Stephen Lawrence' broadcast on 26 July 2006, Mark Daly exposed a possible link between a police informer and the Stephen Lawrence Inquiry.[19] If Mark Daly's allegations are to be believed, he had uncovered a corrupt detective sergeant who had had a key role in the failed investigation of the murder of Stephen Lawrence. While the Stephen Lawrence Inquiry was working in Hannibal House struggling to find evidence of corruption, just up the road a Detective Constable called Neil Putnam was being questioned by police about his own and other officers' alleged corruption. Neil Putnam was charged with corruption and he turned informer. Putnam was convicted in November, 1998, and served a five year jail sentence but not before he gave information on "a number of serving police officers [who] were convicted of offences of 'corruption' and received substantial prison sentences".[20] Those convicted were not directly related to the Stephen Lawrence case. In Mark Daly's second BBC *Panorama* programme, Putnam states on film that he asked to meet Sir William Macpherson to pass on information to the Inquiry about a Detective Sergeant Davidson, someone who was roundly condemned by the Inquiry for his bungled handling of three key witnesses to the murder.[21]

Doreen Lawrence saw the programme before it was broadcast and on 25 July, 2006 and registered a complaint against the Metropolitan Police with the Independent Police Complaints Commission. The IPCC spent a year investigating a range of allegations:

1) Allegations that the officers, who had debriefed Neil Putnam, had failed to record or act upon information he had given them concerning 'allegations of corruption' in the original Stephen Lawrence murder investigation.
2) The Metropolitan Police Service had failed to advise The Stephen Lawrence Inquiry of the concerns regarding a witness, Detective Sergeant John Davidson.
3) The 'allegation of corruption' involving Davidson and Clifford Norris the father of one of the suspects implicated in the murder of Stephen Lawrence.[22]

The IPCC concluded that:

> We have found no evidence in support of the 'allegations' made during the programme. The former member of the CPS [Crown Prosecution Service] does state that he believes he was advised of an 'association between Clifford Norris and John Davidson' however, he was unable to find any document to source this fact.

> During the course of the IPCC investigation comment was made by a number of former senior officers from the MPS that, "CIB3 were determined to investigate any 'allegations of corruption' and had there been evidence to suggest 'corruption' affected the Stephen Lawrence murder investigation they would have investigated the 'allegations' with rigour".[23]

In May 2012 a further IPCC report into police corruption looked into connections between Putnam and the Stephen Lawrence case because it was "clear that corruption and/or collusion in the original

Stephen Lawrence murder investigation was a long held belief of Mr and Mrs Lawrence and this formed part of the Macpherson Inquiry".[24] The report concluded as follows:

> ... this review has not been made aware of any new evidence or information in respect of the IPCC 2006 independent investigation into the allegations made by Neil Putnam that would lead to a change in the conclusions reached.[25]

As part of his research, I was asked by Mark Daly if the message from DC Putnam that he wanted to meet Sir William got through to the Inquiry. Eight years on from the Inquiry I had no more than a vague memory of being told that there was an informer being questioned at the time, but also that there was no connection to the Lawrence case. If the archive of the Inquiry had been available I, or Mark Daly, could have turned to the correspondence files and notes of meetings to find the answer. It is possible that expensive investigations by the IPCC would not have been needed.

The impact of not publishing the archive

If we believe, as we are told, that the reasons for the unavailability of the material are not sinister but are merely administrative, the outcome of the delay and diversion is the same. Discussion about how to make positive change as a result of the Inquiry's findings and recommendations is diverted to discussion of conspiracies and plots. The authority of the Inquiry's conclusions is undermined; hopes for change are lost; the estimated £3 million cost of the Inquiry is potentially wasted.

Not having access to an inquiry archive does more than feed conspiracies: analysis by academics and journalists is prevented; informed comment is not possible.

A significant conclusion of the Stephen Lawrence Inquiry was that it was no longer acceptable for the police to investigate the police. Allegations of wrongdoing by police services at that time were investigated by a Police Complaints Authority (PCA) which appointed a police force in another part of the country to investigate the force subject to a complaint. The Inquiry's recommendation 58 was:

> That the Home Secretary, taking into account the strong expression of public perception in this regard, considers what steps can and should be taken to ensure that serious complaints against police officers are independently investigated. Investigation of police officers by their own or another Police Service is widely regarded as unjust, and does not inspire public confidence.[26]

Implementation of this recommendation came through the 2002 Police Reform Act and in April 2004 the IPCC replaced the PCA. Although funded by the Home Office, the IPCC is entirely independent of the police, of interest groups and political parties; its decisions are free from government involvement.

In its investigation of the *Panorama* allegations in 2006, the IPCC stated that they had no difficulty in gaining access to the transcripts and to the correspondence, and to any other files they called for.[27] It is most unfortunate that no one else, me included, could get that degree of access. As a result the IPCC was vulnerable to suggestions of a whitewash, with no one outside the IPCC who could support their findings. A year later I asked to see the report, but instead was invited to meet with the IPCC Commissioner Deborah Glass. She assured me that there had been a vigorous exploration of the allegations. Yes, the IPPC had had no problems accessing the correspondence files of the Stephen Lawrence Inquiry. No, there was no connection between DC Putnam and DS Davidson at the time. Points which were reiterated by IPCC Chief Executive, Jane Furniss.[28] Crucially, Commissioner Glass told me, the investigation of DC Putnam did not actually occur until after the end of the Stephen Lawrence Inquiry, so there can have been no possibility of him meeting with us.[29]

I confess I was flummoxed with the outcome of my meeting with the Commissioner. The IPCC seemed to have focused on whether or not Putnam spoke up while the Stephen Lawrence Inquiry was still up and running. My interest was in what follow-up there had been on his allegations. If Putnam had something important to tell us, someone somewhere in the police system should have gone in at once to find out just what information he had, about the case or about Detective Sergeant Davidson. I felt I had been made to look like a conspiracy theorist shown up to have followed a false trail, yet all I had done was asked to view the report to see for myself whether or not Mark Daly's allegations stood up. I assumed that this was precisely what the IPPC had done in their investigation, but the IPCC gave me only a vague assurance when I asked whether their team had done what to me seemed the obvious thing to do. That is, regardless of the confusing dates, followed the whole trail, from the officer whom DC Putnam had asked to pass his message to Sir William Macpherson through all subsequent officers for the names of police officers who had handled the message. I reckoned that, where they found where the trail went dead, they might just find someone who had ensured that the informant's information was never going to get an appropriate response.

After the *Panorama* programme was shown, there were conflicting police statements made about the alleged request from DC Putnam to meet Sir William.[30] Apparently, a senior officer claimed that a letter was sent to the Inquiry about an informer being questioned about corruption. If so, did it get to the Inquiry? Did it mention the possibility that some of the information could be relevant to the Lawrence case? If only all the correspondence files were accessible so that we could verify the alleged letter.

As a result of the withholding of the Stephen Lawrence Inquiry archive, particularly in the first few years following the Inquiry when there was still a great deal of interest, there has been none of the academic analysis one would expect after such an inquiry.

Some of the strongest criticisms of the conclusions of the Stephen Lawrence Inquiry have been around the definition of institutional racism. There were submissions to the Inquiry from academics and a small amount of this material is written into the Report, principally from Dr Robin Oakley, but also from Dr (now Professor) Benjamin Bowling and Professor Simon Holdaway.[31] In the normal run of events, after the end of an inquiry, academics would expect to be able to analyse the evidence of police officers, collected from the transcripts of the Inquiry, and to publish robust research in academic journals and other media. I have personally found it very difficult to defend the concept of 'institutional racism' when it has been so unsupported by later academic analysis.

It has also been impossible to discuss or rebut the criticism of the recommendations made by the Inquiry, because no one has been able to analyse the extent to which those recommendations were based (as they properly should be) on the evidence presented to the Inquiry and on the Inquiry's conclusions. The absence of academic analysis because of the lack of access to the detail of the Inquiry must make this one of the most serious examples of undermining the agenda for change set by the Inquiry and its recommendations.

SIX

Defining 'institutional racism' and the challenge to 'double jeopardy'

Two outcomes of the Stephen Lawrence Inquiry turned out to be controversial beyond all expectation. They were the discussion and definition of institutional racism (Chapter Four) and recommendation 38 on 'double jeopardy'.

There was no actual recommendation from the Inquiry on institutional racism, but critics and commentators rightly picked up that there was an implicit recommendation that ran through the whole list of 70 recommendations.[1] The Report did accept and offer a working definition of institutional racism, recognising that institutional racism was "apparent" in the handling of the Stephen Lawrence case and in police practice regarding stop and search and the under-reporting of racist incidents.[2] The Inquiry Report stated that "There must be an unequivocal acceptance of the problem of institutional racism and its nature before it can be addressed."[3] Recommendation 38 was "that consideration should be given to the Court of Appeal being given power to permit prosecution after acquittal where fresh and viable evidence is presented"; a recommendation which challenged the 800-year-old rule of *autrefois acquit*.

There was much criticism of the Inquiry's findings and a reluctance to change.[4] In an interview after the Inquiry, Sir William Macpherson acknowledged these difficulties. He was asked if the line taken by Condon, and perhaps his successor, demonstrated a desire to marginalise Macpherson's findings rather than embrace them.

> "Yes, and I find that attitude very disappointing. The right thing to do when you're criticised is to accept it and try to improve matters; not to moan about what's been said. I don't think the police have turned their backs

on the report. They've taken many essential steps, but they are still prepared to whine ... about other aspects."[5]

Defining institutional racism

Britain is, thankfully, no longer a nation that accepts overt discrimination; since the 1965 Race Relations Act, discrimination on the grounds of colour, race, or ethnic or national origins in public places has been against the law. Gone are the days when landlords could legally and openly state that they accepted 'no blacks, no Irish, no dogs'.[6]

The Lawrence Inquiry found no overt racism in the words or actions of the officers involved in the murder investigations, although did conclude that "in its more subtle form [racism] is as damaging as in its overt form".[7] The rules of policing in themselves are racially neutral, but day-to-day police work is conducted at the discretion of individuals. Officers can choose to give more energy, time and effort to some cases than to others. The Stephen Lawrence Inquiry concluded that there had been "a collective failure" by the police to conduct "an appropriate and professional" investigation.[8] This string of failures led to the conclusion that racism was a factor which played a significant part in that failure. In the Report, we felt obliged to list the episodes which showed the institutional racism in action: "those areas which were affected by racism, remembering always that that emotive word covers the whole range of such conduct", as Sir William Macpherson put it.[9] Summarising these six key episodes took up a whole page of the Report:

> In this case we do not believe that discrimination or disadvantage was overt. There was unwitting racism in the following fields:
>
> i. Inspector Groves' insensitive and racist stereotypical behaviour at the scene. He assumed that there had been a fight. He wholly failed to assess Duwayne Brooks as a primary victim. He failed thus to take advantage of the help which Mr Brooks could have given. His conduct in going to the Welcome

Inn and failing to direct proper searches was conditioned by his wrong and insensitive appreciation and conclusions.

ii. Family Liaison. Inspector Little's conduct at the hospital, and the whole history of later liaison was marred by the patronising and thoughtless approach of the officers involved. The treatment of Mr & Mrs Lawrence was collective, in the sense that officers from the team and those controlling or supervising them together failed to ensure that Mr & Mrs Lawrence were dealt with and looked after according to their needs. The officers detailed to be family liaison officers, Detective Sergeant Bevan and Detective Constable Holden, had (as Mrs Lawrence accepted) good intentions, yet they offended Mr & Mrs Lawrence by questioning those present in their house as to their identity, and by failing to realise how their approach to Mr & Mrs Lawrence might be both upsetting and thoughtless.

This sad failure was never appreciated and corrected by senior officers, in particular Mr Weeden [the Senior Investigating Officer], who in his turn tended to blame Mr & Mrs Lawrence and their solicitor for the failure of family liaison. The failure was compounded by Mr Barker in his Review.

iii. Mr Brooks was by some officers side-lined and ignored, because of racist stereotyping particularly at the scene and the hospital. He was never properly treated as a victim.

iv. At least five officers, DS Davidson, DC Budgen, DC Chase, DS Bevan and DC Holden simply refused to accept that this was purely a racist murder. This (as we point out in the text) must have skewed their approach to their work.

v. DS Flook allowed untrue statements about Mr & Mrs Lawrence and Mr Khan to appear in his statement to Kent. Such hostility resulted from unquestioning acceptance and repetition of negative views as to demands for information

which Mr & Mrs Lawrence were fully entitled to make. DS
Flook's attitude influenced the work which he did.

vi. The use of inappropriate and offensive language. Racism
awareness training was almost non-existent at every level.[10]

Sadly, of the police officers who gave evidence to the Stephen
Lawrence Inquiry, most appeared to me not to have tried hard enough
to find the killers of Stephen Lawrence.[11]

It can be difficult to state unequivocally if a particular action by an
employer or a professional is a manifestation of institutional racism.
For one thing, not every action can be easily measured. Disparities
in the practice of stop and search, or in recruitment, retention and
progression of staff from minority backgrounds can be measured
(although still not that easily assessed). When thinking about
whether the failures in the policing of the Stephen Lawrence case
were motivated by racism with little in way of quantitative or even
qualitative data, I found it helpful to use a test coined by Rabbi Hugo
Gryn: 'the reverse discrimination test'. Mr Panton, the barrister
acting for Greenwich Council, applied the same concept to assess
whether racism operated in the Stephen Lawrence Inquiry:

[I]f the colour of the victim and the attackers was reversed the
police would have acted differently:

In my submission history suggests that the police would have
probably swamped the estate that night and they would remain
there, probably for the next however long it took, to ensure
that if the culprits were on that estate something would be
done about the situation.[12]

Mr Panton's submission echoes the suggestion made by Doreen
Lawrence at the end of her statement to the Inquiry that "if it had
been the other way around that night" somebody would have been
arrested regardless of whether they had done it or not.

There are two good reasons *not* to define institutional racism.
First, as suggested by Doreen Lawrence's in the final paragraph of

Chapter One, those on the receiving end of it know perfectly well when it is there. Mr and Mrs Lawrence needed no definition to identify the problem. They knew within three or four days of the murder of their son that the police investigating the murder were not trying hard enough. They also believed that the collective failure of those officers was connected to the fact that the family is black.[13] Second, those who feel defensive about the existence of institutional racism are likely to spend hours poring over the details of which bits of their work may or may not fit different aspects of the wording. Without a definition to pick over, perhaps they could get on with addressing the issue itself.

The Inquiry Report also acknowledged that we had to "grapple with the problem"[14] of institutional racism in recognition of the difficulty we had in finding words to describe the concept. The Report's chapter on racism (Chapter 6) is the longest in the Report. It took 64 paragraphs before we felt able to offer our own definition:

> The collective failure of an organisation to provide an appropriate service to people because of their colour, culture or ethnic origin. It can be seen or detected in processes, attitudes and behaviour which amount to discrimination through unwitting prejudice, ignorance, thoughtlessness and racist stereotyping which disadvantages minority ethnic people.[15]

After the definition, the Report states that:

> ... without recognition and action to eliminate such racism, it can prevail as part of the ethos or culture of the organisation.

Then there is a classic example of the vivid language used by Sir William Macpherson:

> "It is a corrosive disease."[16]

Addressing institutional racism

Sir Herman (now Lord) Ouseley told the Inquiry that it would be useless to address racism only in one corner of one institution[17] – in this case, the police in South-East London. He argued that only if pursued in all institutions in the country will significant change occur. After his presentation to the Inquiry, I took him aside and suggested that he was spitting in the wind: "No government will ever take on institutional racism in all institutions of the country. Let's hope that, by dealing with it in the police round here, the ripples of good practice will start similar changes in the rest of the police, and then outwards to other institutions." My assessment was wrong and Lord Ouseley was right.

In February 1999 at the launch of the Stephen Lawrence Inquiry Report in parliament, the then Prime Minister, Tony Blair, as well as the Home Secretary, Jack Straw, accepted that institutional racism exists in all institutions. They went further, to embrace multiculturalism and diversity as parts of the agenda of the New Labour government and "to make sure these appalling events lead to a change in race relations within our society".[18] So, just because the terms of reference of the Inquiry referred only to the policing of racist incidents, no institution or organisation could assume that this was a problem only for someone else to deal with. All of us must look to our "processes, attitudes and behaviour"[19] whatever our area of work, to deal with unwitting as well as witting discrimination.

What does this mean for leaders of white-led organisations, as employers as well as providers of services? First, I suggest that, even with the best will in the world, we cannot get it all right. Particularly in relation to clients from minority communities (as well as to staff below the 'glass ceiling' of promotion to senior posts), a white-led local or central government department, or factory, or department store, or my old NHS group practice, is bound to be affected by bias. At the most simple level, individuals connect most easily with people with whom they are most comfortable, usually those most like themselves.

Sadly, because we are human, when confronted with an accusation that our actions are racist we tend to be defensive. We give what we really know are rather feeble excuses: we deny what we are doing, we blame others – other staff who are sloppy, or our patients being disruptive at the end of a hard week, or staff applying for senior jobs who are not bright enough, not trying hard enough. Or we blame black people. This is exactly what the police did with Mr and Mrs Lawrence. Within four days of the murder, senior and junior officers were complaining that the parents of the murder victim were "bombarding" the investigation with questions in a way that was diverting officers from following up leads (see Chapter One).[20]

In our visits to six inner city areas in Part Two of the hearings, the Stephen Lawrence Inquiry found that in all of these locations black people were four to six times more likely to be stopped by police.[21] In each I asked senior officers how much statistical confounding factors could account for those disparities. They all accepted that it could be no more than 1%.[22] Allowing for 1% meant that black people were still three to five times more likely to be stopped by police officers than white people.

More recent research has found that police forces are *28 times* more likely to use stop and search powers against black people than white people.[23] Trevor Hall, then the most senior black civil servant at the Home Office, told guests at his retirement party in 2002 that he had been stopped in his car by police 47 times. He has never been charged as a result of any of these and, most importantly, never given been a reason for the stop.[24] I have only ever been stopped once – and that was when I was backing slowly up the hard shoulder of a motorway. Mr Hall and I are of a similar age and similar social class. In my opinion, the only obvious difference between us is the colour of our skin.

In January 2013, Stephen Lawrence's brother, Stuart, a school-boy in 1993 and now a high flyer in his early thirties, brought an action against the Metropolitan Police in relation to the 25 times he has been stopped by police.[25]

The Inquiry found that the police in the Stephen Lawrence investigation neither listened to nor heard the needs of the family nor of the community. They did not listen for the special consequences arising from the fact that this was a racist incident. The Inspector in charge the first night briefed his officers that a black boy had been injured in a fight.[26] There never was any evidence suggesting a fight. Good evidence was available from the officer guarding the scene. She could have reported what Duwayne Brooks had told her about the attack by five white youths, but Inspector Groves did not ask questions because he assumed it was a fight and his officers believed him.[27] All 40 officers started the investigation by looking for the wrong sort of evidence.

Another argument for addressing institutional racism is a very practical one. Research has repeatedly shown that a relatively low 10–30% of white inner city residents do not trust their police, while for black people it is 40–60% distrust.[28] Since a significant proportion of inner city residents do not trust their police, they are unlikely to report crimes. This may lead to them not giving evidence, especially if they fear that they themselves, rather than the perpetrators of the crimes, will end up being charged by the police. This sort of destructive, negative response to black people by police was reported to the Inquiry in every one of the six inner cities we visited.[29] We know that black people are the main victims of inner city crime;[30] they are therefore often the best placed to help the police. Without the co-operation of so many key people, clear-up rates of all crimes are likely to be unnecessarily low. This has a major impact on the lives of all citizens. Large numbers of burglaries, rapes, thefts, assaults and car crimes remain unsolved, and the perpetrators remain on the streets to commit further crimes.

At all levels of the criminal justice system the scope for injustice is high if the particular needs of black and minority ethnic communities and of black and minority ethnic criminal justice staff members are not addressed. At the most basic level this must lead to large amounts of money wasted in payouts to victims of injustice, as well as to staff who succeed in industrial tribunals.

Double jeopardy

The Stephen Lawrence Inquiry also made the recommendation to abolish the rule of 'double jeopardy' in specially selected cases.[31] The Inquiry's Report stirred the legal establishment by suggesting abolition of the ancient law against '*autrefois acquit*'.

The Norman legal French *autrefois acquit* translates as 'acquitted at another time'. The more familiar name for this law, 'double jeopardy', is an appropriate nickname, suggesting a guarantee against being put in jeopardy a second time. Simply put, the rule is that 'once acquitted or convicted of a crime, a person shall not be tried again for the same crime'.[32] This is also included in the 1966 United Nations International Covenant on Civil and Political Rights (which came into force in 1976), which states that "No one shall be liable to be tried or punished again for an offence for which he has already been finally convicted or acquitted in accordance with the law and penal procedure of each country."[33]

Although this rule is well established, the facts of the Stephen Lawrence case led to concern about cases in which the suspects had been previously acquitted, particularly due to lack of evidence. Having successfully escaped from being twice arrested and now with the certainty of protection by the 800-year-old 'sacrosanct' law, the suspects in the Stephen Lawrence case must have felt that they really were 'untouchable'. Looking back, it does seem that the failure to get convictions in the Stephen Lawrence murder case was not because there was insufficient evidence, but because of the collective failure of the police to make any significant effort to find it. None of us could stomach the idea that three men who appeared to be part of a joint enterprise to commit murder, could never be tried for it simply because the police officers who could have ensured their conviction had bungled the case.

The forensic possibilities of DNA analysis were evolving. We thought about the possibility that in the future some new evidence could be discovered that definitely linked one or other of those acquitted in 1993 to Stephen Lawrence and his murder. Surely the law would be an ass if it could not bring them to trial if new evidence was found? We were unanimous that we must consider all options to find a way to bring them to justice, no matter how impossible the way might seem at first. Faced with this conclusion, we had to question the rule of *autrefois acquit*.

Never having been a practising lawyer, I turned to Liberty[34] for help. It was about a year since I had been elected to the Council of Liberty, so I asked its chair and its director, then Sadiq Khan and

John Wadham (both lawyers) if we could table double jeopardy for discussion at the next Liberty Council meeting. To my surprise they not only agreed, but made it the only item on the agenda. All but one of the 15 members turned up (an uncommonly high turn-out) – I felt like Daniel in the lion's den. At the end I asked for a vote to accept the limited change proposed. I lost by 1 to 13. I had failed to persuade a single Council member of what seemed to me to be the obvious merit of the decision made by Sir William Macpherson and his three Advisers.

Later, John Wadham stated that it was the policy of Liberty that:

> The protection from double jeopardy is a fundamental part of our criminal justice system and we increase the chances of innocent people being convicted if we remove it. People who have been arrested and prosecuted, who will have been locked up in prison for months before they face trial, should be free once they have been acquitted by a jury. It cannot be right to force them to go through this all over again.[35]

Only then did I realise the significance of the high turn-out at Liberty Council. The Council is the forum which thrashes out Liberty's policies, and I had unwittingly stumbled into ensuring that Liberty had a policy on double jeopardy and that the policy would be the opposite of the recommendation of the Inquiry.

Despite this setback, in the interest of justice, we could not ignore the real possibility that new DNA techniques might one day throw up fresh evidence sufficient to convict one or more of the five. Recommendation 38 was the result of the Inquiry's discussions. It should be noted though that we were concerned only with retrial when the suspects had been acquitted, cases of previous *conviction* were not relevant to the Inquiry.

Of the 70 recommendations of the Inquiry, 53 recommended "that [something] be done". Those recommendations are straightforward and definite, for example recommendation 65 "That the Home Office and Police Services should facilitate the development of initiatives to increase the number of qualified minority ethnic recruits."[36]

Recommendation 38 is one of only seven in which more tentative opening words are used: "that consideration should be given to". Sir William Macpherson was a recently retired High Court judge and, as such, would have been well aware that any suggestion of changing the law of *autrefois acquit* would meet with stiff opposition, and would need a lot of thought and discussion. Of all the recommendations of the Inquiry this one received the most vitriolic attack. There was a universally hostile reception to this recommendation at the time of the Inquiry Report's publication and the Law Commission's recommendations in 2001.[37] Had it not been for this change in the law in 2003, Gary Dobson could not have been sent for trial and convicted in 2011 of the murder of Stephen Lawrence and would not now be in prison.

At the time, lawyers and academics were outraged that a judicial inquiry would even consider a change to an 800-year-old law written to protect the citizen from the power of the state.[38] Critics failed to notice the subtle ambivalence of the initial wording of the recommendation: this law was as old as the Magna Carta, and it should never be tinkered with ... ever. Baroness Helena Kennedy's opinion was that "The [double jeopardy] rule exists as a protection of our liberty. The state should not be able to retry people until it gets the result it wants, and to do so is oppressive."[39]

I believe that some of the worries about changing the law on double jeopardy are justifiable. Recommendation 38 could be viewed as part of a long history of chipping away at civil rights and liberties in this country. My own additional concern, in the light of the institutional racism that we found to have contributed to the failings in the Stephen Lawrence case, is that the new law will be used against black people more than it will against white (although as of January 2013 that has not been the case).

Implementing the recommendation

Implementation of recommendation 38 was by way of its referral to the Law Commission. The Law Commission is an independent statutory body responsible for reviewing the law in England and Wales and recommending reform, so was the appropriate body to work out the details. In due course the proposals of the Law Commission were enacted as part of the 2003 Criminal Justice Act.[40]

The new rule is not for any case. It is carefully constructed to be used only for offences where the balance of justice cries out for it, which was exactly how the Stephen Lawrence Inquiry wished it to be. Sections 40–42 of the Act set out the limits of what is proposed:

> 40. This Part of the Act reforms the law relating to Double Jeopardy, by permitting retrials in respect of a number of very serious offences, where new and compelling evidence has come to light. At present the law does not permit a person who has been acquitted or convicted of an offence to be retried for that same offence – this risk of retrial is known as 'Double Jeopardy'.

> 41. The Government considers that the law should be reformed to permit a re-trial in cases of serious offences where there has been an acquittal in court, but compelling new evidence subsequently comes to light against the acquitted person. This is in line with, but drawn more widely than, Recommendations of the Law Commission and those set out in Lord Justice Auld's review of the Criminal Courts, published in 2001. Examples of new evidence might include DNA or fingerprint tests, or new witnesses to the offence coming forward. The measures amend the law to permit the police to re-investigate a person acquitted of serious offences in these circumstances, to enable the prosecuting authorities to apply to the Court of Appeal for an acquittal to be quashed, and for a re-trial to take place where the Court of Appeal is satisfied that the new evidence is highly probative of the case against the acquitted person. [...]

> 42. The new arrangements will apply only in respect of serious offences. They do not include all offences for which life imprisonment is the maximum punishment,

because this would catch a number of common law offences which may not have such serious consequences, and for which a life sentence would rarely be imposed.[41]

The new rule also takes account of the concern voiced by Baroness Kennedy that the state should not be able to retry people until it has the result it wants:

> The measures provide safeguards aimed at preventing the possible harassment of acquitted persons in cases where there is not a genuine question of new and compelling evidence, by requiring the personal consent of the Director of Public Prosecutions (DPP) both to the taking of significant steps in the re-opening of investigations – except in urgent cases – and to the making of an application to the Court of Appeal.
>
> The DPP will take into account both the strength of the evidence and the public interest in determining whether a re-investigation or application to the Court is appropriate.[42]

The recommendation in action

By the time Gary Dobson was arrested in 2010, the new law had been used in two cases without demur (the cases of William Dunlop in 2006 and Mark Weston in 2010). William Dunlop had confessed after being acquitted of murder in 1991, but the case of Mark Weston was the result of new evidence and was precisely the scenario we anticipated might one day allow one or more of those acquitted of the murder of Stephen Lawrence to be tried again.

In 2006, the Metropolitan Police began a new search for forensic evidence in the Stephen Lawrence case, and were able to use new sophisticated techniques. Microscopic examination of every inch of every article of clothing and other effects collected from the homes of the suspects seven years earlier took three years. The DNA evidence used in the case consisted of three tiny spots of blood. Gary Dobson and David Norris were arrested in September 2010.[43]

Before arresting Dobson and Norris in 2010, the police needed the Court of Appeal to agree to quash Gary Dobson's acquittal in 1993. This case took almost a year to come to a decision. The Court was asked by Dobson's lawyers for bail while the appeal process worked its way through the next months, but bail was refused, and he and David Norris were held in custody for over a year up to and during the trial. It seems remarkable to me that there was little media coverage of the incarceration of these notorious men at all during that year, but a High Court injunction on confidentiality was in place, which meant a prison sentence for anyone who broke the silence.

During this period, much time and energy within the Crown Prosecution Service (CPS) was also taken up with preparing for counter-arguments that might be brought up by the defence barristers, and the CPS is justifiably proud that every argument raised by lawyers for Dobson and Norris had been anticipated by the prosecutors.[44] I am not the only person who watched or read about the case day after day, horrified by how officers investigating the case in 1993 put clothing into paper bags, storing valuable evidence in ways that could have led to cross-contamination. The prosecution case looked to be falling apart. However, the prosecutor remained cool and not a single word was said in defence for which the CPS did not have their counter-argument ready.

What seems odd is the apparent silence during and in the wake of the retrial of Dobson of the vocal legal voices that had poured such scorn on recommendation 38. What happened to the hostility in 1999 towards such a heinous breach of the 800-year-old law? The nearest any comments came to criticism were those made by an independent researcher and journalist in Canada:

> This is the second time double jeopardy has been thrown out of the window. We can be sure it will not be the last, and that at some time in the not too distant future attempts will be made to weaken the criteria for prosecution after acquittal. Which will open the door to prosecuting the same person for the same alleged offence over and over again until the jury returns the *right* verdict.[45]

But there was nothing from those who were hostile to the proposed change of law in 1999. To ask why this was so is not an irrelevant question. The hostility that the Stephen Lawrence Inquiry received in 1999 about the recommendation on double jeopardy may have undermined the authority of the whole Inquiry in the eyes of many lawyers who were otherwise sympathetic to the cause of tackling racism.[46]

SEVEN

Unprofessional policing and timid leadership

In my opinion, the Stephen Lawrence Inquiry revealed to public gaze a catalogue of failures by the Metropolitan Police. Failure was piled on failure, and after each exposure there was no apparent confronting of the causes, no reviewing of policies and no improving of practice. Rather, when taken together, a pattern may be detected of tacit agreements at all levels to deny wrongdoing and blame the 'few bad apples'. A conclusion of the Inquiry reads:

> There can be no excuses for such a series of errors, failures, and lack of direction and control. Each failure was compounded. Failure to acknowledge and to detect errors resulted in them being effectively concealed. Only now at this Inquiry have they been laid bare.[1]

This is not the appropriate response of a thoroughly professional organisation. Sadly, other examples of unprofessional policing practice hit the headlines in 2012. One was the investigation into the Hillsborough football stadium disaster, which exposed wrongdoing on the part of large numbers of officers. The Chief Constable of West Yorkshire Police, Sir Norman Bettison, resigned after being accused of making up false stories to blame Liverpool supporters for the 1989 Hillsborough disaster while he was serving with South Yorkshire Police.[2]

Hillsborough, the Stephen Lawrence case and others including the Leveson Inquiry demonstrate what I have come to believe as a serious lack of the positive leadership that is needed to drive through the necessary changes at an institutional level.

There are a few key examples in policing communities on which I will draw in this chapter to examine the impact of good and bad leadership. The first example is the poor direction and control of the Stephen Lawrence case itself. Next are the disparities in stop and search, followed by examples of good and bad policing with Muslim communities. The final example will be some of the policing tactics during the riots of 2011 and 2012.

Poor leadership in the Stephen Lawrence case

The Report of the Inquiry provides a very short summary of the sorry tale of the original case:

> Those violent seconds in 1993 have been followed by extraordinary activity, without satisfactory result. From the Lawrence family's point of view there has been a sequence of disasters and disappointments.
>
> Three of the prime suspects were taken to trial in 1996 in a private prosecution which failed because of the absence of any firm and sustainable evidence. The trial resulted in the acquittal of all three accused.[3]
>
> The question of the early arrests of the suspects is, as we see it, central to the whole of this Inquiry. [...] We reached the conclusion ... that there was a fundamental error made in the judgement and decision making both by [Mr Crampton, the Senior Investigating Officer for the first three days], by his successor Mr Weedon [sic], and by his supervisor Mr Ilsley.[4]

Mike Mansfield QC, acting for the Lawrence family, made several allegations that corruption impeded progress of the investigation. One of these allegations was the 'incompetence' of Mr Crampton in not making a connection between David Norris and his father, the notorious local criminal Clifford Norris:

> Mr Crampton indicated emphatically to this Inquiry that he did not ... make the connection in his own mind between the young 17-year-old David Norris, who was named by several

informants, and the villainous Clifford Norris. Mr Mansfield regularly returned to the suggestion that it was inconceivable that such a connection was not made. Mr Crampton was equally positive that he did not make the connection, although he accepted that he knew about the existence of Norris and his notoriety.[5]

Within two weeks of the murder Stephen's parents, Neville and Doreen Lawrence, held a press conference to complain that the police were not doing enough to apprehend Stephen's killers. The then Commissioner, Sir Paul Condon responded that:

> Twenty-five officers are working full-time on the case and the inquiry [investigation] is continuing with a dedicated team of officers pursuing the task diligently and with total professionalism. We refute any suggestion that this is not so.[6]

In my opinion, almost every page of the 335 in the Inquiry's Report offers evidence to contradict Sir Paul's denial.

Fifteen days after the murder on 6 May 1993, Detective Constable (DC) Budgen reported to the 16:00 police team meeting that information had come earlier that day from police informant 'James Grant' that the Acourt brothers "are fascinated by knives. Tried to buy one. Usually hide them under floorboards."[7] On that same evening Nelson Mandela appeared in public with Mr and Mrs Lawrence (see Chapter One).

At 05:30 and 06:30 of the next day, forced entry was made to the homes of the Acourt brothers and of Gary Dobson; all three were arrested. A similar entry was made to the home of David Norris, but only his mother was there (Norris's arrest, and that of Luke Knight, was made later). Norris's home (like those of the other three) was searched for evidence of murder by stabbing. No floorboards were lifted at any of the three homes, even though all the officers involved in the arrests were present at the meeting the previous evening when the information from Grant had been given out.[8]

That morning DC Budgen was stationed at the home of the Acourt brothers. He told the Inquiry that he "had stayed in a bedroom with Jamie Acourt while the searching took place, and that detailed searching was the responsibility of the qualified search team. He had expected a detailed search, including the lifting of floorboards."[9] Even then, the information reported by DC Budgen about knives under floorboards was not acted upon. On the day of the arrests the detectives had no more information than they had had two weeks before. They had already missed the opportunity to arrest in the vital first 48 hours. The mass of information that had come in by then fully justified the arrest of all five according to the rules outlined in the 1984 Police and Criminal Evidence Act. Senior police officers on the scene at the time told the Inquiry under oath that a decision not to arrest was made on the Sunday after the murder (which happened on Thursday evening). The Inquiry was unable to find any evidence of a discussion about arresting, let alone a clear decision. Rather, "a marked lack of co-ordination and attention to detail seem to have been the features of these early hours".[10]

So what motivated the police to make the dawn raids on 7 May? The Deputy Assistant Commissioner (DAC) in charge of that area of London at the time was David Osland. He was the only officer who was willing to "accept that external pressures might have played their part in the ultimate decision".[11] That is the nearest we had from the police leaders to an acknowledgement of the effect of the banner headlines around Nelson Mandela's meeting with the Lawrences.

There was no hard evidence gained from the searches. All that the detectives could hand to the CPS was the identification provided by Duwayne Brooks who was so shaken by the events of that night that his evidence was easy to tarnish as unreliable. The CPS had little option but to discontinue proceedings against all five in turn during 1993 and 1994. No trial meant they walked free.

When Sir Paul Condon finally gave evidence to the Inquiry (see Chapter Four and Appendix C), he quickly set out his stall, outlining the transformational leader he planned to be when he was appointed Commissioner just a few months before Stephen Lawrence was murdered:

> I chose fairness, justice and equality as the theme of my first speech when I became Commissioner. Within days literally of becoming Commissioner I pledged myself and the Metropolitan Police to fairness, justice and equality. As early as 1994 I sought the Commission for Racial Equality and other partnership help to move forward our understanding and analysis of many of the significant issues facing the Met. For example, stop and search and disproportionality.... I supported the formation of the Black Police Officers Association ... and pledge my personal support to them. In 1996, after extensive consultation with the community in London, I published the five year plan for the Met which recognises diversity, policing diversity, as one of the most significant challenges facing the Met. Chairman, I have always acknowledged that the police service in London is in a pivotal position of power, of trust and influence and I recognise my responsibility to discharge that task.[12]

I have no reason to disbelieve that the Commissioner had these fine aspirations for recognising diversity; that he also genuinely wanted to challenge the racism which he clearly abhors. How sad he must have felt to be here, five years later, trying hard to keep to those initial commitments. Is it that the deep wells of racism were too deeply embedded to be dealt with? Sir Paul Condon's statement continued for some time (see Appendix C), reflecting on "our past mistakes, our failures, the challenges we face" and outlining his "ambitious programme of reform".[13] Unfortunately, much of his statement contained nothing of substance, in my view; faces in the public section of the chamber began to lengthen with boredom during his speech. This all seemed a long way from the incisive leader Sir Paul had set out to be in 1993.

Another key point in the Commissioner's speech was when he stated "I may not have been here, Chairman, but I have listened."[14] Until Sir Paul pointed it out, I had not appreciated that he had not managed even a half hour at the back of the hall during any of the 59 days of hearings during the previous six months. DAC John Grieve was there for most, if not all, of the Part One hearings. Of course the Commissioner would not have been able to come every day and it was appropriate that DAC Grieve should do so as the eyes and ears of the Commissioner. But DAC Grieve does not have to prove to anyone that he has "heard the anger, the frustration, the confusion" and "the desire for reform";[15] he had been there to hear it. He demonstrably connected appropriately and professionally with the appalling revelations from the officers being questioned.

For those who know the catalogue of police failures in the Stephen Lawrence case, there is an obvious parallel with the yawning absence for seven months of the Commissioner himself until day 3 of Part Two. Mr Weeden, the Senior Investigating Officer who took over the case on the Monday after the Thursday of the murder, and was in charge of the investigation for over a year, was severely criticised for not managing to meet with Mr and Mrs Lawrence at any time in that first year.[16]

When pushed to acknowledge the failings of the police in the case and of the leadership shown, Sir Paul Condon's responses were vague or gave a general outline of positive changes already made, or of plans and programmes for the future. An example demonstrates the problem:

> THE CHAIRMAN: Commissioner, Mr & Mrs Lawrence [and] their advisers very early on during the investigation, in the very early days of the murder investigation detected, as it seems to us, that things were going wrong from the hours after the murder was committed and certainly during the first week when no arrests were made. Following your acceptance that things went badly wrong, what is the area upon which you put your finger as the real ground for acceptance that things went wrong?

> SIR CONDON: I think the acceptance is in the clear failure to bring Stephen's brutal racist thugs who murdered him to justice. I think that is the single most important test of the manifestation of that failure. The Inquiry have had the benefit of the independently supervised Police Complaints Authority report from Kent, you have had the opportunity to examine witnesses here and you have had the opportunity to form judgements across, where things could and indeed should have

been done better. I mean, I am at your disposal if you wish to draw me to any aspects of that.[17]

The Stephen Lawrence Inquiry drew the Commissioner's attention to the review by Chief Superintendent Barker, instigated by DAC Osland then acknowledged and approved by the Commissioner (see Chapter Four). The review was set up as a "review of undetected major crimes"[18] following the CPS's decision in July 1993 not to prosecute Neil Acourt and Luke Knight. The Lawrence Inquiry found this review to have been a spectacular disaster: "factually incorrect and inadequate", "flawed and indefensible".[19]

The exchange between the Judge and the Commissioner was significant enough to be chronicled in the report:

> CHAIRMAN: What still troubles me, Commissioner, is that it seems to me that that review is simply accepted at face value by everybody who saw it, not only yourself because you saw it, but particularly perhaps the senior officers who ought to have been responsible for those who made the vital wrong decisions in the early hours. I do not understand how they could have accepted it if they had been doing their job properly.

> COMMISSIONER: If I may respond to that. With the benefit of hindsight, several years on I understand the force of what you are saying. .... Faced with a report that seemed to be diligent, that contained a number of recommendations that seemed to be acknowledging flaws, that is arguing for reform that had been carried out by a middle ranking officer, then I think that did lead people to take that report as it was set out. Now, I accept with the benefit of hindsight that can be challenged and people must make a judgment around that.[20]

Our final Report disagreed with Sir Paul Condon's reliance on hindsight: "Our judgment must be that at the time, without the need of hindsight, the Review should have generated questions from senior officers."[21]

At this point in the exchange Assistant Commissioner (AC) Dennis O'Connor was moved to come to the rescue of his boss:

> MR O'CONNOR: Chairman, if I may add a little to that, having some responsibility for the way forward. Our view is, to I think help answer your question, our view is this: that the nature of leadership associated with those inquiries has to change. The leadership is relied too much on trust; it needs to be far more challenging, ie less acceptance, more drill down, more probing; and part of the reason for Mr Grieve's appointment is that that challenge in leadership can take place outside of the line command directly, coldly and clinically, that is part of Mr Grieve's remit.[22]

AC O'Connor was a great deal more concise and to the point and acknowledged the need for *leadership* to change. I remember at this stage feeling that I would much rather engage with DAC Grieve or AC O'Connor than to listen to more of the circular arguments of the Commissioner.

The Lawrence Inquiry itself, and Mike Mansfield QC on behalf of the Lawrence family, looked hard for evidence of corruption to account for the unbelievably poor performance of the police investigating Stephen's murder. However, no concrete evidence of it could be found in 1998/99. In the end, the conclusion of the Inquiry was that:

> There was undoubtedly evidence of corruption or attempted corruption of a vital witness in the Stacey Benefield stabbing case, in which the suspect David Norris was accused. The strong inference is that Clifford Norris, David Norris' father, was behind that corruption and that he was closely involved in trying to pervert the course of justice by bribing Stacey Benefield and another witness involved in the case named Matthew Farman....

> In the Stephen Lawrence case there is no evidence of such interference with witnesses. The 'Norris factor' is said to have involved the pulling of punches and the deliberate slowing

down and 'fudging' of the investigation, so that the suspects, and in particular the suspect David Norris, were protected and ineffectively pursued during the whole of the first investigation.

No contact during the investigation between Clifford Norris or his agents and any AMIP [Area Major Incident Pool] police officer directly involved in the investigation has been alleged. We are asked to conclude by inference and because of earlier or indirect association that the influence of Clifford Norris must have been at work from the earliest days after Stephen Lawrence's murder and right through to the Barker Review. We are asked to conclude that the influence must in particular have governed or affected the decisions of the more senior officers almost from the start and that such influence must have been widespread [...]

The problems in seeking to establish that there was collusion or corruption by inference are obvious . It is right that we should say at once that no collusion or corruption is proved to have infected the investigation of Stephen Lawrence's murder. It would be wrong and unfair to conclude otherwise. It seems to us sensible to record this conclusion at once, so that the text of this Report can be read with this in mind. [23]

It was suggested in the BBC *Panorama* investigations that, with all their experience and in-depth knowledge of London criminals, the police must have known pretty soon who killed Stephen Lawrence.[24] The Lawrence family have continued to suspect that corruption was at play in the early investigations into Stephen's murder.[25] In 2012, the Metropolitan Police continue to be under scrutiny in connection with corruption. Only one day after publishing their own report into corruption following allegations made in the *Guardian* and *Independent* newspapers, which found no evidence of wrongdoing,[26] the Home Secretary, Theresa May, ordered a further review and required the Metropolitan Police to hand over all documentation.[27] We await the outcome.

'Golden threads'

The language of policing in Britain is riddled with jargon. One example is the concept of a 'golden thread', which describes good practice embedded in policing from top to bottom, from community to international level.[28] The golden thread is often used specifically in relation to good connections with local communities and positive race relations. The argument is that 'golden threads' do not need specific training but should be woven into all training and practice. For example, reports into policing around the time of the Inquiry found that "forces have suggested that the profile of community and race relations training is maintained by a 'Golden Thread' approach ... that runs through all training. Evidence suggests that this is not the case."[29]

Even Sir Paul Condon confessed to the Stephen Lawrence Inquiry that:

> The golden thread approach from which you have heard from other agencies who have been before you which was adopted in the wake of Lord Scarman's report has not been successful, certainly not as successful as I would like. It has tended to reduce down to training for fairness and when faced with difficult definitions, difficult situations, complex chaotic environments, the police training has to distill down to treat everyone the same, treat everyone fairly.[30]

He continues with further emphasis on the 'complexity' (my most hated of excuses) to say that:

> In the complexity of cities like London the challenge is to treat everybody as individuals, not just the same and although this thread of fairness is noble and honourable, in itself it is not enough and the new training must embrace with vigour the notion of treating people as individuals.[31]

There has been much debate about whether racial equality training should be a 'golden thread' through all police training or if it would be better as focused and separate courses.[32] A special report on police training published just after the Stephen Lawrence Inquiry concluded that:

> ... training in community and race relations must be a 'golden thread' running through all aspects of police training. [...] We recognise that such an approach will not be successful in isolation as there is a danger that the golden thread will be too fine. There is therefore a need for dedicated training in community and race relations. A dual approach should be taken by all forces.[33]

But still in 2005, six years after these two reports were published, the Commission for Racial Equality quoted a senior manager in the police as saying "whilst there was a 'golden thread' of race equality in most of our courses, this 'thread' could be thicker in places".[34]

Any 'golden thread' of race equality was absent in all the examples of unprofessional policing in this chapter, as in the Stephen Lawrence case. I have, however, observed a different and new golden thread: it is a thread of timidity when faced with complex problems. It is a difficult thread to find, because leaders do not decide to be timid; there is no training for it; there is no monitoring that shows that it happens.

This timidity may have led to unprofessional actions, which can seriously damage the reputation of a profession far beyond the incident itself. The inevitable negative publicity also drives down the morale of the whole service, especially of the many good people in the profession. There have been high profile 'mistakes' in other professions which have led to negative publicity and then to poor staff morale, particularly in social work for example.[35] This may also drive those individuals who have made mistakes and poor decisions into a mindset of aggressive denial. However, poor leadership and the denial, or even covering up, of failure by senior staff in the face of overwhelming evidence can be more insidious than the blatant actions of one individual. Bad practice from the top down inevitably undermines trust and confidence in the individuals and in the organisation.

Stop and search

Stop and search powers have been granted to all accredited police constables under several Acts of Parliament since the 1824 Vagrancy Act. The intention is that the police should act on intelligence about local crime, and no doubt most do, but there has been little in the law or guidance to prevent an officer from abusing those powers. The high levels of disparity in the number of black people searched compared with white reflect the large amount of discretion police officers have to stop and search anyone. Without accountability officers can choose who they will stop and who will be left in peace. Inevitably there will be some officers who make decisions based on their preconceptions, particularly towards identifiable groups they do not usually mix with.

A year prior to the Stephen Lawrence Inquiry, the crime prevention charity Nacro argued that:

> nothing has been more damaging to the relationship between the police and the black community than the ill judged use of stop and search powers. For young black men in particular, the humiliating experience of being repeatedly stopped and searched is a fact of life, in some parts of London at least.[36]

The Stephen Lawrence Inquiry agreed and was critical of unacceptable disparities in stop and search between black and white citizens as discussed earlier (Chapter Six). We saw these disparities as clear evidence of 'institutional racism'.[37] They were (and still are) discriminatory against black and minority ethnic citizens, and provide measurable evidence of 'institutional racism' in action. The Inquiry's recommendations 60–63 were designed to curb the stop and search powers of police officers and to bring racist, unprofessional and arbitrary stops under control. Recommendation 61 reads:

> That the Home Secretary, in consultation with Police Services, should ensure that a record is made by police officers of all "stops" and "stops and searches" made under any legislative

provision (not just the Police and Criminal Evidence Act). Non-statutory or so called "voluntary" stops must also be recorded. The record to include the reason for the stop, the outcome, and the self-defined ethnic identity of the person stopped. A copy of the record shall be given to the person stopped.[38]

For some months after the launch of the report of the Inquiry senior and junior officers claimed that they could not stop black people any more, for fear of being called racist:

> There was a sharp, albeit short-lived, drop in the total number of stop searches following the publication of the Inquiry report but disproportionality actually increased during this period. The idea that police officers might be scared of using their stop search powers for fear of being branded racist was one I became familiar with whilst carrying out the evaluation of the implementation of Recommendation 61 from the Inquiry....[39]

The Stephen Lawrence Inquiry team had grappled with the need for very simple, easy to operate recommendations. With strong leadership from the top, we were convinced that constables on the street would be able to do what the Inquiry asked of them. It is regrettable that about a year after the end of the Inquiry, the Metropolitan Police were piloting a form to record stop and search information that was on two sides of A4 paper and had 37 questions. It took an average of 22 minutes to complete. Officially the rationale for such a long form was this: while recording 'stops', there is an opportunity to seek further intelligence and information on local crimes. The result is obvious: from a simple idea, the form to put the new recommendation in practice is too long to collect any useful information on local crime or on stops. The outcome of such a long form is that the recommendation is unworkable. Ben Bowling and colleagues conclude:

> ... the police response to the Inquiry report has primarily been a defensive one driven by a need to protect

their organisational self-image and uphold a sense of innocence/virtue. This, it seems to me, is both a deeply personal and political response, which represents a huge barrier to achieving progressive change.[40]

Why would any police service want to curb a recommendation that could improve the professionalism of its officers? To understand why requires recognition of the role of power. People rarely like giving up power and recommendation 61 was correctly interpreted by police officers as an attempt to curb their powers and their discretion.[41]

After all those sincere apologies and commitments to change given throughout the Inquiry hearings (see Chapter Four), police leaders only needed to put our recommendations into practice and the benefits would surely follow. In fact, a survey of police officers conducted at the time of the implementation of recommendation 61 found widespread support within the police for increased accountability providing it was not at the cost of significantly increased bureaucracy.[42] But what happened was that police leaders proposed and condoned the long, bureaucratic pilot forms. I believe that recommendation 61 was undermined more than any other of the 70 in the Report. This was leadership backwards, not forwards. It is no surprise that, more than a decade after the Stephen Lawrence Inquiry, even now that better recording systems are in place,[43] disparities in stop and search by the Metropolitan Police are double what they were.[44] Some officers have learned how to do some stops (with or without searches) less offensively, but there are still too many blatantly discriminatory stops, some of which are still done with unnecessary aggression.[45]

Crucially there is also little recognition of the damage to public trust created by every inappropriate, arbitrary or aggressive stop. The word spreads very quickly through communities that the police 'have done it again'. Years of hard work building trust and confidence within black and minority ethnic communities can be wiped out by one inappropriate, badly conducted stop.[46]

An earnest young of man from a black Caribbean background told me recently that he had been stopped and searched four times in the previous year:

"They did it with respect Dr Stone. It wasn't aggressive. They've got a job to do. I don't have a problem with being stopped."[47]

I wish more of the young black men I meet were as positive as him. People can accept that it is probably necessary to do stops and searches where the carrying of knives is prevalent. Sadly, many young black men still believe that a lot of stops are just for fun, and not really looking for knives or anything else relevant to local crime:

"You can tell they're not real. It's the tone of their voice. Their swaggering. And their aggression. They try to wind you up, and then they have you for interfering with the course of justice."

"It's a crime isn't it? Wasting police time? 'Cos that's what they're doing. Instead of winding us up they should be off following up crimes. Why don't they get prosecuted for wasting police time?"[48]

That's a good question. I had no answer, but it deserves one.

Engagement with Muslim communities

Strong leadership can, and does, make a positive difference to community relations. In the weeks following the London bombings of July 2005 the police acted appropriately and professionally. There could have been serious outbursts of anti-Muslim prejudice, verbal abuse and violence against British Muslims in the wake of the reports that the bombers were British born and British educated Muslims. The usual effect of public demonising of a group or a country that is seen as Muslim is an increase in anti-Muslim rhetoric, hostility and violence, which spills over into violence against all minority ethnic groups. Such responses in 1990, at the start of the first Gulf War, offered a bleak precedent for Britain. The Islamophobia Commission of the Runnymede Trust reported that:

> At the time of the Gulf War there was a 100% increase in racist attacks in Bradford. A senior police officer was quoted as saying that 'dark skinned people were attacked because they were considered to be supporters of Saddam Hussein'. There is frequently amongst racist offenders a seamless convergence of anti-Muslim, anti-foreigner,

> anti-Asian, anti-immigrant and anti-black hostilities. [...]
> Islamophobia may feed and be fed by hostilities which
> have nothing to do with Muslims. A black person or a
> Hindu may be attacked or abused on the street because
> Britain is in dispute with a country which happens to
> be Muslim.[49]

Following the 9/11 attacks in the USA many Sikhs have been killed,
having been confused with Muslims because of their turbans and
beards.[50]

As the ghastly story of the London bombings unfolded on
our television screens, fear of a backlash against British Muslim
communities grew.[51] There were initial reports of increasing violence
directed towards Muslims,[52] but a wider, sustained backlash did not
happen; there was very little retaliation against Muslims or other
minority ethnic groups.[53] I believe that this success was due mainly
to strong leadership from government ministers and from within the
Metropolitan Police force, which is to be commended. The then
Prime Minister Tony Blair, the then Home Secretary Charles Clarke
and other key ministers were united in asserting that these terrorist
actions were made by a handful of extremists. At the same time they
repeatedly exonerated the vast majority of the two million Muslims
who live in and contribute to this country. Prime Minister Tony
Blair also had the courage to recognise the needs of the majority of
British Muslims for protection by and engagement with the police:

> What we are confronting here is an evil ideology.... It is
> not a clash of civilisations – all civilised people, Muslim
> or other, feel revulsion at it. [...] We must join up with
> our Muslim communities to take on the extremists. [...]
> Muslims believe in democracy just as much as any other
> faith and, given the chance, show it.
>
> The spirit of our age is one in which the prejudices
> of the past are put behind us, where our diversity is our
> strength. It is this which is under attack. Moderates are
> not moderate through weakness but through strength.

Now is the time to show it in defence of our common
values.[54]

Even Tony Blair's most ardent critics should be able to recognise the
powerful effect his words had in preventing an explosion of anti-
Muslim prejudice and violence.

This constructive leadership played out in more than just words.
A month after the bombings I was invited to the Central Mosque
in Regents Park for an awards ceremony. Present in uniform were
a police sergeant and a constable; the sergeant was given an award
for his support of the mosque and its members.

One of the Imams explained to me that, since the bombings, the
police had offered daily protection by a uniformed officer stationed
not just outside, but inside the mosque if that was the wish of the
mosque's director. The sergeant and his constable were so warmly
welcomed that initial suspicion on both sides was soon replaced by
genuine friendship. Both sides got to know each other and barriers
between them, born of ignorance, melted away. The outcome was
confident, appropriate and professional community policing, which
was in turn rewarded by the goodwill of the community.

I wish that this small example of professional policing had become
far more widespread. If it had, maybe police officers would have
gained the confidence and trust to be able to go into mosques
and remove violent fanatics, with the support of the local Muslim
community. Regretfully, the lessons of gaining confidence and
engaging with people from minority communities were quickly
lost. They were also almost certainly undermined as a result of the
disastrous shootings some months later of Jean Charles de Menezes
and of two innocent Muslims in Forest Gate.

The shooting of Jean Charles de Menezes, a Catholic Brazilian,
two weeks after the London bombings in July 2005, is well known.
The case was high profile in the media and has been the subject of
an inquiry[55] and other analysis,[56] so I will not repeat it here. The
Forest Gate saga is less well known.

Shootings at Forest Gate

On 2 June 2006 a 23-year-old British Muslim, Mohammed Abdulkahar was shot by police at his home in Forest Gate, East London. Thankfully he clattered down the stairs towards the police a fraction slower than expected or he may have been shot dead, instead of being wounded in the shoulder. He and his brother Abdul Koyair were arrested on suspicion of terrorist activities but were later released without charge when no evidence was found.[57] This terrible mistake could all too easily have ended with another death of an innocent man at the wrong end of an armed police officer's gun.

A senior Muslim police officer, Chief Superintendent Dal Babu, said to me that if only the firearms squad had had a few Muslim officers in it, the situation would never have got to the point of shooting anyone in that house in Forest Gate, while the most senior Muslim police officer, Ali Dizaei, called for "more rigorous analysis" of community intelligence.[58] After the shootings of Jean Charles de Menezes and Mohammed Abdulkahar, imaginative close engagement with Muslim communities was quietly dropped. Research carried out around this time found that there was "a belief that police are not really interested in the Muslim communities' problems" and that a lack of trust in the police was partly derived from a perceived failure of the police to have an impact upon the problems that really matter to communities.[59] Thankfully, more recent research following up on the above study has found that although there still remained "opportunities for improvement", trust in the police from Muslim communities has recovered following a low in the wake of the London bombings and the Forest Gate shootings,[60] and that "Muslim communities have a higher level of trust and confidence in the police than the general population."[61] The Metropolitan Police have also recently announced the creation of the London Muslim Communities Forum to help build better relations with London's Muslim communities.[62] Let us hope that this is moving police leadership forwards, and not backwards.

Policing protests and riots

A more recent example of poor, or timid, leadership is the way protesters have been dealt with. In 2009, during the chaos of the demonstrations against the G20 summit meeting in London, police officers were filmed pushing, shoving and generally acting aggressively towards protesters. This excessive use of force led to the death of Ian Tomlinson, who was not a rioter but just happened to be walking in the area at the time. Police officers at all levels are genuinely appalled about what happened to Ian Tomlinson and the officer responsible has recently been sacked following a disciplinary panel.[63]

Watching the TV footage of what happened to Ian Tomlinson I realised that hundreds of officers policing the protests did not have their 'collar' numbers displayed on their shoulders, which officers are required to do whenever they are in uniform. It dawned on me that years ago I had seen police officers go into crowd control without identification numbers: during the miners' strikes of the 1980s, when officers were caught on camera perpetrating unacceptable violence. Their identification numbers are the primary means by which an officer can be held accountable by the public, so what reason can there be for removing or hiding these numbers other than in the expectation of breaking the law and not wanting to get caught? The accountability of the police officers during the miners' strikes has recently come under the spotlight, with accusations of "widespread collusion" and new calls for an inquiry.[64]

I find it quite shocking that the same tactic of removing identification numbers was adopted 40 years later. It is explained away now, as it was then, by the 'few bad apples' theory.[65] In all these cases, where were the senior officers who should have snapped at the frontliners "put your number back on at once"? The Hillsborough Independent Panel suggested that it is not possible for so many officers to act and plan to act in ways that evade accountability, unless it is considered normal or acceptable practice by their superior officers as well.[66]

Even before the G20 summit in London the police had been criticised for their heavy handed approach with protesters,[67] but in the aftermath there was a widespread "erosion of public confidence in the police".[68] Two years later, in 2011, there was yet another policing disaster exacerbated by poor relations with the local community. The initial protests in North London following the shooting of Mark Duggan were remarkably peaceful. But within a few days dreadful riots broke out, at first in London, but then in one UK city after another.

In much of the TV footage of these riots the police were seen standing by, lined up in full riot gear and clearly outnumbering rioters and looters, just watching them as they stepped through shop windows smashed by the earlier protesters. They looked over at the police, who did not seem interested; at first warily and then with increasing confidence the protesters turned into looters, calmly taking away TVs and other goods.

Most of the looting was caught on the many commercial as well as police CCTV cameras, so it was possible for looters to be tracked down within the following few days and arrested. But it felt somehow wrong for the police to stand by watching as people stole under their noses; the public saw the police response as slow and inadequate.[69] Letting the looters 'get away with it' also led to an escalation of rioting and looting: to an attitude of "just rob everything, police can't stop it".[70] Arguments have been made that by this time officers were so exhausted, or so outnumbered that they could not face going in to arrest the looters, or were not prepared as they would have been for a planned protest.

My response to these excuses is to rebut each of them. First, officers should keep themselves fit enough to do their job. Early in 2012 it was reported that 64% of officers are overweight.[71] Allowing this degree of unfitness to be the norm is unprofessional on the part of the individuals, as well as by their superiors. Second, I can see nothing that is appropriate or professional in a policing tactic which encourages officers to stand around and do nothing while people commit serious crime under their noses. It certainly avoids an Ian Tomlinson disaster, but that does not make it acceptable. It sends out a signal to other people that the police are not interested. My final rebuttal is a general comment: not having a strategy or plan in place to deal with unexpected events, such as the riots of 2011, is clearly a sign of poor leadership.

It appears to me that senior and junior police officers have reacted to each of the three disasters discussed above by doing anything but accept they got it wrong and work out how to do the job better next time. That police leaders have not been willing to condemn or attempt to reduce the damaging effects of unprofessional policing of the public, especially Britain's black, Muslim and ethnic minority populations, has been shown by the examples above to be shallow and self-destructive. These are not the responses of a thoroughly professional organisation. The professional responses would be to look at what the operation aimed to achieve, look at where things went wrong, say sorry, work out how to achieve it without the awful mistakes made, then train frontline officers how to do it properly next time. The lessons learnt from the Inquiry should have led to stronger leadership and better trained officers able to deal effectively with challenging circumstances within all our communities.

Looking to the future, there are bound to be more public outbursts about the way that the police interact with groups of their fellow human beings. Policing is a difficult job and, sadly, police services are likely to be seen getting it wrong again on more occasions. The only way to escape the past is to create a future committed to appropriate and professional policing of *all* communities. There is an alternative to timidity as a response to public exposure of fallibility and wrong doing. Appropriate and professional leadership is needed to find methods to continue firm and fair policing in all the areas discussed in this chapter.

EIGHT

Final reflections

I noted in the Introduction a convention whereby people inside an inquiry do not tell people outside about anything that was said or is being done. A senior civil servant explained to me another convention, one that constrains panel members after, not during, an inquiry. It is that the people who write recommendations should not be involved in the implementation of them. The reason he gave was that recommendations need to be implemented by people who will not be biased by having been involved in writing them. I explained this convention to a senior businessman and he fell about laughing. He was adamant that he would never waste the time and money invested in the person who writes his reports without it being part of the contract for the author to give a certain amount of time to supervising the implementation.

I had rather hoped that this convention was already on its way out in 1999, at the end of the Stephen Lawrence Inquiry. I already had one set of recommendations to implement: the 60 proposed by the Runnymede Trust's Commission on British Muslims and Islamophobia,[1] whose report had been launched by Jack Straw in October 1997. Add to these the 22 recommendations of the David Bennett Inquiry[2] and the 70 recommendations from the Stephen Lawrence Inquiry,[3] and the total of 152 is enough to last me for the rest of my lifetime. It never occurred to me that I might not be involved in implementation. These final reflections provide ideas that I hope will be implemented with or without me.

Better access to inquiry archives

For me, the most frustrating story which cries out for an explanation is the absence from public scrutiny of the transcripts, the correspondence files and the rest of the archive for more than five years. I do not buy the explanations that point to civil service lethargy. The Stephen Lawrence Inquiry was not a 'quick-fix' little investigation into a distant corner of a government department's activities. It was one of the biggest and one of the most public inquiries into one of the most significant institutions in the country – the Metropolitan Police Service.

The Inquiry was initiated in a blaze of publicity by the Home Secretary. When the Report was launched it was on the day of Prime Minister's questions, and both the Prime Minister and the Home Secretary made major speeches to parliament welcoming it. Both accepted all the recommendations, and spoke of the commitment of the government to their implementation.[4] Valuable documentation gathering dust on departmental shelves should not have been an option after the Inquiry finished. When the transcripts and then most of the correspondence files were finally released, there was no fanfare and no publicity; they just materialised at The National Archives. My own notes remain missing. It is important that the remaining correspondence files are released into the archive quickly, and that research is undertaken to establish how and to what extent the withholding of the archive has damaged the possibilities for the police and other services to gain from "the lessons to be learned for the investigation of prosecution of racially motivated crimes".[5] The lack of public scrutiny of the Inquiry's conclusions and recommendations, and the inability of journalists and academics to analyse and comment, is surely one of the most damaging blows to the effectiveness of the Inquiry.

Addressing institutional racism

The most fundamental concern of this book, however, is that the main aim of the recommendations of the Stephen Lawrence Inquiry – to eliminate racism within the police – has not been achieved. Sadly, the British police are still charged with being institutionally racist.[6] Research 10 years on from the Inquiry Report found racism to still be rife within the police,[7] while a recent investigation into police records by the *Independent on Sunday* has shown that complaints of racism against the police have more than doubled in the past decade.[8] Despite the fact that "the vast majority of the complaints submitted by alleged victims of racial abuse have been rejected, because the police themselves have ruled either that they are untrue, or that they cannot be substantiated" it has been reported that 120 Met officers were found guilty of racist behaviour between 1999 and 2011.[9] This must be addressed and challenging racism must be put firmly on the agenda, supported from the top with strong leadership.

As discussed in Chapter Six, disparities in stop and search between white and black citizens also remains shockingly high.[10] This has a corrosive effect on the community, ultimately making policing more difficult. When police officers act "appropriately and professionally" (the words we constantly use throughout the Report of the Inquiry), stop and search disparities should reduce and black and white people will be stopped on the streets in more or less equal numbers; similarly, crimes will be investigated with equal vigour and fairness, without reliance on stereotypes or, worse, prejudice. It is then, and only then, that a new trust will develop between the police and their communities, and between the communities and their police.

A common denial of institutional racism is that it is a complex issue, as we saw earlier in the book. I strongly disagree. Enough has been written and enough has been said about it in the past 14 years to clarify what it is and why it is damaging to society. There is no excuse for carrying on doing what is wrong. Just stop it!

There is also no need to look for yet more recommendations, for example to address racist stereotyping, institutional racism or disparities in employment and in stop and search. Just assess year on year the implementation of the recommendations of the Stephen Lawrence Inquiry.

Improving police leadership

The Stephen Lawrence Inquiry exposed weak leadership in the lack of control or direction over the initial investigation, and an acceptance of sloppy police work. Seventy recommendations were in the Report, and had there been a clear, unwavering response from senior officers, we would have seen far greater improvements in race equality today. Chapter Seven shows how strong leadership can be equally damaging if moving in the wrong direction – leading backwards not forwards.

Before and after the Stephen Lawrence Inquiry, Sir Paul Condon had the opportunity to demonstrate strong leadership and push forward on issues of racism within the police. It appears to me that he failed to do so and this was a lost opportunity at a crucial time.

The new Commissioner of the Metropolitan Police, Bernard Hogan-Howe, has promised:

- Zero tolerance of racist officers.
- Positive action to fast-track the recruitment of black people into senior police posts using "lateral entry" to hire them.
- The introduction of CCTV into the Met's 6,000 vehicles, including police vans, where some people have died.
- The conclusion of a review by May of controversial police stop and search, which has "disproportionately" targeted black people, particularly males, with changes to include fewer "but more intelligent" stops and the better training of officers.[11]

These promises are commendable. However, his critical friends, inside and outside the police service, have had 31 years of promises with almost no positive outcomes. After the failures of so many promises, plans and strategies, Bernard Hogan-Howe will have to work hard to earn our trust and confidence in his pledges. What will begin to turn the tide in his favour will be targets set for measurable outcomes in each of the four areas listed above.

However, these promises do show a fresh sensitivity to the impact of policing on black communities. They must be welcomed, and the hope has to be that they will counter much of the long-standing negative perceptions held by black people. Let us hope that Mr Hogan-Howe has begun to turn the Metropolitan Police onto a new course of justified pride in its professionalism. Policing practice must not disadvantage any identifiable group in society, but should welcome the diversity of Britain, embrace the differences and ensure that police officers are able and willing to work in appropriate ways with people from different backgrounds from their own.

Recruitment, training and promotion of black and minority ethnic police officers

The moral argument for addressing institutional racism is to do with equity and fairness, but there are also very practical reasons for it. We ignore the extra skills and diverse experience of black and minority ethnic people at our peril. The resignation of Chief Superintendent Dal Babu after 30 years in the Metropolitan Police highlighted the continuing problems. He says in a recent interview that "It's about having that cultural understanding ... do you understand the cultural aspects that might be misinterpreted as being aggression within a particular community? ... Do you understand when communities are praying on a particular day?"[12] To be promoted to just below, or certainly above, the glass ceiling black and minority ethnic people, like women, will have had to overcome prejudice and discrimination repeatedly. By the time they are promoted, they will have developed understandings and new ways of thinking that can only be of added benefit to employers. It is an indictment that the strategic command course for the next generation of chief constables has no black or minority ethnic officers this year.[13]

Our organisations are bound to fail if we go on promoting to the most senior posts only white men who have not had those benefits, and who tend to the narrow monocultural way of thinking, as demonstrated by the police investigating team in the Stephen Lawrence case. Dal Babu sums it up: "[m]y sadness is we have gone from 1% to 5% black and ethnic minority officers in 30 years. We have not managed to replicate the communities we serve."[14]

Improving the quality of police leadership starts at the top, but it is vital that this encompasses all senior officers. I would like to see serious questions being asked of our police commissioners and all senior officers in respect of their commitment to addressing racism within their forces in promotion and appointment processes. We need to ensure that the right people are leading, and in the right direction.

A move to a more ethnically diverse police force will require a relinquishing of power from some people and groups, which is understandably challenging. It also requires all those who currently have power – overt or subtle – due to their position, gender and ethnicity to make this happen day to day.

Ensuring a truly independent inquiry

It is vital that an inquiry be independent and not have interference from any person, group or organisation. It is particularly important for public trust that this is so. If there is even a hint of interference, the validity of the findings and the support for the recommendations can easily be undermined. Central to this is the independence of the core inquiry team. In Chapter Three I raised the challenges that can arise of the secretary being seconded from a department involved in the case.

I have been told by Home Office ministers and senior civil servants that seconded officials are trained to draw the boundary between the inquiry and loyalty to their government department. I am assured that, while on secondment, the confidentiality of the inquiry is paramount. I had private discussions with two senior Home Office insiders concerning the independence of secretaries to inquiries. Both offered the usual mantra that the boundaries of independence around the secondee would be maintained as tightly as could be. One, however, added that if the sensitivity of what the inquiry was likely to uncover was great enough, the secretary would be invited every week to his department to pass on information about what the inquiry was thinking and what the latest exposure was likely to be.

I recognise that any secretary to an inquiry who is there by virtue of secondment from his civil service job is perhaps put in an impossible position. There is, of course, potential for conflict of interest, which must be a huge burden to anyone in such a role. An independent inquiry must be able to rely on all those involved to be impervious to any outside influence, especially among the dozen or so core individuals.

Putting pressure on a civil servant to breach his loyalty to the inquiry, if this could be true is thoroughly unprofessional behaviour by senior Home Office staff. It is they who are much more culpable than the poor Grade 7 official, alone and unsupported.

Whatever did or did not happen that led to the cancellation and reinstatement of the Birmingham visit, I now firmly believe that for an inquiry to be truly independent it must appoint its own secretary. Inquiry chairs are able to call on expert advisers, and should be able to enlist their support to ensure selection of a secretary who has an understanding of the sensitivities surrounding the inquiry and experience of working with those communities whose trust is key to the inquiry's success.

The chair of any inquiry should resist the lure of 'donations in kind' when they come in the form of a secretary seconded from the civil service. There are two tempting benefits that come with this: one is the saving of money, since a secondee customarily remains on the payroll of the government department while on secondment; second is the convenience of having staff support from the very beginning. If an independent secretary is to be appointed, a secondee could be appointed in the interim, but only to cover for the time it takes to appoint and brief an independent secretary appointed by the chair and his or her advisers, thus overcoming the issues of speed and instant support discussed in Chapter Two.

Ensuring an open and accountable police force

In 1997, in desperation, Mr and Mrs Lawrence referred the failure of the first murder investigation to the Police Complaints Authority (PCA). As was customary at the time, the PCA commissioned another police force to do the review. They chose Kent Police. The Kent Report "found no evidence to support the allegation of racist conduct by any Metropolitan Police Officer involved in the investigation of the murder of Stephen Lawrence".[15] Usually such investigations are carried out by forces from distant areas, not by neighbouring forces where there may be a possibility that individual officers know one another.

Sir William Macpherson expressed the unanimous view of the panel in paragraph 44.14 of the Inquiry Report:

> We have heard regularly during our Part 2 meetings of disquiet
> as to the perceived lack of independence of PCA inquiries and

procedures. This does not in any way mean that the members of the PCA are personally subject to criticism. But since PCA inquiries, certainly in major cases, are conducted with or through other police forces, the perception is that such investigations of police by police may not be seen to result in independent and fair scrutiny and that justice is not seen to be done by such investigation.[16]

The choice of Kent Police to undertake the PCA investigation of its huge neighbour, the Metropolitan Police, is more than odd. Before joining the Metropolitan Police as Commissioner in 1993, Paul Condon had been Chief Constable of Kent Police. The lead Kent officer for this PCA review was Robert Ayling, who had been Paul Condon's Deputy Chief Constable. This created an extra cause for concern with regard to genuine independence, in that Mr Ayling was being invited to investigate the work of his old boss. These associations invite criticism that there might have been, at minimum, a risk of collusion.

The Inquiry recommended that openness and accountability be improved within the police service.[17] This led to the establishment of the Independent Police Complaints Commission (IPCC). This has been a great improvement on the PCA, but right from the start it has needed adequate resources to be able to employ and train its own independent staff for "serious complaints". Instead, its funds have been cut to the bone in the last two years.[18] The coalition government is now proposing its abolition. My personal view is that no new organisation is likely to do a better job than the IPCC. I would rather see injection of the funds necessary for it to undertake its role effectively. That way there would be no hiatus for a year or more while a new organisation is set up. It is hard to see how any new structure could be more independent than the existing IPCC.

Despite the Inquiry's findings, the police are still primarily policed from within. In 2012, amid concerns that racism allegations were not being handled correctly within the Metropolitan Police, the IPCC announced that "all complaints of a racist nature against Met Officers will bypass the force's internal complaints procedure and will be automatically referred to the independent body".[19] Shortly after, in June 2012, London Mayor Boris Johnson ordered another review into racism in the police, this time into the impact of the 2008 Race and Faith Inquiry.[20]

Community engagement

Central to addressing issues of discrimination is engaging with excluded communities. The Stephen Lawrence Inquiry Report emphasised the damage that was caused as a result of this missing dimension; from the poorly managed family liaison with the Lawrence family through to a lack of understanding of the impact that excluding Birmingham from the Inquiry visits would have on broader race relations. Many of the issues raised in the reflections above have a significant impact on black and minority ethnic communities, and on the credibility of the Inquiry and its recommendations. They also have an impact on the ability of the police force to effectively do their job.

The Stephen Lawrence Inquiry interviewed 'race awareness' trainers employed by the police, as well as the senior officers who managed their contracts and were responsible for payments to them. Their view of the training for which they were responsible was pretty jaundiced. They all confessed that the police had gained little from the work, despite the millions of pounds spent on it over the years.

What might work better would be a programme for all police officers, from whatever background and no matter what rank, to spend one week a year on paid leave as a full-time volunteer at a community centre or project that is run by, and provides for, people whose backgrounds are different from their own.

I can think of no better way than this to develop 'cultural awareness'.

The costs would be minimal, for a few paid co-ordinators and for incidental expenses of the volunteers. Instead of paying for expensive professional trainers, police services would be paying for one week of the annual salary of each of the officers seconded. Since the officers have to go on training schemes anyway, there would be almost no extra cost to police budgets. Net savings would be considerable. For the community organisations, there would be a modest cost for existing staff taking the time necessary to supervise the volunteers.

On the other hand, they would have a guaranteed stream of volunteers who would probably be more reliable than most.

Final thoughts

Sadly, the lessons that had been revealed by the Stephen Lawrence Inquiry are still not being implemented. Strong leaders are needed to make change happen.

Sir William's final word on the Inquiry?

> "It was the hardest thing I have ever had to do. It was not at all an easy case to conduct. Many people would have failed to conduct it at all."[21]

Afterword[1]

Following publication of *Hidden Stories*, in 2013–14 I revisited each of the six areas where the Lawrence Inquiry had taken place: Bristol, Birmingham, East London, Manchester, Bradford and West London. Over 500 people attended these events. I shared my experiences of being a part of the Lawrence Inquiry and what I believed to be an attempt by Home Office civil servants to undermine the Inquiry itself. In turn, members of the audience shared their own experiences of racism and covert surveillance.

Role of civil servants during the Inquiry

In February 2014, before the release of his report, I had a conversation with Mark Ellison QC. I asked how he had got on with the Stephen Lawrence Inquiry files at The National Archive at Kew as part of his review.[2] I said I knew that the files were difficult to access as they were not indexed. He looked puzzled and told me the Home Office people were very helpful, that they had given him access to all their files and he had no difficulty finding any of the information he sought. I asked whether he had been pointed in the direction of the National Archive at Kew. He replied that he had not. He had seen all the files in the Home Office.

To me, this revelation was a bombshell. From the answer to Parliamentary Questions,[3,4] I had been led to understand that all the records of the Lawrence Inquiry were now contained in 41 files at The National Archives at Kew. Ellison, it seemed, had been shown only papers from the Inquiry at the Home Office.

As we were both certain that the documents we had seen were originals, it suggests that the Lawrence Inquiry records have been divided in two. Part are housed in The National Archives and a hitherto unknown part housed in the Home Office. This might explain why notes I made during the Lawrence Inquiry, for example, are missing from The National Archives. It seemed that Ellison had not been told about the papers in The National Archives,[5] while I, needless to say, had never been informed about the remainder at the Home Office.

In June 2014 I made a formal complaint[6] to the Home Secretary that senior Home Office civil servants could have undermined the Inquiry from the outset on four counts, three of which have already been raised in this book.[7] The fourth count set out my belief that there are two archives of the Inquiry: the public one at The National Archives and one that is private.

The reply from Mark Sedwill, Permanent Secretary at the Home Office, in August 2014 informed me that the Inquiry papers were split into four sections, and that one section – the evidence files – were still held by the Home Office:

> You made a related complaint about the archive now being in two parts. This is unavoidable as the evidence files still held at the Home Office contain information which should not be in the public domain while the investigation into the murder of Stephen Lawrence continues.[8]

It seems bizarre that the Home Office should guard any papers of a live police investigation, in particular such a high profile case as the Stephen Lawrence case. We take it for granted that they must be being held in a secure environment. Why has it been necessary to take files from the Metropolitan Police and hold them in the Home Office?

In the interests of transparency and open government, archives of public inquiries are public material. They should be publicly available as soon as possible after the end of the inquiry concerned. The Hutton Inquiry (2003–04) addressed the issues surrounding the death of the weapons inspector David Kelly. Transcripts and reports were available to the public within weeks of the end of the inquiry.

Mark Sedwill's letter also states that the material was made available to Mark Ellison and that 'Mr Ellison has confirmed to us that he considered the material as part of his Review'.[9]

Covert police surveillance

During my visits to the areas where the Inquiry had been held, I met with a number of people who shared their personal experiences of racism and covert surveillance by the police.

Janet Alder, the sister of Christopher Alder who died in police custody, attended our Bradford event. She informed a shocked audience how she learnt that she and her barrister were under surveillance for trying to establish the truth about the death of her brother.[10]

The experience of Mohammed Amran was voiced by his legal adviser. Mohammed had been informed that he was the potential victim of an alleged smear campaign by the West Yorkshire Police while he was due to give evidence at the Lawrence Inquiry back in 1998.[11]

In West London we heard from Sukhdev Reel, who told us that she had arrived from a meeting with the police who had informed her of the extent of surveillance on her during her campaign to establish the truth about the murder of her son Ricky.[12]

In 2013, in the course of preparation for the event in Manchester, I learnt that surveillance had been undertaken on members of the public attending the Lawrence Inquiry while it sat in Manchester. I spoke to Charles Critchlow, former president of the Black Police Association, who told me that in 1998 he alerted senior officers in Greater Manchester Police to the serious implications of a circular from Special Branch, which requested information and intelligence on members of the public attending the Stephen Lawrence Inquiry.[13] Sixteen years later, the concerns he had raised and escalated were echoed in the revelations of the Ellison Review regarding covert police surveillance during the Stephen Lawrence case.[14] Four months later I had the pleasure of awarding Charles with an award for Exemplary Conduct in a Public Office, in recognition of his 'vigilance, integrity and courage in defending the human rights of individuals attending the public session of the Stephen Lawrence Inquiry held in Manchester'.[15]

Racism

In the course of my 'tour', the bravery of a number of people who have challenged racism in the area of employment, both in the criminal justice system and education, was shared with the audiences; from the account in Bradford of Kashif Ahmed,[16] former West Yorkshire police officer, to the experiences of David McLeod[17] in Bristol and Gurpal Virdee[18] in West London. Their accounts were harrowing and deeply moving and we applaud their bravery in challenging racism.

A recent freedom of information request to UK police forces has revealed that hundreds of police officers who have had complaints of racism against them upheld in the past five years have avoided dismissal.[19] Surely if a police officer is found to be acting in racist ways at work it must always be considered gross misconduct and lead to dismissal.

During the Lawrence Inquiry we made three recommendations (55, 56, 57) asking the Metropolitan Police if there were any ways in which it might be possible to stop officers escaping from the results of their misconduct by retiring on medical or other grounds. Commissioner Condon told us he was working on it and was hoping to have some recommendations on it soon. That was in 1998. Theresa May, the Home Secretary, announced on 22 July 2014 that she would take on this challenge by introducing legislation to ensure that police officers cannot resign or retire to avoid misconduct hearings.[20] The new regulations came into force on 12 January 2015.[21] Furthermore, as a result of the independent review by Mark Ellison into allegations of corruption in the Stephen Lawrence case and the coalition government's response to it, a new criminal offence has been created. Section 26 of the Criminal Justice and Courts Act 2015 makes it an offence for a police officer to exercise the powers and privileges of a constable in a way that is corrupt or otherwise improper. The legislation supplements the existing common law offence of misconduct in public office.

Stop and search

The importance of accountability was a strong theme at all of the events. We heard disturbing accounts in Manchester of the reality of stop and search for young black men and the knock-on effect of this on their education.

Recent statistics reveal that per 1,000 of the population, black people are 6.0 times more likely to be stopped and searched compared with white people. Asian people and those from mixed ethnic groups were just over two times more likely to be stopped and searched than white people.[22] In relation to section 60 of the Criminal Justice and Public Order Act 1994, black people are 29 times more likely to be stopped and searched than white people.[23]

Section 60 stop and searches

Notwithstanding the dismal headline figures mentioned in the previous paragraph, there are encouraging glimmers that the situation is improving. The most striking statistical indication of this is the fall in the number of stops, especially under section 60 of the Criminal Justice and Public Order Act 1994, in the Metropolitan Police area, where the majority of section 60 stops take place.

Commissioner Bernard Hogan-Howe must take much of the credit for this. In July 2012 he announced his intention to reduce section 60 stops by half (as part of a number of measures to limit and regulate stops).[24] Latest statistics reveal that in the year ending 31 March 2014 there were 3,944 section 60 stops.[25] This figure represents a fall of around a quarter compared with the previous year. Of this number, 5% led to an arrest. It is encouraging that the number of section 60 stops has decreased since its peak in the year ending 31 March 2009. The decrease has been attributed to police forces using the power in a more focused way.[26]

While overall stop and search numbers have reduced in the past few years there are still 11% more stop and searches taking place than a decade previously.[27] Available data indicates that stop and search has become more targeted as illustrated by an increase in arrest rates.[28] This suggests a more outcomes-focused approach.

It may be that there is a recognition at last at the highest levels of government of the damage caused to society by the overuse – and disproportionate use – of stop and search.

Best Use of Stop and Search Scheme

On 26 August 2014 the Home Secretary launched the Best Use of Stop and Search Scheme. The scheme is part of a range of measures that are aimed at contributing to a reduction in the overall use of stop and search, leading to better and more intelligence-led stop and searches and more effective outcomes. As of 1 December 2014 35 forces implemented the scheme, which involves the following;

- Increase transparency by recording all outcomes of stop and search and whether there is a connection between the grounds for the search and the outcome;
- Restrict the use of section 60 'no suspicion' powers;
- Give members of the public the opportunity to observe stop and search in practice; and
- Introduce a community complaints trigger – ensuring that complaints are properly monitored and scrutinised.[29]

Whether all this activity translates to fundamental changes in practice remains to be seen. And even as one form of abuse of powers is at last reined in, another may rear its head. For example, while there has been attention given to curbing section 60 stop and search powers, there has been no equivalent drive from government to limit the much greater potential for abuse of the powers to stop and search under schedule 7 of the Terrorism Act 2000. Schedule 7 allows:

- detention for up to nine hours without arrest;
- the confiscation of belongings for seven days;
- the taking and retention of DNA samples.

Shockingly, as with section 60, there is no need for officers to have reasonable suspicion before stopping and detaining someone under schedule 7. Schedule 7 stops, like other stops, are disproportionately used against people from minority ethnic communities. As with other stops, schedule 7 stops are disproportionately used against people from minority ethnic groups, with Asians reported to have been detained in higher numbers.[30] This seems to be like a reappearance of the old discredited 'sus' laws coming in by the back door. Of course, these are just the tip of the iceberg of constantly proliferating so-called anti-terrorism laws with sweeping, ill-regulated powers. As terrorism is such an emotive subject today, political figures are frightened of appearing to obstruct measures that are deemed to protect people from it.

Recruitment, retention and progression of black and minority ethnic police officers

The small proportion of black and minority ethnic police officers remains pitiful. At higher grades it may even be reducing, following a number of high-profile retirements. In his examination of witnesses to the Home Affairs Committee into leadership and standards in the police, the Chair of the Committee, Keith Vaz, raised the following question with Mike Fuller (previously Chief Constable of Kent Constabulary):

> Mr Fuller, you are an example of the success. You were the first black chief Constable. You served for six years in Kent and on your appointment you said that the perception of the glass ceiling has been broken, yet since your appointment nobody else has been appointed and there are no black or Asian people on the strategic command course. There are no ACPO-rank black or Asian people. It seems to have gone back to 1994, if you like.[31]

In response to concerns made by the Committee, the government outlined the following:

> The Chief Executive of the College [of Policing] and chief constables have agreed to an extension of the

deadline for expressions of interest from BME officers to the Senior Police National Assessment Centre (PNAC), which for successful candidates leads to the Strategic Command Course (SCC). The Chief Executive has confirmed he will speak with the chief constable of any BME candidate who nominates herself/himself in this extended period. He has also confirmed that the College will work towards having a new process in place next year to ensure greater participation of BME officers in the senior PNAC and SCC processes for admission to chief officer rank, as part of the wider programme of work.[32]

It is important that this and future governments' responses are monitored very carefully by groups such as the National Black Police Association.

I support the Northern Ireland experiment on recruitment of people from minority communities, which was echoed by comments made by the Metropolitan Police Commissioner Hogan-Howe who said in March 2014 that he supported a 50:50 recruitment process, whereby one black or minority ethnic officer is recruited for every white officer recruited,[33] but this is certainly not yet taking place.

In the light of these developments it was deeply saddening for me to learn of the case of PC Carol Howard from the Metropolitan Police. PC Howard, a firearms officer in the Diplomatic Protection Group, initiated proceedings against her employer on the grounds of race, sex discrimination and victimisation. PC Howard was successful in her action.[34]

PC Howard's case has been the catalyst for an investigation by the Equality and Human Rights Commission into unlawful discrimination, harassment and victimisation of Metropolitan Police personnel, which was launched on the 22 September 2014. The focus of the investigation is the Met's fairness at work and misconduct proceedings. The Commission will present its findings later on this year.

PC Howard's case is truly shocking, and it is important that individuals take forward cases of discrimination to employment tribunals if they believe that they have been aggrieved. Furthermore, my experience has shown that it is important that employment tribunal cases are settled in court and in public, rather than in court and in secret. This will result in:

- police services accepting responsibility for making mistakes and learning from them;
- saving huge amounts of money from out of court settlements, which can then be fed back into policing;
- no gagging clauses.

Change will happen when discussion is in the open.

There is a powerful business case for equality. If the police discriminate less, less money will have to be spent on tribunals to redress the inequities of discrimination. This should hardly be the motivating reason, but any tool that will help to focus minds should be employed.

Final thoughts

Over the years my work has shown me that understanding and addressing racism is best brought about through a sustained grassroots approach, in which communities come together with the purpose of improving the quality of life for all. At every meeting in the cities where the Stephen Lawrence Inquiry was held, the commitment of the people we met and spoke with who want to work together to eradicate racism in the UK was loud and clear. I met and heard of the wonderful work of voluntary sector organisations with dedicated volunteers who support victims of racism and racial violence, groups like the Newham Monitoring Project in London and Stand Against Racism & Inequality (SARI) in Bristol. This is becoming ever more important as we are seeing a worrying rise of right wing political parties in the UK and Europe. Their rise is sadly mirrored by a rise in the numbers of hate crimes, both of a racial and religious nature. With a continued anti-immigrant rhetoric in the UK and Europe and no clear messages from our political leaders of the caustic and dangerous nature of these outbursts we need to seek out and support those individuals and groups who are willing to challenge this corrosive and divisive rhetoric and speak up for tolerance and understanding.

The meetings reinforced my belief that when we are trying to campaign for change, talking about 'racism' may not be ideal. Unfortunately, people find it too difficult to cope with the idea their behaviour might be 'racist'. It puts people's backs up and they react in a defensive and therefore intransigent way. Instead we get more traction by concentrating on 'professionalism'. It is not professional to act in a racially discriminatory or insensitive way. By taking this tack, we may achieve more of the changes we desire.

Notes

Preface

1   BBC News (2013) 'IPCC to supervise Stuart Lawrence race case investigation', 10 January, www.bbc.co.uk/news/uk-england-london-20978774.

2   Macpherson, W., Cook, T., Sentamu, J. and Stone, R. (1999) *The Stephen Lawrence Inquiry: Report of an inquiry by Sir William Macpherson of Cluny*, Norwich: The Stationery Office, chapter 47.

3   Ibid, 46.1.

4   Lord Scarman made a number of recommendations to the police force, including efforts to recruit more ethnic minorities into the police force and changes in training and law enforcement. He stressed the importance of tackling 'racial disadvantage' and 'racial discrimination'. The inquiry recommended 'urgent action' to ensure that racial disadvantage did not become an "endemic, ineradicable disease threatening the very survival of our society". Scarman L.G. (1981) *The Brixton disorders 10–12 April 1981: Report of an inquiry*, London: HMSO.

5   EHRC (Equality and Human Rights Commission) (2012) *Race disproportionality in stops and searches under section 60 of the Criminal Justice and Public Order Act 1994*, Manchester: EHRC.

Introduction

1   Statement from Neville and Doreen Lawrence, 4 May 1993.

2   Macpherson, W., Cook, T., Sentamu, J. and Stone, R. (1999) *The Stephen Lawrence Inquiry: Report of an inquiry by Sir William Macpherson of Cluny*, Norwich: The Stationery Office, 46.1.

3   Ibid, chapter 47.

4   See for example *The Times*, 4 January 2012.

5   Rollock, N. (2009) *The Stephen Lawrence Inquiry 10 years on: A critical review of the literature*, London: Runnymede Trust.

[6] Stone, R. (2009) *Independent review of the Stephen Lawrence Inquiry 10 years on*, London: Uniting Britain Trust.

[7] Stephenson, P. (2009) Speech to the conference to mark the 10th anniversary of the Stephen Lawrence Inquiry.

[8] Smikle, T.C. (2009) *NBPA Report: 10yr anniversary of the Stephen Lawrence Inquiry Report*, Tamworth: National Black Police Association, pp 20–1.

[9] BBC News (2011) 'Profile: Sir Paul Stephenson', 17 July.

[10] *The Guardian* (2012) 'Met police racists will be driven out vows Bernard Hogan-Howe', 13 April.

[11] The Diversity Group (2012) 'Met must improve racial diversity, admits Hogan-Howe', 9 January.

[12] Ibid.

[13] BBC News (2012) 'Stop and search overhaul planned by the Met', 13 January.

[14] Lawrence, D. (2012) 'Met police haven't changed over racism', Interview on LBC Radio, 12 April.

[15] Rollock, 2009, op cit; Stone, 2009, op cit.

[16] Macpherson et al, 1999, op cit.

[17] Letter from Councillor Roy Benjamin to Stephen Wells, 18 September 1998.

[18] Notes from meetings with Muhammad Idrish and Maxie Hayes, 3 July 2012.

[19] Hankin, A. (2012) 'Overwhelmed: probe into Hillsborough cover-up by the police "too big for IPCC"', *Mirror*, 23 October.

Chapter One

[1] The Leveson Inquiry is a judicial, two-part public inquiry into the culture, practices and ethics of the British press and police with regard to phone hacking. Part one was completed with the publication of the Leveson Report; part two cannot take place until current police investigations and any subsequent criminal proceedings have been completed.

[2] Macpherson, W., Cook, T., Sentamu, J. and Stone, R. (1999) *The Stephen Lawrence Inquiry: Report of an inquiry by Sir William Macpherson of Cluny*, Norwich: The Stationery Office, chapter 1.

3 Hewitt, R. (2005) *White backlash and the politics of multiculturalism*, Cambridge: Cambridge University Press, see chapter 3 'Greenwich and its racial murders', pp 35–55.

4 Transpontine (2012) 'Racist murder in South East London', 8 January.

5 Lee Jasper, evidence presented to the Stephen Lawrence Inquiry as reported in *The Economist* (1999) 'Stephen Lawrence's legacy', 28 January.

6 Kerr, W. (1993) 'Stephen Lawrence's family expresses frustrations', BBC News, 4 May.

7 Kerr, W. (1993) 'Stephen Lawrence's family meet Nelson Mandela', BBC News, 6 May.

8 Macpherson et al, 1999, op cit, 13.24–13.29.

9 Ibid, 14.52.

10 Ibid, 18.8–18.14.

11 Ibid, 14.46.

12 Transcripts of the Inquiry, Part One, day 32, p 6052.

13 Ibid, Part One, day 3, pp 202–3.

14 Ibid, pp 194–218.

15 Ibid.

16 Macpherson et al, 1999, op cit, chapter 13.

17 Ibid, 26.37.

18 Ibid, 14.66.

19 Ibid, 14.66.

20 Ibid, chapter 11; see also Transcripts of the Inquiry, Part One.

21 *The Independent* (1993) 'Student murder charges dropped: teenagers freed as CPS find insufficient evidence to provide a realistic prospect of conviction for "racially motivated" attack', 30 July.

22 Macpherson et al, 1999, op cit, 46.21.

23 Ibid, chapter 19.

24 Ibid, 15.13.

25 Ibid, 28.27.

26 Ibid, 5.5–5.7.

27 Ibid, chapter 41.

28 Transcripts of the Inquiry, Part One, day 1, p 5.

29 Ibid, Part One, day 3, pp 208, 210.

30 Macpherson et al, 1999, op cit, chapter 46.

Chapter Two

[1]   Macpherson, W., Cook, T., Sentamu, J. and Stone, R. (1999) *The Stephen Lawrence Inquiry: Report of an inquiry by Sir William Macpherson of Cluny*, Norwich: The Stationery Office, 3.1.

[2]   Ibid, 45.1.

[3]   *The Observer* (1998) 'Father may ask Lawrence judge to step down', 15 March.

[4]   Transcripts of the Inquiry, Part One, day 1, p 6.

[5]   Ibid, pp 3–14.

[6]   BBC News (1998) 'Home Secretary to meet Lawrence parents', 16 March.

[7]   Personal communication. I remember this conversation well but I have no notes from this time as they remain in the Home Office, unreleased into the public archive.

[8]   See opening statements in Transcripts of the Inquiry, Part One, day 2, pp 25–34.

[9]   BBC News (1998) 'Lawrence family to return to inquiry', 17 March.

[10] Scarman L.G. (1981) *The Brixton disorders 10–12 April 1981: Report of an inquiry*, London: HMSO.

[11] See, for example, Deech, R. (2011) 'My legal hero: Lord Leslie Scarman', *The Guardian*, 20 January.

[12] *Concise Oxford Dictionary, Ninth edition.*

[13] Blofeld, J., Sallah, D., Sashidharan, S., Stone, R. and Struthers, J. (2003) *Independent Inquiry into the death of David Bennett*, Cambridge: Norfolk, Suffolk and Cambridgeshire Strategic Health Authority.

[14] Transcripts of the Inquiry, Part One, day 2, pp 16–17.

[15] Ibid, pp 26–9.

[16] See, for example, Ellis, F. (2012) 'The Macpherson Report: "anti-racist" hysteria and the Sovietization of the United Kingdom', drfrankellis.blogspot.com/2012/04.

[17] Prime, J., Foust-Cummings, H., Salib, E.R. and Moss-Racusin, C.A. (2012) *Calling all white men: Can training help create inclusive workplaces?*, New York: Catalyst.

[18] Macpherson et al, 1999, op cit, 6.34.

Chapter Three

[1] *Daily Mail* (1997) 'Murderers: *The Mail* accuses these men of killing. If we are wrong, let them sue us', 14 February.

[2] Macpherson, W., Cook, T., Sentamu, J. and Stone, R. (1999) *The Stephen Lawrence Inquiry: Report of an inquiry by Sir William Macpherson of Cluny*, Norwich: The Stationery Office, 42.27.

[3] Personal communication during the Inquiry.

[4] For anyone who wishes to read the transcripts, the five appeared over two days. The day and page numbers are: Jamie Acourt, day 50, p 9721; Neil Acourt, day 50, p 9800, David Norris, day 50, p 9886 (recalled day 51); Luke Knight, day 51, p 9973; Gary Dobson, day 50, p 10015.

[5] See Hughes, M. (2012) 'Stephen Lawrence murder: how justice took years to catch up with Gary Dobson and David Norris', *The Telegraph*, 3 January.

[6] Transcripts of the Inquiry, Part One, day 51, pp 10088–9.

[7] Bagehot, W. (1998) 'Six young Britons', *The Economist*, 4 July.

[8] See Macpherson et al, 1999, op cit.

[9] Transcripts of the Inquiry, Part One, day 50, pp 9742–3.

[10] The Nation of Islam in Britain is a small offshoot of the American organisation led by Louis Farrakhan. It is effective in taking young black men away from crime, drugs and violence. Their version of Islam is not recognised by other Muslims. Their uniforms are sharp two-piece suits and red bow ties.

[11] BBC News (1998) 'Scuffles suspend Lawrence Inquiry', 29 June.

[12] Ibid.

[13] BBC News (1998) 'Violence disrupts Lawrence Inquiry', 29 June.

[14] Transcripts of the Inquiry, Part One, day 50, pp 9761–2.

[15] Ibid, p 9762.

[16] Ibid, p 9765.

[17] Ibid, p 9766.

[18] Ibid, p 9768.

[19] Ibid.

[20] Ibid, p 9770.

[21] Ibid, pp 9770–2.

[22] Ibid, p 9912.

[23] Ibid, day 51, p 9948.

[24] Ibid, pp 9941–3.

[25] Ibid, p 9966.

[26] Statement from Neville and Doreen Lawrence at the Stephen Lawrence Inquiry, 29 June 1998.

[27] See also Bagehot, W., 1998, op cit.

[28] Statement from Jamie Acourt, Neil Acourt, Gary Dobson, Luke Knight and David Norris at the Stephen Lawrence Inquiry, 30 June 1998.

[29] BBC News (1998) 'Violence erupts at Lawrence Inquiry', 30 June.

[30] Hughes, M. (2012) 'Stephen Lawrence murder: how justice took years to catch up with Gary Dobson and David Norris', *The Telegraph*, 3 January.

[31] BBC News (1998) 'Scuffles suspend Lawrence Inquiry', 29 June; BBC News (1998) 'Violence disrupts Lawrence Inquiry', 29 June.

[32] Transcripts of the Inquiry, Part Two, day 1, pp 2–3.

[33] See Appendix B for the full press release.

[34] Letter from Muhammad Idrish to Sir William Macpherson, 9 September 1998; see Appendix B.

[35] Letter from Stephen Wells to Muhammad Idrish, 14 September 1998; see Appendix B.

[36] Letter from Birmingham: Councillor Roy Benjamin to Stephen Wells, 18 September 1998; see Appendix B.

[37] Letter from Stephen Wells to Muhammad Idrish, 14 September 1998; see Appendix B.

[38] Letter from Stephen Wells to Muhammad Idrish, 28 September 1998; see Appendix B.

[39] Interview with Muhammad Idrish, 3 July 2012.

Chapter Four

[1] Macpherson, W., Cook, T., Sentamu, J. and Stone, R. (1999) *The Stephen Lawrence Inquiry: Report of an inquiry by Sir William Macpherson of Cluny*, Norwich: The Stationery Office.

[2] *The Guardian* (1998) 'Lawrence family spurns Met chief's personal apology over racist murder: when sorry is not enough', 2 October.

[3] Macpherson et al, 1999, op cit, chapter 30.

4 Transcripts of the Inquiry, Part One, day 45, pp 8568–9.

5 Ibid, p 8570.

6 Ibid, pp 8570–71.

7 Ibid, p 8572.

8 The NT3 boxes at The National Archives are mainly typed correspondence. My own internal handwritten notes and my computer disks are, at the time of writing, still in the Home Office's long-term storage.

9 *The Telegraph* (2009) 'Obituary: Edmund Lawson QC', *The Telegraph*, 11 May.

10 Note from Ed Lawson QC to Sir William Macpherson; see Appendix B.

11 BBC News (1998) 'Lawrence family unimpressed with police apology', 17 June.

12 Transcripts of the Inquiry, Part Two, day 3, p 279.

13 Ibid, p 286.

14 Ibid.

15 BBC Newsnight (2001) 'A black police officer at odds with his bosses', 8 May.

16 Transcripts of the Inquiry, Part Two, day 3, pp 286–7.

17 Rollock, N. (2009) *The Stephen Lawrence Inquiry 10 years on: A critical review of the literature*, London: Runnymede Trust.

18 Stone, R. (2009) *Independent review of the Stephen Lawrence Inquiry 10 years on*, London: Uniting Britain Trust.

19 Dhani, A. and Kaiza, P. (2001) *Police service strength: England and Wales, 31 March 2011*, Home Office Statistical Bulletin 13/11, London: Home Office, p 14.

20 Transcripts of the Inquiry, Part Two, day 3, pp 280–1.

21 EHRC (Equality and Human Rights Commission) (2010) *Stop and think: A critical review of the use of stop and search powers in England and Wales*, Manchester: EHRC; EHRC (2012) *Race disproportionality in stops and searches under section 60 of the Criminal Justice and Public Order Act 1994*, Manchester: EHRC.

22 Transcripts of the Inquiry, Part Two, day 3, pp 288–9.

23 Ibid, pp 289–91.

24 Ibid, pp 306–7.

25 Ibid, pp 307–8.

26 Ibid, pp 309–10.

[27] Ibid, pp 311–12.

[28] Ibid, day 1, p 57.

[29] Ibid, day 3, pp 317–18.

[30] For example, BBC News (1998) 'Black officers tell of police racism', 28 September.

[31] Transcripts of the Inquiry, Part Two, day 3, pp 319–22.

[32] Ibid, p 322.

[33] Ibid, pp 326–9.

[34] Ibid, p 329.

[35] Bennetto, J. (2009) *Police and racism: What has been achieved 10 years after the Stephen Lawrence Inquiry Report?*, London: Equality and Human Rights Commission; Rollock, 2009, op cit.

[36] Transcripts of the Inquiry, Part Two, day 3, pp 333–5.

[37] Ibid, pp 335–9.

[38] See Appendix C for the full transcript of the Commissioner's submission and questioning.

[39] Transcripts of the Inquiry, Part Two, day 3, pp 340–67.

[40] BBC News (1998) 'Lawrence Inquiry shakes trust in the police', 16 June.

[41] Riddell, M. (2000) 'The *New Statesman* interview – Sir William Macpherson', *New Statesman*, 21 February.

[42] Casciani, D. (2009) 'Phillips clears police of racism', BBC News, 19 January.

[43] Phillips, T. (2009) Speech to the Stephen Lawrence Conference, London, 24 February.

[44] Baldwin, T. and Rozenberg, G. (2004) 'Britain "must scrap multiculturalism"', *The Times*, 3 April.

[45] Muir, H. (2009) 'Trevor Phillips: a career in crisis', *The Guardian*, 28 July; Cameron, D. (2011) Speech to the Munich Security Conference, 5 February.

[46] Finney, N. and Simpson, L. (2009) *'Sleepwalking to segregation'? Challenging myths about race and migration*, Bristol: The Policy Press.

Chapter Five

[1] Macpherson, W., Cook, T., Sentamu, J. and Stone, R. (1999) *The Stephen Lawrence Inquiry: Report of an inquiry by Sir William Macpherson of Cluny*, Norwich: The Stationery Office.

[2] www.the-hutton-inquiry.org.uk, available through The National Archives.

[3] At time of publication these can be found at www.archive.official-documents.co.uk/document/cm42/4262/4262.htm.

[4] See *Hansard*, HC Deb, 29 March 1999, vol 328, c 778.

[5] www.blink.org.uk.

[6] Chouhan, K. and Jasper, L. (2000) *A culture of denial*, London: 1990 Trust.

[7] *Hansard*, 19 October 2004, c 602w.

[8] *Hansard*, 25 January 2005, c 293w.

[9] *Hansard*, Cm 111129, 29 Nov 2011, c 803W.

[10] richardstonesli.wordpress.com.

[11] Macpherson et al, 1999, op cit, 6.34.

[12] Ibid, chapter 46.

[13] Transcripts of the Inquiry, Part One, day 51, pp 11056–8.

[14] Personal communication.

[15] Macpherson et al, 1999, op cit, 46.3.

[16] Unpublished draft of the Stephen Lawrence Inquiry Report.

[17] 'The secret policeman', BBC *Panorama*, first aired 21 October 2003.

[18] CRE (Commission for Racial Equality) (2005) *The police service in England and Wales: Final report of a formal investigation by the Commission for Racial Equality*, London: CRE.

[19] 'The boys who killed Stephen Lawrence', a *Panorama* programme for the BBC, first aired 26 July 2006.

[20] IPCC (Independent Police Complaints Commission) (2007) *Investigation report: IPCC independent investigation into complaints following* 'The boys who killed Stephen Lawrence', London: IPCC, 6.

[21] Macpherson et al, 1999, op cit, chapter 19.

[22] IPCC, 2007, op cit, p 5.

[23] Ibid, p 32.

[24] IPCC (2012) *Investigation report: IPCC independent investigation into complaints following* 'The boys who killed Stephen Lawrence', London: IPCC, p 24.

[25] IPCC (2007), op cit, pp 26–7.

[26] Macpherson et al, 1999, op cit, recommendation 58.

[27] IPCC, 2007, op cit.

[28] IPCC (2012) 'IPCC Review of 2006 investigation into allegations of corruption in the Stephen Lawrence murder investigation', Press release, 31 May.

[29] Personal communication with Deborah Glass.

[30] See for example, Gillard, M. and Flynn, L. (2012) 'The copper, the Lawrence killer's father, and secret police files that expose a "corrupt relationship"', *The Independent*, 6 March.

[31] Macpherson et al, 1999, op cit, 6.31, 6.33 and 6.37.

Chapter Six

[1] See Lea, J. (2002) 'The Macpherson Report and the question of institutional racism', *The Howard Journal of Criminal Justice*, vol 39, no 3, pp 219–33.

[2] Macpherson, W., Cook, T., Sentamu, J. and Stone, R. (1999) *The Stephen Lawrence Inquiry: Report of an inquiry by Sir William Macpherson of Cluny*, Norwich: The Stationery Office, 6.45.

[3] Ibid, 6.48.

[4] Boris Johnson was very critical of the Stephen Lawrence Inquiry Report in a series of articles in *The Telegraph*; his opinions are summarised in Johnson, B. (2003) *Lend me your ears*, London: Harper Collins. Also see for example, Upton, J. (1999) 'The smallest details speak the loudest', review of *The Macpherson Report* and Brian Cathcart's, *The case of Stephen Lawrence*, Viking, London, 1999, in *The London Review of Books*, vol 21, no 13, 1 July, p 9; Innes, M. (1999) 'Beyond the Macpherson Report: managing murder inquiries in context', *Sociological Research Online*, vol 4, no 1.

[5] Riddell, M. (2000) 'The *New Statesman* interview – Sir William Macpherson', *New Statesman*, 21 February.

[6] Such signs, displayed in the windows of boarding houses in England in the 1950s, are reported to have been a common sight, http://news.bbc.co.uk/1/hi/magazine/6681337.stm.

[7] Macpherson et al, 1999, 6.4.

[8] Ibid, 6.34 and 46.27.

9   Ibid, 46.28.

10 Ibid.

11 Ibid, chapter 46.

12 Ibid, 46.26.

13 Kerr, W. (1993) 'Stephen Lawrence's family expresses frustrations', BBC News, 4 May.

14 Macpherson et al, 1999, op cit, 6.34.

15 Ibid.

16 Ibid.

17 Transcripts of the Inquiry, Part Two, day 4, pp 454–70.

18 BBC News (1999) 'New era of race relations', 24 February.

19 Macpherson et al, 1999, op cit, 6.34.

20 Ibid, 14.66.

21 Administrative papers of the Inquiry, transcripts from the regional meetings (The National Archives NT3).

22 Ibid.

23 EHRC (2012) *Race disproportionality in stops and searches under section 60 of the Criminal Justice and Public Order Act 1994*, Manchester: EHRC.

24 Trevor Hall had noted a similar statistic shortly after the Inquiry Report, as quoted in *The Economist* (1999) 'Stephen Lawrence's legacy', 28 January.

25 BBC News (2013) 'IPCC to supervise Stuart Lawrence race case investigation', 10 January, www.bbc.co.uk/news/uk-england-london-20978774.

25 Macpherson et al, 1999, op cit, chapter 11.

26 Ibid, 11.12–11.13.

27 Moon, D. and Flatley, J. (eds) (2011) *Perceptions of crime, engagement with the police, authorities dealing with antisocial behaviour and Community Payback: Findings from the 2010/11 British Crime Survey*, Supplementary Volume 1 to Crime in England and Wales 2010/11, London: Home Office; Roberts, D. (2011) *Reading the riots: Investigating Britain's summer of disorder*, London: Guardian Books.

28 Administrative papers of the Inquiry, op cit.

29 MoJ (Ministry of Justice) (2011) *Statistics on race and the criminal justice system 2010*, London: MoJ.

30 Macpherson et al, 1999, op cit, recommendation 38.

[31] See *Connelly v DPP*, [1964] AC 1254.

[32] 1966 United Nations International Covenant on Civil and Political Rights, see Klug, F. (2010) *Commonsense: Reflections on the Human Rights Act*, London: Liberty.

[33] UN (United Nations) General Assembly (1966) *International covenant on civil and political rights*, 16 December, UN Treaty Series, vol 999, p 171, www.unhcr.org/refworld/docid/3ae6b3aa0.html.

[34] For those not familiar with the distinction between Liberty, Justice, and other similar organisations with short snappy names, this is the one that used to be called the National Council for Civil Liberties (NCCL). Soon after the end of the Stephen Lawrence Inquiry I was elected to the Council of Liberty.

[35] Liberty (2001) 'Double jeopardy breaches a key protection in our justice system', Press release.

[36] Macpherson et al, 1999, op cit, recommendation 65.

[37] See Dyer, C. (1999) 'Double jeopardy rule to be reviewed', *The Guardian*, 3 July; BBC News (2001) 'Fears over justice reforms', 21 June; *Daily Mail* (2001) 'Double jeopardy rule may be scrapped', 6 March.

[38] See Dyer, 1999, ibid; BBC News, 2001, ibid; *Daily Mail*, 2001, ibid; Liberty, 2001, op cit; Gabb, T. (2002) 'Why the double jeopardy rule should not be changed', *Libertarian Alliance*, no 67, 26 June; Helm, T. (2002) 'Justice Bill is a con trick, says Labour QC', *The Telegraph*, 10 November; *The Telegraph* (2002) 'Blunkett to unveil law reforms', 21 November.

[39] Linton, M. and Kennedy, H. (2001) 'Second time unlucky?', *The Guardian*, 17 July.

[40] *Daily Mail* (2005) 'Double jeopardy to be scrapped under court reforms', 30 March.

[41] 2003 Criminal Justice Act, Part 10, pp 40–2.

[42] Ibid, p 41.

[43] BBC News (2011) 'Stephen Lawrence pair face murder trial', 18 May.

[44] CPS (Crown Prosecution Service) (2012) 'Statement on conviction of David Norris and Gary Dobson for the murder of Stephen Lawrence', Press statement, 3 January.

[45] Baron, A. (2012) 'Stephen Lawrence – the compounding of an injustice', *Digital Journal,* 4 January.

[46] See Steel, J. (2001) 'Two years on, Macpherson Report still splits opinion', *The Telegraph,* 20 February; Hume, M. (1999) 'Macpherson Report: keeping our wits about us', *LM magazine,* issue 119, April.

Chapter Seven

[1] Macpherson, W., Cook, T., Sentamu, J. and Stone, R. (1999) *The Stephen Lawrence Inquiry: Report of an inquiry by Sir William Macpherson of Cluny,* Norwich: The Stationery Office, 46.23.

[2] Conn, D. (2012) 'Hillsborough: Norman Bettison stands down from West Yorkshire police', *The Guardian,* 24 October.

[3] Macpherson et al, 1999, op cit, 2.1, 2.3.

[4] Ibid, chapter 39.

[5] Ibid, 13.57.

[6] Reported in Brown, M. (1993) 'Stephen Lawrence: the boy who didn't see black and white', *The Telegraph,* 7 May.

[7] Macpherson et al, 1999, op cit, 23.2.

[8] Ibid, 23.9.

[9] Ibid, 23.9.

[10] Ibid, 11.59.

[11] Ibid, 29.25.

[12] Transcripts of the Inquiry, Part Two, day 3, pp 279–80.

[13] Ibid, p 280.

[14] Ibid, p 281.

[15] Ibid.

[16] Macpherson et al, 1999, op cit, chapter 14.

[17] Transcripts of the Inquiry, op cit, pp 298.

[18] AMIP Guidelines, *Reviews of unsolved cases,* section 8.1.

[19] Macpherson, 1999, op cit, 46.21.

[20] Ibid, 28.55.

[21] Ibid, 28.56, emphasis added.

[22] Transcripts of the Inquiry, op cit, pp 303–4.

[23] Macpherson et al, 1999, op cit, 8.7–8.11.

[24] 'The secret policeman', a *Panorama* programme for the BBC, first aired 21 October 2003; 'The boys who killed Stephen Lawrence', a *Panorama* programme for the BBC, first aired 26 July 2006; see also Chapter Three.

[25] Miller, D. (2012) 'Stephen Lawrence's mother demands new public inquiry into son's murder after fresh claims of police corruption', *Daily Mail*, 23 April.

[26] Dodd, V. (2012) 'Stephen Lawrence murder: Met police report finds no evidence of corruption', *The Guardian*, 31 May; IPCC (Independent Police Complaints Commission) (2012) *Review report: IPCC independent investigation into complaints following* 'The boys who killed Stephen Lawrence', London: IPCC.

[27] Dodd, V. (2012) 'Stephen Lawrence: Theresa May orders review into police corruption claims', *The Guardian*, 1 June; Peachey, P. (2012) 'After 19 years, Stephen Lawrence police face corruption investigation', *The Independent*, 12 May.

[28] Home Office (2010) *Policing in the 21st century: Reconnecting police and the people*, Cm 7925, London: Home Office.

[29] HMIC (Her Majesty's Inspectorate of Constabulary) (1997) *Equal opportunities and community and race relations: Minimum effective training levels*, p 44.

[30] Transcripts of the Inquiry, op cit, p 282.

[31] Ibid.

[32] See for example, HMIC (Her Majesty's Inspectorate of Constabulary) (1997) *Equal opportunities and community and race relations: Minimum effective training levels*.

[33] Home Affairs Select Committee (1999) *Fourth report: Police training and recruitment*, London: The Stationery Office, p 169.

[34] CRE (Commission for Racial Equality) (2005) *The police service in England and Wales: Final report of a formal investigation by the Commission for Racial Equality*, London: CRE, p 121.

[35] For example the cases of Victoria Climbié and of Baby Peter Connolly.

[36] NACRO (1997) *Policing local communities: The Tottenham experiment*, London: NACRO, p 3.

[37] Macpherson et al, 1999, op cit, 46.31.

[38] Ibid, chapter 47, recommendation 61.

39 Bowling, B., Parmar, A. and Phillips, C. (2003) 'Policing ethnic minority communities', in T. Newburn *The handbook of policing*, Cullompton: Willan, p 540.

40 Ibid.

41 Stop and Search Action Team (2004) *Strategy 2004/05*, London: Home Office.

42 Shiner, M. (2006) *National implementation of the recording of police stops*, London: Home Office.

43 The current stop and search policy is that the record of a search must always include: "A note of the self defined ethnicity, and if different, the ethnicity as perceived by the officer making the search ... The date, time and place the person or vehicle was searched ... The object of the search ... the grounds for suspicion ... the identity of the officer carrying out the search." Home Office (2011) *Code of practice for the exercise by police officers of statutory powers of stop and search: Police officers and police staff requirements to record public encounters*, PACE Code A 2011, London: Home Office.

44 EHRC (Equality and Human Rights Commission) (2012) *Race disproportionality in stops and searches under section 60 of the Criminal Justice and Public Order Act 1994*, Manchester: EHRC.

45 Ibid.

46 Rosenbaum, D., Schuck, A., Costello, A., Hawkins, D. and Ring, M. (2005) 'Attitudes toward the police: the effects of direct and vicarious experience', *Police Quarterly*, vol 8, no 3, pp 343–65.

47 Personal communication; community consultation run by Race On the Agenda (ROTA) in South London in 2012.

48 Personal communication, ibid.

49 Runnymede Trust (1997) *Islamophobia: A challenge for us all*, London: Runnymede Trust.

50 Bailey, D. (2012) 'Factbox: Violent anti-Sikh incidents in the US since 2001', *Chicago Tribune*, 5 August.

51 For example, Dilowar Hussain, director of the East London Mosque expressed concern that the mosque might be attacked, as reported in *The Times* (2005) 'London has stood together', 8 July.

52 IRR (Institute of Race Relations) (2005) 'Anti-Muslim backlash intensifies', 28 July, www.irr.org.uk/news/anti-muslim-backlash-intensifies/

[53] Doughty, S. (2006) 'Race crime backlash after 7/7 did not materialise, admits DPP', *Daily Mail*, 4 December.

[54] Blair, T. (2005) Speech to the Labour Party Conference, 16 July, as reported by BBC News 'Blair speech on terror', 16 July.

[55] IPCC (2007) *Stockwell One: Investigation into the shooting of Jean Charles de Menezes at Stockwell underground station on 22 July 2005*, London: IPCC; IPCC (2007) *Stockwell Two: An investigation into complaints about the Metropolitan Police Service's handling of public statements following the shooting of Jean Charles de Menezes on 22 July 2005*, London: IPCC.

[56] Punch, M. (2010) *Shoot to kill: Police accountability, firearms and fatal force*, Bristol: The Policy Press; Squires, P. and Kennison, P. (2010) *Shooting to kill? Policing, firearms and armed response*, Oxford: Wiley-Blackwell.

[57] BBC News (2006) 'Raid police apologise for "hurt"', 14 June.

[58] BBC News (2006) 'Officer demands critical analysis', 14 June.

[59] Innes, M., Roberts, C., Lowe, T. and Abbott, L. (2007) *Hearts and minds and eyes and ears: Reducing radicalisation risks through reassurance-oriented policing*, Cardiff: Universities' Police Science Institute, p 4.

[60] Innes, M., Roberts, C. and Innes, H. with Lowe, T. and Lakhani, S. (2011) *Assessing the effects of Prevent policing: A report to the Association of Chief Police Officers*, Cardiff: Universities' Police Science Institute.

[61] ACPO (2011) 'New research indicates Muslim communities welcome engagement', Press release, 10 April.

[62] Mayor's Office for Policing and Crime (2012) 'London Muslim Communities Forum launched', Press release, 27 March.

[63] Walker, P. (2012) 'Ian Tomlinson case: PC Simon Harwood sacked for gross misconduct', *The Guardian*, 17 September.

[64] BBC News (2012) 'Miners' strike policing: Labour calls for Orgreave inquiry', 22 October.

[65] El-Enany, N. (2012) 'Simon Harwood is just the latest police officer found not guilty', 19 July.

[66] Hillsborough Independent Panel (2012) *Hillsborough: The report of the Hillsborough Independent Panel*, London: The Stationery Office.

[67] Joint Select Committee on Human Rights (2009) *Demonstrating respect for rights? A human rights approach to policing protest*, 23 March.

[68] McVeigh, T., Syal, R. and Hinsliff, G. (2009) 'G20 protests: how the image of the UK police took a beating', *The Observer*, 19 April.

[69] Davies, C. (2011) 'Boris Johnson heckled in Clapham Junction over London riots', 9 August.

[70] Lewis, P. and Quinn, B. (2011) 'London riots: how did the Metropolitan Police lose control of the capital?' *The Guardian*, 8 August.

[71] Winsor, T. (2012) *Independent review of police officer and staff remuneration and conditions, Final report*, London: The Stationery Office.

Chapter Eight

[1] Runnymede Trust (1997) *Islamophobia: A challenge for us all*, London: Runnymede Trust.

[2] Blofeld, J., Sallah, D., Sashidharan, S., Stone, R. and Struthers, J. (2003) *Independent Inquiry into the death of David Bennett*, Cambridge: Norfolk, Suffolk and Cambridgeshire Strategic Health Authority.

[3] Macpherson, W., Cook, T., Sentamu, J. and Stone, R. (1999) *The Stephen Lawrence Inquiry: Report of an inquiry by Sir William Macpherson of Cluny*, Norwich: The Stationery Office, chapter 47.

[4] *Hansard*, HC Deb, 24 February 1999, c 380, 390–404, www.publications.parliament.uk/pa/cm199899/cmhansrd/vo990224/debindx/90224-x.htm.

[5] Macpherson et al (1999), op cit, 3.1.

[6] See for example, *The Telegraph* (2009) Police 'still institutionally racist', 15 February; *The Independent* (2012) "Metropolitan police still institutionally racist', 6 April; *The Guardian* (2012) 'Police watchdog launches review of Met racism complaints', 16 April.

[7] Rollock, N. (2009) *The Stephen Lawrence Inquiry 10 years on: A critical review of the literature*, London: Runnymede Trust; Stone, R. (2009) *Independent review of the Stephen Lawrence Inquiry 10 years on*, London: Uniting Britain Trust.

[8] Brady, B. (2012) 'Police "in denial" over rise in racism complaints', *Independent on Sunday*, 6 May.

[9] Ibid.

[10] EHRC (Equality and Human Rights Commission) (2012) *Race disproportionality in stops and searches under section 60 of the Criminal Justice and Public Order Act 1994*, Manchester: EHRC.

[11] Wadsworth, M., Lucas, J. and Simpson, S. (2012) 'Hogan-Howe faces community backlash', *The Voice*, 21 April, www.voice-online.co.uk/article/hogan-howe-faces-community-backlash.

[12] *The Telegraph* (2013) 'Senior Met Police chief quits with race crisis parting shot', 4 February, www.telegraph.co.uk/news/uknews/law-and-order/9846515/Senior-Met-Police-chief-quits-with-race-crisis-parting-shot.html.

[13] Laville, S. (2013) 'Senior Asian police officer retires after promotion snub over media skills', *The Guardian*, 4 February, www.guardian.co.uk/uk/2013/feb/04/senior-asian-policeman-quits-met.

[14] Ibid.

[15] PCA (Police Complaints Authority) (1997) *Report by the Police Complaints Authority on the investigation of a complaint against the Metropolitan Police Authority by Mr N. and Mrs D. Lawrence* (the Kent Report), Cm 3822, London: The Stationery Office, 14.28.

[16] Macpherson et al, 1999, op cit, 44.14.

[17] Ibid, recommendations 1–5.

[18] Laville, S. and Walker, P. (2013) 'Police funds 'should be diverted to improve under-resourced IPCC', *The Guardian*, 1 February.

[19] Evans, M. (2012) 'IPCC to handle all Met Police racism complaints', *The Telegraph*, 16 April.

[20] *Information Daily* (2012) 'UK police: London Mayor Boris Johnson announces review into police racism', 6 June.

[21] Riddell, M. (2000) 'The *New Statesman* interview – Sir William Macpherson', *New Statesman*, 21 February.

Afterword

[1] Written with Sam Wishaw.

[2] Mark Ellison QC was commissioned by the Home Secretary to undertake a review into the following: (1) Was there evidence providing reasonable grounds for suspecting that any officer associated with the initial investigation of the murder of Stephen Lawrence acted corruptly?(2) Were there any further lines of

investigation connected to the issue of possible corrupt activity by any officer associated with the initial investigation of the murder of Stephen Lawrence? (3) Was the Macpherson Inquiry provided with all relevant material connected to the issue of possible corrupt activity by any officer associated with the initial investigation of the murder of Stephen Lawrence? (4) What was the role of undercover policing in the Lawrence case, who ordered it and why? Was information on the involvement of undercover police withheld from the Macpherson Inquiry, and if it had been made available what impact might that have had on the Inquiry? (5) What was the extent of intelligence or surveillance activity ordered or carried out by police forces nationally in respect of the Macpherson Inquiry, Stephen Lawrence's family or any others connected with the Inquiry or the family? (6) What was the extent, purpose and authorisation for any surveillance of Duwayne Brooks and his solicitor?

3   *Hansard* 19 October 2004, c 602w.

4   *Hansard* 25 January 2005, c 293w

5   Though more recently he has suggested that he had seen them , perhaps out of a concern not to distract from or undermine his report. He was certainly adamant that he had not when we first spoke about it.

6   Letter from Richard Stone to Theresa May, Home Secretary, 3 June 2014; see Appendix D.

7   (1) Attempting to have a planned visit of the Inquiry to Birmingham in 1998 cancelled; (2) withholding transcripts of the hearings from 1999–2005; (3) withholding the correspondence files from 1999–2011) (see Chapter Three).

8   Reply from Mark Sedwill, Permanent Secretary, 1 August 2014 (page 1); see Appendix D.

9   Reply from Mark Sedwill, Permanent Secretary, 1 August 2014 (page 2); see Appendix D.

10 IPCC (Independent Police Complaints Commission) (2013) ' Investigation into surveillance following death of Christopher Alder', 26 July, www.ipcc.gov.uk/news/investigation-surveillance-following-death-christopher-alder#sthash.TVeIDNw2.dpuf

11 www.theguardian.com/uk-news/2013/jul/05/norman-bettison-mohammed-amran-allegations

12 Williams, R. (2014) "'The police were spying on me rather than looking for Ricky's killers" – Sukhdev Reel', *The Guardian*, 27 August

13 *Hansard*, 18 July 2013, c WA150, www.publications.parliament.uk/pa/ld201314/ldhansrd/text/130718w0001.htm

14 Ellison, M. (2014) *The Stephen Lawrence Independent Review: Possible corruption and the role of undercover policing in the Stephen Lawrence case*, HC1094, London: Home Office.

15 Reflecting Our Communities (2014) National Black Police Association 14th annual training conference and AGM, 29-31 October, London, www.nbpa.co.uk/wp-content/uploads/2011/08/NBPA-Booklet.pdf

16 BBC 'File on 4' (2012) 'Police racism' [transcript], http://news.bbc.co.uk/1/shared/bsp/hi/pdfs/05_06_12_fo4_policeracism.pdf

17 BBC News (2014) 'Bristol City Council accused of racism by black development worker', 12 November, www.bbc.co.uk/news/uk-england-bristol-30026180

18 Lakhani, N. (2012) "'If you complain about racism, your career is finished," says Met detective Gurpal Singh Virdi', *The Independent*, 9 May

19 BBC News (2014) 'Racism probe police officers "avoid sack"', FOI research reveals', 30 December, www.bbc.co.uk/news/uk-england-30398621

20 *Hansard* 22 July 2014, c 1265

21 www.gov.uk/government/news/new-regulations-prevent-police-officers-retiring-or-resigning-to-avoid-dismissal

22 Ministry of Justice (2013) *Statistics on Race and the Criminal Justice System 2012*, London:

23 Hurrell, K. (2013) *Race disproportionality in stops and searches 2011-12*, Equality and Human Rights Commission, Briefing Paper 7.

24 *The Telegraph* (2012) 'Random stop and search to be halved, Met chief orders', 13 January.

25 'Police powers and procedures England and Wales year ending 31 March 2014', Home Office, 16 April 2015, www.gov.uk/government/statistics/police-powers-and-procedures-england-and-wales-year-ending-31-march-2014

26 Ibid.

27 Stop and Search factsheet produced by Stop Watch, stop-watch. org/get-informed/factsheet/stop-and-search

28 Ibid.

29 'Launch of government's Best Use of Stop and Search Scheme', 1 December 2014, www.gov.uk/government/news/launch-of-governments-best-use-of-stop-and-search-scheme

30 Schedule 7 factsheet produced by Stop Watch, stop-watch.org/ get-informed/factsheet/schedule-7

31 Home Affairs Committee (2013) Minutes of evidence, HC67-II, 23 April, www.publications.parliament.uk/pa/cm201314/cmselect/ cmhaff/67/130423.htm

32 HM Government (November 2013) *The government response to the third report from the Home Affairs Committee session 2013-14 HC 67: Leadership and standards in the police*, Cm 8759

33 BBC News (2014) 'Met Police chief backs 50:50 recruitment', 27 March, www.bbc.co.uk/news/uk-england-london-26765540

34 www.judiciary.gov.uk/wp-content/uploads/2014/09/et-howard. pdf

APPENDIX A

Timeline of key events

22 April 1993	Stephen Lawrence is stabbed to death in an unprovoked attack by white youths
23 April 1993	Suspects identified
4 May 1993	Family hold press conference to express frustrations that police are not doing enough to catch killers
7 May-23 June 1993	Suspects arrested and two charged
29 July 1993	Crown Prosecution Service drops charges against two of the five suspects
22 December 1993	Inquest halted as family barrister claims new evidence
16 April 1994	Crown Prosecution Service refuses to prosecute, saying new evidence is insufficient
September 1994	Private prosecution launched by Doreen and Neville Lawrence against the suspects
December 1994	Police surveillance of Gary Dobson's flat
18-25 April 1996	Private prosecution fails
13 February 1997	Inquest verdict of unlawful killing "in a completely unprovoked racist attack by five youths"
	Doreen and Neville Lawrence make a formal complaint against the Metropolitan Police
14 February 1997	*Daily Mail* newspaper names the five suspects on its front page; invites them to sue
20 March 1997	Police Complaints Authority investigation
15 December 1997	Police Complaints Authority report identifies "significant weaknesses, omissions and lost opportunities". The report finds no evidence to support the allegation of racist conduct by any Metropolitan Police officer involved in the investigation
31 July 1997	Public inquiry announced
16 March 1998	Stephen Lawrence Inquiry opens
16 March-21 September 1998	Inquiry Part One: 'quasi-judicial' hearings; evidence from 88 witnesses about the murder investigation
8 September-21 January 1999	Inquiry Part Two: 'lessons to be learned'; visits to six inner cities for meetings with local organisations and individuals; further submissions of evidence but hearings no longer quasi-judicial

---

17 July 1998	Assistant Commissioner Johnston apologises to family on behalf of the Metropolitan Police
1 October 1998	Metropolitan Police Commissioner Sir Paul Condon apologises to family
October 1998	PC Charles Critchlow (Greater Manchester Police), raises concerns with senior officers about a request by Special Branch for information and intelligence regarding groups or individuals likely to attend the Stephen Lawrence Inquiry
24 February 1999	Stephen Lawrence Inquiry Report published. It concludes that the police investigation was 'marred by a combination of professional incompetence, institutional racism and a failure of leadership by senior officers'
5 May 2004	Crown Prosecution Service announce insufficient evidence to prosecute anyone for Stephen's murder
April 2005	Double jeopardy scrapped
25 and 26 July 2006	Doreen and Neville Lawrence make formal complaints to the Independent Police Complaints Commission against the Metropolitan Police following private screening of BBC *Panorama* documentary
26 July 2006	BBC *Panorama* documentary 'The boys who killed Stephen Lawrence' alleges police corruption helped shield the killers from conviction
	Independent Police Complaints Commission asks the Metropolitan Police to review evidence before it investigates
14 October 2007	Independent Police Complaints Commission report published; finds no evidence of police corruption
8 November 2007	Police confirm they are investigating new evidence
February 2009	Stephen Lawrence Inquiry Report 10-year anniversary
7 September 2010	Gary Dobson and David Norris arrested
October 2011	Operation Herne launched to review and investigate the use of undercover officers by the former Metropolitan Police Special Demonstration Squad
14 November 2011	Trial begins
3 January 2012	Gary Dobson and David Norris both found guilty of the murder of Stephen Lawrence
2 April 2012	Independent Police Complaints Commission reviews its 2007 investigation; finds no new evidence

31 May 2012	Review by Metropolitan Police finds no new evidence of police corruption
1 June 2012	Home Office announces new inquiry looking into claims of police corruption in the murder investigation
11th July 2012	Home Secretary Theresa May announces an independent review of alleged police corruption during the Stephen Lawrence murder investigation, to be conducted by Mark Ellison QC
24 June 2013	Channel 4 *Dispatches* documentary 'The police's dirty secret' reports on allegations by an undercover police officer that he was part of an operation to 'smear' the family of Stephen Lawrence in 1993
8th July 2013	John Grieve, former Deputy Assistant Commissioner of the Metropolitan Police, admits authorising the secret recording of a meeting involving himself, Duwayne Brooks and his lawyer in May 2000
6th March 2014	Publication of *The Stephen Lawrence Independent Review: Possible corruption and the role of undercover policing in the Stephen Lawrence case*. Mark Ellison's findings reveal that the family of Stephen Lawrence were spied on by an undercover Metropolitan Police officer during the murder investigation
12 February 2015	The Criminal Justice and Courts Act 2015 comes into force, making it an offence for a police officer to exercise the powers and privileges of a constable in a way that is corrupt or otherwise improper
12 March 2015	Theresa May announces a statutory inquiry into undercover policing led by Lord Justice Pitchford

APPENDIX B

Correspondence regarding Part Two hearings

THE INQUIRY INTO THE MATTERS ARISING FROM
DEATH OF STEPHEN LAWRENCE

Chairman: Sir William Macpherson of Cluny
Secretary: Stephen Wells

Hannibal House
Elephant & Castle
London SE1 6TE

Telephone No:
Fax No:

Friday, August, 28, 1998   Press Release
(For immediate release)

Part 2 hearings
- venues and dates

The Stephen Lawrence Inquiry today announced the venues and dates for meetings to be held as part of the second stage of the inquiry. The meetings will be open to the public.

During Part 2 the Inquiry wants to identify lessons to be learned for the future investigation and prosecution of racially motivated crimes. It will be inviting interested groups and individuals to the meetings to expand on written submissions already received.

The meetings will be held in:

London - Hannibal House, Elephant and Castle
September 24-25 and October 1-2

London - Victoria Hall, (Town Hall complex), New Broadway, Ealing
October 8

Manchester - Jarvis Piccadilly Hotel, Piccadilly Plaza
October 13

London - York Hall, Old Ford Rd, Bethnal Green
October 15

Bradford - Stakis Hotel, Hall Ings
October 21

Bristol - Hilton National Hotel, Redcliffe Way
November 3

mtc/2

Notice of visits for the Part 2 hearings omitting Birmingham (page 1)

The meetings, which will run from 10am to 4.30pm, will be chaired by the Inquiry chairman Sir William Macpherson of Cluny. His advisers, Tom Cook, former Deputy Chief Constable of West Yorkshire; the Bishop for Stepney, the Right Reverend Dr John Sentamu; and Dr Richard Stone, chairman of the Jewish Council for Racial Equality will also be at the meetings.

Leading organisations and individuals will be invited to make presentations at the Hannibal House meetings. The other meetings will focus on contributions from local organisations and individuals.

The Inquiry has received 85 written submissions for Part 2. Submissions included examples of good practice, concerns about current policy and practice and proposals for change.

Sir William wishes to stress that Part 2 of the Inquiry is not an investigation into the current relationship between the police and ethnic minorities. "Primarily we wish to be constructive for the future - we are looking for positive recommendations concerning the investigation and prosecution of racially motivated crimes in order to be able to report in accordance with our terms of reference."

It is hoped that Sir William's report will be presented to the Home Secretary by the end of the year.

Notes to editors

1) The Inquiry's terms of reference are:

> **"To inquire into matters arising from the death of Stephen Lawrence on 22 April 1993 to date in order particularly to identify the lessons to be learned for the investigation and prosecution of racially motivated crimes."**

2) The Part 1 hearings, into matters arising from the death of Stephen Lawrence, began at Hannibal House on March 16, 1998 and finished on July 20. The Inquiry heard 56 days of evidence from 88 witnesses, two thirds of whom were serving police officers, ex-police officers or police employees.

3) The nine parties with legal representation at the Inquiry will make closing oral submissions for Part 1 on September 16, 17, 18 and 21.

Contact: Mike Booker
        Press Officer
        Tel:
        Mob:

Notice of visits for the Part 2 hearings (page 2)

19/9

ASIAN RESOURCE CENTRE

অ অ্যা অ্যা অ্যা ৴

101 Villa Road, Handsworth, Birmingham B19 1NH

Tel: (0121) 523 0580
(0121) 551 4518
Fax: (0121) 554 4553

Our ref:　　Your ref:　　Date: 9|9|98.

Sir William Macpherson
ROOM 313
Hannibal House
Elephant & Castle
London
SE1 6TE.

From:
Muhammad Idrish
Coordinator.
0121 551 0691.

Dear Sir,

Re: The Inquiry: Stephen Lawrence: lessons to be learnt.

We were given to understand that the Second part of your Inquiry will travel round the country to to take evidence from organisations & Individuals involved in and have experience of Race anti-Racist work. However I am disappointed to know that you do not plan to visit Birmingham.

It is a fact that, Birmingham's total population of 961,000 consists of 207000 Black people (21%) according to 1991 census. Within 0-17 age group Black population constitute 35% of the total.

Black population of Birmingham Suffers from acts of Racism same way as Black people in other part of the country but it has got its own unique characteristics. Never forget the fact that notorious Enoch Powell Bloo River of Blood Speech was made in Birmingham — Its ghost still haunts us.

We demand that your inquiry comes to Birmingham and listen to us.

Thanks,
yours Surely
Md. Idrish

P.S. enclosed is our annual report to give you an idea as to who we are!

REGISTERED CHARITY No. 511682

Muhammad Idrish's letter to Sir William Macpherson, 9 September 1998

THE INQUIRY INTO THE MATTERS ARISING FROM THE DEATH OF STEPHEN LAWRENCE

Chairman: Sir William Macpherson of Cluny
Secretary: Stephen Wells

Hannibal House
Elephant & Castle
London SE1 6TE

Telephone No:
Fax No:

1. Chairman } to see
2. Dr Stone }
Back to me in due course.

14 September 1998

Muhammad Idrish
Co-ordinator
Asian Resource Centre

Handsworth
Birmingham B19 1NH

Dear Mr Idrish

PART 2 - VENUES AND DATES

Thank you for your letter of 9 September to the Chairman of this Inquiry. Sir William has seen your letter, and has asked me to reply on his behalf in these terms. Maxie Hayles has also written to Sir William, and I replied to him in similar form.

Firstly, may I say that our not coming to Birmingham is a matter simply of diary availability of the Inquiry team - in particular, we have to be sensitive to Dr Richard Stone's (one of Sir William's advisers) position as a senior member of the Jewish faith, at a time when there are many Jewish festivals necessary for him to attend; the availability of suitable venues in Birmingham at the time when we might have been able to visit Birmingham; and the need to maintain the momentum of the Inquiry.

As to the first reason just given, you, I am sure, would wish us to be sensitive to the community and faith-based commitments of the Inquiry team; and, as to the third reason, we are conscious that the Inquiry must now proceed quickly towards the consideration of its recommendations and its report to the Home Secretary, so that the reform and change process can begin as soon as possible. However, it was the second problem - the availability of venues - which effectively scupper our chances of coming to Birmingham during the period we had available. Staff here were at great pains to attempt to secure a suitable venue in Birmingham, and even moved provisional bookings in other cities to see if a better result could be achieved. I can assure you that Sir William and I were both disappointed not to be visiting Birmingham.

Letter confirming no Birmingham visit (page 1), 14 September 1998

We do, of course, understand your disappointment in turn. However, you should not overlook the fact that we are consulting in public interested organisations in two areas of London with significant black populations - Ealing (which includes Southall) to the west of London; and Tower Hamlets (which draws in areas such as Newham) to the east of the capital. We are also travelling to Bristol, Manchester and Bradford; cities which, like Birmingham, have significant black populations and where the concerns and advice of the black community can be heard by the Inquiry. Furthermore, Andrew Houseley, Richard Stone and the inquiry team are seeking to find an opportunity to hear from representative organisations in Birmingham of the matters which concern you there, and to hear ideas for tackling those concerns. We will be in touch as matters proceed.

I hope this letter allays some of your fears, concerns and disappointment. If you would like a further word in the light of this letter, please be in touch. In the meantime, I have made sure that Sir William and Dr Stone have seen the report you enclosed with your letter.

Yours sincerely

STEPHEN WELLS

Letter confirming no Birmingham visit (page 2), 14 September 1998

COUNCILLOR ROY BENJAMIN,
Chair of Equalities,
THE COUNCIL HOUSE,
VICTORIA SQUARE,
BIRMINGHAM, B1 1BB

TEL. NO.:
MOBILE:

18 September 1998

Mr S Wells
Secretary of the Inquiry

Hannibal House
Elephant & Castle
London   EC1 6TE

Dear Mr Wells,

Re: Stephen Lawrence Inquiry – Part Two Hearings

I am writing to request that you reconsider your decision to not hold a full inquiry session in Birmingham as part of your second stage hearings schedule.

I have sought to gather together the rather unfortunate series of events which seem to have culminated in an impression being created that somehow there was no suitable venue available in Birmingham. Having this year hosted the European Home and Justice Ministers conference; G8; Eurovision and the International Lions Convention – not to mention a host of other large events, it seems somewhat inconceivable that the inquiry was unable to find space in Britain's second city.

The process used by your office for approaching Birmingham was, I have to say, somewhat perfunctory. According to my information, only the Birmingham Convention and Visitors Bureau (BCVB) was contacted, furthermore according to staff at BCVB the first contact was only made on July 27th and in addition no indication was given which enabled the staff to distinguish your request from any other run of the mill enquiry. Given the terms of reference for your Part Two Hearings and given local Government's pivotal role in seeking to tackle racially motivated crime, I am surprised that no letter or contact was made with the City Council via either the Chief Executive or the leader of the council. I can assure you that had that single connection been made then this situation could have been avoided. Nevertheless, I do hope you will reconsider your decision. Birmingham is the regional focus for the Midlands. Over 20% of all black and ethnic minority people live in this region. The levels of racial attack/racial harassment is high and continues,

Letter from Councillor Benjamin to Stephen Wells (page 1), 18 September 1998

AF

THE INQUIRY INTO THE MATTERS ARISING FROM THE DEATH OF STEPHEN LAWRENCE

Chairman: Sir William Macpherson of Cluny
Secretary: Stephen Wells

Hannibal House
Elephant & Castle
London SE1 6TE

Telephone No:
Fax No: 28 September 1998

Muhammad Idrish Esq
Co-Ordinator
Asian Resource Centre

Handsworth
Birmingham B19 1NH

Dear Mr Idrish

PART 2 OF SIR WILLIAM'S INQUIRY: MEETING IN PUBLIC IN BIRMINGHAM

As you know, I have written to you recently explaining the Inquiry's difficulties in finding a suitable venue in Birmingham on a date appropriate to the Inquiry's business. I am pleased now to be able to write to say that Sir William has found it possible to extend his period of consultation, and we now expect to hold a meeting in public, along the lines of those already convened in London, Bristol, Bradford and Manchester, in the National Indoor Arena on Friday, 13 November. I will provide you with fuller details when they are available.

Yours sincerely

STEPHEN WELLS

Letter to Muhammad Idrish from Stephen Wells confirming Birmingham venue, 28 September 1998

THE INQUIRY INTO THE MATTERS ARISING FROM THE DEATH OF STEPHEN LAWRENCE

Chairman: Sir William Macpherson of Cluny
Secretary: Stephen Wells

Hannibal House
Elephant & Castle
London SE1 6TE

Telephone No:
Fax No: 28 September 1998

Councillor Roy Benjamin
Chair of Equalities
The Council House
Victoria Square
Birmingham B1 1BB

Dear Councillor Benjamin

PART TWO HEARINGS OF THIS INQUIRY

Thank you for your letter of 18 September, about the Inquiry's difficulties in arranging a meeting in public in Birmingham. As you will probably now know, Sir William has extended his period of consultation, and we now intend to hold a meeting in the Olympian Suite in the National Indoor Arena on Friday, 13 November.

Without wishing to go over the history, I have to say in defence of the Inquiry that considerable energies and efforts were expended in trying to arrive at a suitable arrangement in Birmingham, alongside arrangements being made at the same time for two meetings in London and three others (in Bristol, Bradford and Manchester). It was on advice that we approached the Birmingham Convention and Visitors' Bureau, contact being made as soon as possible once the Chairman had made his rulings about the format of Part 2 of his Inquiry and once he and Inquiry staff could concentrate on Part 2 upon the summer recess of Part 1. I can assure you that my staff and I tried very hard indeed to find a suitable venue on a date suitable for us, bearing in mind the demand for facilities in the other cities during the time that was available to us, and allowing for the other commitments of Sir William's advisers and their need to observe festivals arising in their faiths. I am pleased to say that, with the help last week of Birmingham City Council, we have been able to secure a public venue.

As with the other provincial locations, Sir William intends to hold a private Reception for senior local figures, during the evening of Thursday, 12 November. I have yet to find a venue for that, or even for our own overnight accommodation(!), but we are pressing ahead.

Yours sincerely

STEPHEN WELLS

Letter to Cllr Benjamin from Stephen Wells confirming Birmingham venue, 28 September 1998

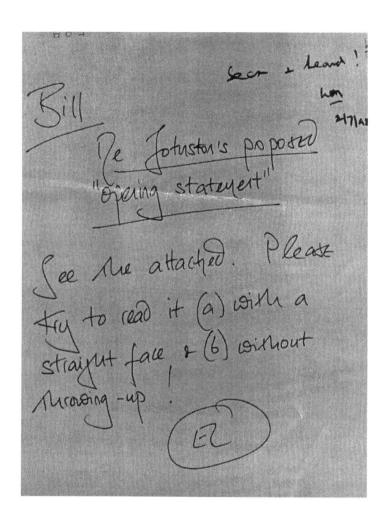

Note from Ed Lawson QC to Sir William Macpherson

THE INQUIRY INTO THE MATTERS ARISING FROM THE DEATH OF STEPHEN LAWRENCE

Chairman: Sir William Macpherson of Cluny
Secretary: Stephen Wells

Hannibal House
Elephant & Castle
London SE1 6TE

Telephone No:
Fax No: 15 February 1999

The Rt Hon Jack Straw MP
The Home Secretary
Home Office
50 Queen Anne's Gate
London SW1H 9AT

Dear Home Secretary —

On 31 July 1997 you asked me to inquire into the matters arising from the death of Stephen Lawrence, in order particularly to identify the lessons to be learned for the investigation and prosecution of racially motivated crimes.

The three people appointed to support me in my task were Mr Tom Cook, the Rt Revd Dr John Sentamu and Dr Richard Stone. They have acted as full members of a team in all respects. I am pleased to tell you that the Inquiry Report, which I deliver to you today, is accepted by all three "Advisers" in its entirety. The Report therefore sets out our unanimous views, based upon the evidence and material put before us during both parts of the Inquiry.

I take personal responsibility for all that is set out in the Report.

Yours sincerely,

SIR WILLIAM MACPHERSON OF CLUNY
CHAIRMAN

MR TOM COOK

THE RT REVD DR JOHN SENTAMU
BISHOP FOR STEPNEY

DR RICHARD STONE

Report delivered to Home Secretary - covering letter

APPENDIX C

Transcript of Sir Paul Condon's presentation and questioning at the Inquiry on institutional racism

Part Two, day 3

THE CHAIRMAN: Ladies and gentlemen, we welcome you
< 3>   to the second batch of public hearings dealing with
< 4>   Part 2 of the Stephen Lawrence Inquiry; and as this
< 5>   has a very different attendance today, I just want to
< 6>   make a few preliminary observations to help us before
< 7>   we embark on today's hearings.
< 8>   These hearings are to help us to make
< 9>   recommendations for the future investigation and
<10>   prosecution of racially related crimes. Those words
<11>   come, of course, from the terms of reference which
<12>   Mr Straw gave to us as long ago as July 1997. We
<13>   will of course be very much influenced by all we
<14>   heard in Part 1 but these hearings are not repeats of
<15>   Part 1 and while we echo back to some extent, we do
<16>   that only to assist us in making representations. A
<17>   large part as most people know, I think, of the
<18>   recommendations are contained in written documents
<19>   which have been submitted. We have more than 90 from
<20>   organisations and individuals and the purpose of
<21>   these hearings is to allow particularly those who
<22>   play or will play a part in implementing any
<23>   proposals we make, to add to what they have given in
<24>   their written submissions to us. It is not a free
<25>   for all, as everybody understands that I know, but we

P-277

< 1>   will be hearing today from the Metropolitan Police
< 2>   Service representatives and later from the Police
< 3>   Federation. That is this afternoon's hearings. We
< 4>   will, as you know, also be making visits out of
< 5>   London to various places later on in the month of
< 6>   October and early November.
< 7>   We have today the Metropolitan Police Service.
< 8>   The attendance is, as I see in front of me, the
< 9>   Commissioner, Sir Paul Condon. Mr Dennis O'Connor,
<10>   who is Assistance Commissioner of South West London
<11>   and the holder of Race and Community Relations Policy
<12>   Portfolio and Deputy Assistant Commissioner John
<13>   Grieve, who is head of the Race and Violent Crime
<14>   Task Force which has recently been set up.
<15>   Commissioner, what we have done in the past last
<16>   week is to ask those who appear to say what they wish
<17>   by way of introduction and then all of us will
<18>   question you or your brothers who sit with you and
<19>   you can decide who answers the questions amongst
<20>   yourselves. I hope that is a sensible way of going
<21>   ahead.
<22>   SIR CONDON: Ladies and gentlemen, Chairman, thank
<23>   you very much for giving me the opportunity to appear
<24>   before this Inquiry. I will only speak for a few
<25>   minutes and neither of my colleagues will at this

P-278

< 1>   stage and clearly we want to devote most time to your
< 2>   questions.
< 3>   I believe, Chairman, that it is right and just
< 4>   as Commissioner that I should be here today, that I
< 5>   should experience the anger and frustration felt by
< 6>   many in the community about the tragic death of
< 7>   Stephen. Most of all it is my duty to be here to
< 8>   recognise the courage and dignity of Mr & Mrs
< 9>   Lawrence. I deeply regret that we have not brought

<10> Stephen's racist murderers to justice. I would like
<11> to personally apologise again today to Mr & Mrs
<12> Lawrence for our failures. Also, I do not forget
<13> Duwayne Brooks and his needs and the sense that he
<14> should have been given more support.
<15> Chairman, I chose fairness, justice and equality
<16> as the theme of my first speech when I became
<17> Commissioner. Within days literally of becoming
<18> Commissioner I pledged myself and the
<19> Metropolitan Police to fairness, justice and
<20> equality.
<21> As early as 1994 I sought the Commission for
<22> Racial Equality and other partnership help to move
<23> forward our understanding and analysis of many of the
<24> significant issues facing the Met. For example, stop
<25> and search and disproportionality, as early as 1994

P-279

< 1> we were speaking and encouraging partnership
< 2> activity.
< 3> I supported the formation of the Black Police
< 4> Officers Association and had the honour to speak at
< 5> their inaugural meeting and pledge my personal
< 6> support to them. In 1996, after extensive
< 7> consultation with the community in London, I
< 8> published the five year plan for the Met which
< 9> recognises diversity, policing diversity, as one of
<10> the most significant challenges facing the Met.
<11> Chairman, I have always acknowledged that the
<12> police service in London is in a pivotal position of
<13> power, of trust and influence and I recognise my
<14> responsibility to discharge that task.
<15> My Part 2 submission to you, sir, sets out an
<16> ambitious programme of reform and I will refer to it
<17> later but if I may briefly set the scene by
<18> describing our past mistakes, our failures, the
<19> challenges we face together with society.

<20> I may not have been here, Chairman, but I have
<21> listened. I have heard the anger, the frustration,
<22> the confusion, the desire for reform and change that
<23> has emerged from this vital inquiry. This Inquiry
<24> has focused not just the police service but society
<25> generally and has challenged us all to reform, to

P-280

< 1> innovate, to move forward. I accept that a central
< 2> concern of this Inquiry is around racism in the Met
< 3> and I will return to that in a few moments.
< 4> I acknowledge that society and the police
< 5> service, in particular, have not done enough to
< 6> combat racist crime and harassment. The skills and
< 7> resources that have been applied successfully to many
< 8> other areas have not routinely been brought to bear
< 9> on the issues of combating racial crime and I think
<10> there is clearly scope for far more to be done and it
<11> will be done and it must be done.
<12> This Inquiry, sir, has expressed concern about
<13> the disproportionate application of police powers to
<14> some minority ethnic groups and particularly stop and
<15> search. Race or stereotypes clearly have an
<16> opportunity to be played out in the exercise of that
<17> discretion and I will say more about that in a
<18> while.
<19> The academic analysis which you have had
<20> revealed to you, and there is far more, reveals the
<21> complexity of the issues of disproportionality and
<22> the limitations of seeking simplistic interpretation
<23> of the data. This is a complex issue and I know is
<24> central to many of your thoughts. My plea is that a
<25> superficial analysis that does not ignore the

P-281

< 1> complexity of this situation will not actually take
< 2> us forward.

< 3>   Chairman, we have not been as effective as a
< 4>   service as I would wish in cases involving
< 5>   allegations of racist behaviour, discrimination by
< 6>   police officers. I have stood up around London from
< 7>   virtually my first few days in office and some of the
< 8>   people in this room will have heard me. I have said
< 9>   with no pride but with honesty there are racists in
<10>   the police service.
<11>   I have always set out my determination, the
<12>   determination of the police service to deal with
<13>   these people. All fair minded officers support this
<14>   campaign. I have campaigned in recent years for
<15>   changes to the disciplinary procedures. This has not
<16>   been popular but I do believe honestly and sincerely
<17>   that reform is necessary if we are able to deal
<18>   effectively with individual malpractice. I have
<19>   given evidence to the Home Affairs Select Committee,
<20>   I am confident that next year significant reform will
<21>   better enable us to deal with individual malpractice
<22>   in whatever form it manifests itself.
<23>   Chairman, London is becoming increasingly
<24>   diverse and I accept that our officers are not fully
<25>   equipped to deal with the increasingly rich diversity

P-282

< 1>   of the wonderful city they police. The golden thread
< 2>   approach from which you have heard from other
< 3>   agencies who have been before you which was adopted
< 4>   in the wake of Lord Scarman's report has not been
< 5>   successful, certainly not as successful as I would
< 6>   like. It has tended to reduce down to training for
< 7>   fairness and when faced with difficult definitions,
< 8>   difficult situations, complex chaotic environments,
< 9>   the police training has to distill down to treat
<10>   everyone the same, treat everyone fairly. That is a
<11>   noble ambition but it is not enough. In the
<12>   complexity of cities like London the challenge is to

<13> treat everybody as individuals, not just the same and
<14> although this thread of fairness is noble and
<15> honourable, in itself it is not enough and the new
<16> training must embrace with vigour the notion of
<17> treating people as individuals. Nor has the trickle
<18> down approach of training been particularly
<19> successful. You have heard of the graduates of the
<20> SSU, of training at Turvey of the Holyroode and
<21> elsewhere. Again, good people doing good things but
<22> not in sufficient numbers or sufficient ways to
<23> dramatically impact this complex environment.
<24> Those, Chairman, I think are some of the
<25> mistakes, the challenges, the frustrations of the

P-283

< 1> past and, if I may, I will briefly set out and
< 2> elaborate on our proposals for reform. I have set
< 3> out in my Part 2 submission a programme, which is not
< 4> just merely aspirational or borne out of necessity,
< 5> it has behind it I think a programme of timed
< 6> implementation of specific product which you may wish
< 7> to explore with us subsequently and I think it is an
< 8> innovative programme, the like of which we have not
< 9> seen anywhere in the world. We have looked for
<10> inspiration elsewhere, we have looked for best
<11> practice elsewhere. There are elements of these
<12> issues but I honestly believe we have put together a
<13> programme for reform that, with your help and others,
<14> will truly be, I think, inspirational in moving
<15> forward these issues.
<16> It has three many ingredients: Investigation,
<17> prevention and ensuring we have a truly anti-racist
<18> police service.
<19> In regards to investigation, Chairman, I have
<20> established a racial and violent crime task force
<21> which in my experience is unique. I have put it
<22> under the command of Deputy Assistant Commissioner,

\<23\> John Grieve who is with me today; a man who has had
\<24\> outstanding success in dealing with terrorism and
\<25\> will bring his determination his drive his expertise

P-284

\< 1\> to challenging the evil, the peril of racism and its
\< 2\> manifestations. We will build on good practice and
\< 3\> corporate standards. I want to ensure that racially
\< 4\> motivated crime is properly identified, recorded,
\< 5\> investigated and that we have an intelligence led
\< 6\> approach. I want victims and witnesses to be
\< 7\> properly supported. Community safety units will be
\< 8\> established throughout London and will operate to
\< 9\> very detailed standards which you may wish to explore
\<10\> with us later.
\<11\> In relation to prevention, Chairman, the Crime
\<12\> and Disorder Act could not have been better timed.
\<13\> It actually for the first time gives us a statutory
\<14\> framework and puts on others a statutory obligation
\<15\> to have a programme of community safety based on
\<16\> local issues and local consultation. I believe this
\<17\> will for the first time, certainly in London, create
\<18\> a framework for taking forward prevention of racially
\<19\> motivated crime. We have in place the technology, we
\<20\> have in place the techniques, and I invite and
\<21\> encourage you, or indeed members of the Inquiry, to
\<22\> visit John Grieve's unit; talk to the dedicated
\<23\> people who are staffing that unit; see the technology
\<24\> which has been utilised, state of the art, that gives
\<25\> me the confidence to say we can perform.

P-285

\< 1\> The third element, Chairman, is building an
\< 2\> anti-racist police service. I think this has three
\< 3\> important elements and you have already identified
\< 4\> them in this Inquiry:
\< 5\> Training;

< 6>   The Recruitment, Retention and Advancement of

< 7>   minority ethnic officers; and

< 8>   Notions of fairness and positive action in all

< 9>   aspects of policing.

<10>   I would briefly say a few words about each.

<11>   A substantial programme is underway, has been

<12>   underway. We have identified over the last few years

<13>   the weaknesses of the post Scarman approach to

<14>   training: This notion of a golden thread of

<15>   fairness. It improves, but it doesn't do enough. I

<16>   think you are aware of our police and diversity

<17>   training at Lambeth. I hope you have seen our work

<18>   books that we are using at Lambeth. This came out of

<19>   an early project at Hammersmith and a determination

<20>   by us to be at the forefront of training on these

<21>   issues. The lessons coming out of Lambeth will be

<22>   taken forward. It does involve significant lay

<23>   involvement and it will be replicated in 15 other

<24>   locations in London in the next 12 months.

<25>   We have also reviewed all of our training to

P-286

< 1>   make sure these aspirations are incorporated in all

< 2>   of our training.

< 3>   Recruitment. I joined the Met by accident on

< 4>   the first day, (pause) -- literally by accident in

< 5>   becoming a police officer; literally by accident in

< 6>   terms of it was the first day that a colleague from

< 7>   an ethnic minority background joined the Met. So I

< 8>   have seen the development from just one colleague,

< 9>   one courageous colleague through to today.

<10>   When I came back as Commissioner I had the

<11>   privilege to meet again with that colleague on many

<12>   occasions and I had the privilege of celebrating his

<13>   career at his retirement party last year.

<14>   THE CHAIRMAN: I know exactly what the emotions there

<15>   are and what feelings there are, but I hope that

<16>　laughter and reactions of that kind can be avoided so
<17>　that we can hear what is said. You may not agree
<18>　with it and we may not agree with it, but please let
<19>　us all hear what is said without that. It would be
<20>　helpful. Thank you very much.
<21>　SIR CONDON: Sir, I had the privilege of speaking at
<22>　my colleague's retirement party to celebrate his
<23>　courage, the pathfinding endeavours and his
<24>　achievements. The number of colleagues from a
<25>　minority ethnic community has increased by 50% during

P-287

< 1>　my Commissionership and is now at 865 that represents
< 2>　about 3.3% of the strength of the Met. At point of
< 3>　recruitment it varies from 6% to 8% year to year. So
< 4>　we are growing in terms of the number of colleagues
< 5>　from minority ethnic background, but I am impatient.
< 6>　It is not fast enough. It is not rapid enough. My
< 7>　ambition is that the Met should represent the rich
< 8>　diversity of the great city we police and therefore
< 9>　we must make significant progress.
<10>　In 1994 I set up a positive action team. It is
<11>　often forgotten it actually won the gold award from
<12>　the British Diversity Awards for its endeavors to
<13>　recruit colleagues into London. We have a
<14>　Recruitment and Advancement Working Group under lay
<15>　Chairmanship and recommendations for fellowship
<16>　schemes, active career support are being taken
<17>　forward. The notion of supporting and development
<18>　colleagues through fellowships, through role
<19>　modeling, through mentoring (sic). I take particular
<20>　measure in knowing that we now have colleagues from
<21>　minority ethnic backgrounds commanding key police
<22>　stations in London at senior rank on merit, quite
<23>　properly, and others are following in their wake.
<24>　The third limb of an anti-racist police
<25>　strategy, Chairman, is about fairness and fairness

P-288

< 1> issues will be taken forward in a number of ways. I
< 2> have always encouraged lay involvement in every
< 3> aspect of our work to encourage openness,
< 4> understanding and trust, and more and more ways are
< 5> being sought to encourage this openness and
< 6> involvement.
< 7> Informants;
< 8> Stop and search;
< 9> Recruitment and retention.
<10> The penny has not just dropped. All of these issues
<11> have involved significant lay involvement in recent
<12> years and will continue to do so.
<13> I think we are seeking ways to ensure that we
<14> never passively allow racism to unconsciously impact
<15> our policies, our strategies, our tactics or indeed
<16> individuals and I think that is the challenge for
<17> us.
<18> Chairman, if I could mention the complexities of
<19> your task -- if I may give an opinion on some of
<20> those complexities.
<21> Chairman, you and the members of the team have
<22> repeatedly pointed out the significance of words and
<23> phrases. You have raised important issues in your
<24> efforts, to use your words sir, "to grapple" with the
<25> concept of "institutional racism" as applied to the

P-289

< 1> police service. Lord Scarman -- I have had the
< 2> privilege of meeting him many times and discussing
< 3> this issue with him. He opened a police station for
< 4> me literally within walking distance of where we are
< 5> today. He concluded, "the direction and policies of
< 6> the Met are not racist". I maintain this is still
< 7> true to that definition.
< 8> I have serious reservations -- not for me or for
< 9> the Met -- I have serious reservations for the future

<10> of these important issues if the expression

<11> "institutional racism" is used in a particular way.

<12> I am not in denial. I am not seeking weasel words.

<13> I have been the first to be critical of police

<14> officers and the police service to say things which

<15> are unpopular. I am not denying the challenge or the

<16> need for reform, but if you label, if this Inquiry

<17> labels my service as "institutionally racist" (pause)

<18> then the average police officer, the average member

<19> of the public will assume the normal meaning of those

<20> words. They will assume a finding of conscious,

<21> willful, or deliberate action or an action to the

<22> detriment of ethnic minority Londoners. They will

<23> assume the majority of good men and woman who come

<24> into policing to serve their fellow men go home to

<25> their families; go to their churches; go to their

P-290

< 1> voluntary groups; go about their daily lives with

< 2> racism in their minds and in their endeavour. I

< 3> actually think that use of those two words in a way

< 4> that would take on a new meaning to most people in

< 5> society would actually undermine many of the

< 6> endeavors to identify and respond to the issues of

< 7> racism which challenge all institutions and

< 8> particularly the police because of their privileged

< 9> and powerful position.

<10> Racism is a feature throughout society. Racism

<11> is a feature in policing.

<12> I have always seen the challenge personally as

<13> being not to, for the police service, as Scarman

<14> said: "We do not set a social context. We do not

<15> create a social disadvantage. The social or economic

<16> conditions of many of our great cities". The

<17> challenge for policing is never to amplify those

<18> challenges. Never to amplify those problems through

<19> police behaviour, practices or policies. My fear is,

<20> convenient though it may be, to lay the door at the
<21> door of the police service disproportionality or
<22> racism alone, I think would be bound to fail because
<23> whilst it might be popular, in some quarters, and
<24> convenient labeling I think it would miss the
<25> challenge of the great problem. That is not being in

P-291

< 1> denial. The analysis of the challenge and the
< 2> problems I share significantly with the panel from
< 3> what I know of what you have said and heard, but I do
< 4> offer some caution around using those words in new
< 5> and different ways.
< 6> I think this Inquiry has already done immensely
< 7> valuable work in pointing out the perils, the
< 8> challenges for the police and for society. You have
< 9> already mobilised a concern and a momentum for change
<10> which I think we all now seek to build upon. I think
<11> we have come very close to making real progress in
<12> identifying the issues, the remedies, the challenges
<13> and the needs, but I do believe there is better hope
<14> if we go forward on the basis of shared
<15> understandings and analysis.
<16> I am not hiding behind definition. I cannot
<17> wait for the world to settle on words or
<18> definitions. I never have. I have set in train and
<19> built upon four particular things which I think
<20> address the peril that we are seeking to deal with,
<21> regardless of what we have.
<22> Firstly, we are monitoring individual officers
<23> and their use of discretionary powers in more
<24> powerful ways than has ever happened before, anywhere
<25> in the world. Building on the work of 1994; building

P-292

< 1> on what we are doing now. We have more information
< 2> building up on individual use of discretion than any

< 3>   other force in the world.

< 4>   We have developed new training to address the

< 5>   challenges of diversity. I am not just treating

< 6>   people fairly, but treating them as individuals.

< 7>   Had officers at various stages responded to the

< 8>   needs, if I may, of Mr & Mrs Lawrence, of

< 9>   Duwayne Brooks in ways that reflected them as

<10>   individuals, their anxieties, their needs, their

<11>   concerns, their pain, then I think rather than when

<12>   faced with challenge -- just falling back on 'we

<13>   treat everyone the same' -- then I think different

<14>   things would have happened and I think we recognise

<15>   and have built upon the training.

<16>   Thirdly, we are seeking ways to promote the fair

<17>   use of discretion. Everyone can tell you what the

<18>   challenge is, Chairman, no-one will tell you what

<19>   success looks like. I think again there are elements

<20>   of pot psychology around some of the simplistic

<21>   analysis. I think many academics have pointed to the

<22>   dangers of a notion of overemphasis of what some have

<23>   called "democratic suspicion". The notion that in

<24>   50% of the population are women and 50% of stop and

<25>   search should reflect women. That simplicity of the

P-293

< 1>   fallacy of democratic suspicion is very easy to fall

< 2>   into. These are challenging issues. We need the

< 3>   help of this Inquiry and others to begin to define

< 4>   what success might look like in the exercise of

< 5>   fairness and not just fall back on, if you like, a

< 6>   further narrative of what disproportionality looks

< 7>   like superficially.

< 8>   Fourthly, we have taken action to protect those

< 9>   who are particularly vulnerable to racially motivated

<10>   crime and investigate race crimes to the highest

<11>   level, John Grieve's new rule.

<12>   Chairman, thanks primarily to this Inquiry there

<13> is a tangible momentum for change. This Inquiry has
<14> mobilised society in a way that I have not
<15> experienced in my policing. I have campaigned for
<16> many years for a more accountable, an interventionist
<17> form of police authority for the Met. I realise, I
<18> have always realised the importance of lay
<19> involvement in all that we do, to build trust and
<20> confidence, to develop policies and tactics. I have
<21> also argued for a strategic authority for London and
<22> for a Mayor for London. Why? Because many of the
<23> big social and economic issues facing this great
<24> City, facing its rich diversity of people and
<25> activity, puts the police service in the position of

P-294
< 1> having to make the tough choices and set the
< 2> priorities. Disproportionality as an issue has cried
< 3> out for informed debate, not this year or last year,
< 4> but for many many years, a debate within the
< 5> democratic framework of London there has not been a
< 6> democratic framework to enable that debate. For too
< 7> long the police service in London has been left to be
< 8> damned if it takes action and damned if it does not.
< 9> So I therefore welcome the imminent changes to the
<10> governments of London, hopefully to ministerial
<11> priorities, to reflect and support the challenges
<12> facing us and with your help dealing with the
<13> recommendations from this Inquiry. I honesty believe
<14> there is a real momentum for change and you and your
<15> colleagues have added significantly to that
<16> momentum. The Crime and Disorder Act does provide a
<17> timely framework for change, a framework which has
<18> not been present in London for many many years.
<19> The new offences of racially aggravated crimes
<20> are important symbolic and pragmatic additions to our
<21> armory to deal with racism. As I said earlier, I
<22> hope that a ministerial priority will at some stage

<23> acknowledge, encourage and resource a programme for
<24> reform around these significant issues, particularly
<25> in the London context.

P-295

< 1> Chairman, in conclusion I have set out my
< 2> personal sorrow and regret at having failed Stephen,
< 3> his parents, his friends and Londoners. There is a
< 4> sense of shame in the Met about many aspects of this
< 5> tragic case. There is also great anger and
< 6> frustration that at times the acquisitions of this
< 7> Inquiry have not done justice to the courage, to the
< 8> endeavour, to the integrity of the majority of police
< 9> officers, men and women, civilian staff who join, who
<10> stay in the service. Every year in the Met over
<11> 10,000 police officers are injured on duty. During
<12> my time as Commissioner four have been murdered, many
<13> hundreds have been stabbed, shot, broken bones. They
<14> stay in the police service to do good things for
<15> their fellow citizens. They stay in the police
<16> service to serve their fellow men and women. I
<17> believe and hope this Inquiry with your help will be
<18> a real watershed, as Scarman was, on these issues. I
<19> am resolute in my determination to improve our
<20> performance in combating racial crime and violence.
<21> My service wants to succeed in all its endeavours.
<22> People do not come into policing to fail, they come
<23> into policing to succeed, to serve, to help change.
<24> We take pride in having reduced reported crime
<25> to the lowest level for almost a decade in London.

P-296

< 1> We have the biggest survey of Londoners each year
< 2> carried out to professional standards by outside
< 3> bodies. The two crimes which worry Londoners the
< 4> most have been burglary and street robbery.
< 5> Burglary, the crime which worries Londoners the most,

< 6> has been reduced to the lowest level for 20 years in
< 7> London. The same people who felt shame and anger and
< 8> failure in relation to Stephen's tragic death this is
< 9> the same force that fought the IRA on the streets of
<10> London to the point where we help create a climate
<11> for the peace process. We police this great City to
<12> a standard that attracts admiration and emulation
<13> around the world.
<14> I have never known a stronger determination in
<15> my 32 years as a police officer from within all
<16> levels of the service to improve and reform around
<17> this great issue which faces this Inquiry. I
<18> honestly and sincerely hope, Chairman, that with your
<19> help, with the help of your panel, that you will help
<20> us honour Stephen Lawrence's memory with enduring
<21> perform and progress. For that is my intention.
<22> Thank you, Chairman.
<23> THE CHAIRMAN: Do either of your colleagues wish to
<24> make any introductory remarks?
<25> SIR CONDON: I think not, Chairman, I know you

P-297

< 1> realise who they are. Dennis O'Connor is in charge
< 2> of a large part of South London and has been given
< 3> the special task by me to lead on diversity issues
< 4> and has taken forward that programme having served in
< 5> Surrey Police and Kent Police before coming back to
< 6> the Met. John heads up this unit and you are aware
< 7> of it, sir.
< 8> THE CHAIRMAN: Thank you. They can take the
< 9> opportunity to add anything by way of answer to the
<10> questions which we have later.
<11> THE CHAIRMAN: Commissioner, Mr & Mrs Lawrence, their
<12> advisers very early on during the investigation, in
<13> the very early days of the murder investigation
<14> detected, as it seems to us, that things were going
<15> wrong from the hours after the murder was committed

<16> and certainly during the first week when no arrests
<17> were made. Following your acceptance that things
<18> went badly wrong, what is the area upon which you put
<19> your finger as the real ground for acceptance that
<20> things went wrong.
<21> SIR CONDON: I think the acceptance is in the clear
<22> failure to bring Stephen's brutal racist thugs who
<23> murdered him to justice. I think that is the single
<24> most important test of the manifestation of that
<25> failure. The Inquiry have had the benefit of the

P-298
< 1> independently supervised Police Complaints Authority
< 2> report from Kent, you have had the opportunity to
< 3> examine witnesses here and you have had the
< 4> opportunity to form judgements across, where things
< 5> could and indeed should have been done better. I
< 6> mean, I am at your disposal if you wish to draw me to
< 7> any aspects of that.
< 8> THE CHAIRMAN: What worries me is this, looking to
< 9> the future: during the autumn of 1993 -- this is the
<10> only aspect upon which I am harking back you
<11> understand -- and the early months of 1994, I have
<12> looked at all the correspondence, some of which was
<13> signed personally by yourself, assurances were
<14> repeatedly given to members of Parliament and to the
<15> public that the investigation had been properly
<16> handled. I wonder how that squares with your
<17> acceptance now that the investigation went badly
<18> wrong?
<19> SIR CONDON: I think a key and similar point in the
<20> Inquiry came with the review. I think we acknowledge
<21> from myself down the devastating impact that that
<22> review had in the sense of from the early days a
<23> significant number of senior people recognised the
<24> importance of this case, became drawn into it and
<25> that review which, although it made recommendations

P-299

< 1>   for change, 13 of them and so on, by mistakenly

< 2>   conveying the impression that the early stages of the

< 3>   Inquiry had gone well, misled key people. I know all

< 4>   the theories that have been put forward before you,

< 5>   sir, and your Inquiry team. At that time, since that

< 6>   time the Met has solved almost 700 murders. This

< 7>   tragic case quickly came to the attention of senior

< 8>   people because it was clearly a racist murder, of the

< 9>   dignity and the frustration and the understandable

<10>   anger of Mr & Mrs Lawrence. Two days after Stephen's

<11>   tragic death, the Bishopsgate bomb went off in

<12>   London. The Met was under siege from terrorism in

<13>   London, but even with all that going on, with all the

<14>   things that were happening throughout London, people

<15>   were aware there was something specially tragic about

<16>   this case and I think for me one of the greatest

<17>   senses of failure is that despite the early interest

<18>   of a number of senior people locally, the flaws of

<19>   that early investigation were not revealed in a way

<20>   that enabled Mr & Mrs Lawrence to be properly

<21>   informed.

<22>   I remember having the privilege of meeting them

<23>   about a year after Stephen's tragic death and at that

<24>   point, the review had been prepared and in briefing

<25>   Ian Johnston and the others who were working hard on

P-300

< 1>   the second Inquiry, I made it absolutely clear

< 2>   Mr & Mrs Lawrence should made aware of the details of

< 3>   the review. Reviews even at that stage were

< 4>   relatively rare, you have the benefit of Mr Cook's

< 5>   experience on the Panel, reviews were relatively rare

< 6>   things in the sense of only two had been conducted

< 7>   within the Met. Many forces have not carried out any

< 8>   reviews of that nature and so I think the devastating

< 9>   impact of a report which seemed to be something new

<10> and different in police culture which was saying that
<11> here was an Inquiry that had flaws, that needed 13
<12> recommendations, that was being processed, but was
<13> essentially sound, misled key people. I do not say
<14> that in terms of being over defensive but I think
<15> that review was such a missed opportunity to bring
<16> truth to the flaws of that early investigation.
<17> THE CHAIRMAN: You know, I think, what our reaction
<18> to the review was because it was made plain when the
<19> officer involved was giving evidence here. But you
<20> accept now that it was grossly misleading?
<21> SIR CONDON: Yes, I do. I accept that it had a
<22> disproportionate impact on the relationship. The
<23> police service -- I have been the strongest critic of
<24> police failure, police malpractice, police wrongness,
<25> I have never shirked my responsibility from saying

P-301
< 1> those things even though it can be profoundly
< 2> unpopular. Had it, at an early stage, the Met had
< 3> real knowledge of how this case had failed in those
< 4> first few hours, I honestly believe endeavour would
< 5> have been made to bring that to the notice, not just
< 6> of Mr & Mrs Lawrence, but the wider community.
< 7> THE CHAIRMAN: The problem for the future that may
< 8> arise is this, is it not: the AMIP Directive and
< 9> Guide required such reviews should take place as a
<10> matter of course. We understand that apart from this
<11> case the Nickel case was the only one in which there
<12> had ever been a review. What is the policy to the
<13> future as to such reviews?
<14> SIR CONDON: Reviews have been significantly
<15> reformed. In 93 that was very early stages, not just
<16> for the Met but the service as a whole. But if I
<17> may, if I can invite through you John Grieve to just
<18> say something about the investigative process and the
<19> review process.

<20> MR GRIEVE: Sir, you have seen the murder manual that
<21> has been prepared by ACPO for the assistance of the
<22> Metropolitan Police. There are now three stages of
<23> review that are coming in with a list of standard
<24> operating procedures, standards to be achieved in
<25> very considerable detail. It lists very precisely

P-302
< 1> what it is expected that will be achieved in "the
< 2> golden hour", which is a phrase we have adopted from
< 3> the paramedics, the first hour of the inquiry and the
< 4> first five hours of the inquiry. We list in very
< 5> considerable detail, we have that document available
< 6> for you, the activities we would expect to be
< 7> undertaken and the measures, the level to be
< 8> achieved.
< 9> There are three levels of inspection. The first
<10> is self inspection, whereby that list is given to the
<11> officers themselves and they are instructed to
<12> inspect themselves.
<13> The second is where they are inspected by a
<14> cadre of their colleagues and the third is where
<15> there is an inspection which is carried out outside
<16> of the detective group that is dealing with that
<17> particular crime.
<18> THE CHAIRMAN: What still troubles me, Commissioner,
<19> is that it seems to me that that review is simply
<20> accepted at face value by everybody who saw it, not
<21> only yourself because you saw it, but particularly
<22> perhaps the senior officers who ought to have been
<23> responsible for those who made the vital wrong
<24> decisions in the early hours. I do not understand
<25> how they could have accepted it if they had been

P-303
< 1> doing their job properly.
< 2> SIR CONDON: If I may respond to that. With the

< 3> benefit of hindsight, several years on I understand
< 4> the force of what you are saying.
< 5> I think if you put yourselves in the position of
< 6> a service at that time which I say had no or very
< 7> little experience of reviews of that nature being
< 8> carried out. That was not confined to London that
< 9> was the service experience. Faced with a report that
<10> seemed to be diligent, that contained a number of
<11> recommendations that seemed to be acknowledging
<12> flaws, that is arguing for reform that had been
<13> carried out by a middle ranking officer, then I think
<14> that did lead people to take that report as it was
<15> set out.
<16> Now, I accept with the benefit of hindsight that
<17> can be challenged and people must make a judgment
<18> around that.
<19> MR O'CONNOR: Chairman, if I may add a little to
<20> that, having some responsibility for the way
<21> forward. Our view is, to I think help answer your
<22> question, our view is this: that the nature of
<23> leadership associated with those inquiries has to
<24> change. The leadership is relied too much on trust;
<25> it needs to be far more challenging, ie less

P-304

< 1> acceptance, more drill down, more probing; and part
< 2> of the reason for Mr Grieve's appointment is that
< 3> that challenge in leadership can take place outside
< 4> of the line command directly, coldly and clinically,
< 5> that is part of Mr Grieve's remit.
< 6> If today, sir, we had any doubts or
< 7> uncertainties about a case of any significance of
< 8> this nature, we would have no hesitation in deploying
< 9> Mr Grieve with the expertise he would bring to it,
<10> without being inhibited by line command or without
<11> being over trusting in terms of the leadership he
<12> would exercise.

<13> THE CHAIRMAN: The basic decisions made which may be
<14> subject to criticism -- we have not of course made
<15> the decisions yet as you understand, but our reaction
<16> during the evidence must be apparent. The basic
<17> decisions made were leadership and immediate
<18> imaginative decisions by senior officers in the very
<19> early days of the investigation.
<20> Are you satisfied that the high standards are
<21> present at that level in the officers in the
<22> Metropolitan Police, particularly in the CID?
<23> SIR CONDON: Yes, I am, sir, in the sense of -- in
<24> London every year every senior detective solves three
<25> or more murders. The workload on detectives in

P-305

< 1> London is greater than in any other location, but
< 2> despite that pressure they work incredibly hard and
< 3> they have, I think, good success. Again, you have
< 4> the benefit of someone on the panel who can talk to
< 5> you about that.
< 6> In my submission to Part 1 I tried to show for
< 7> you the challenge in the Met compared to some other
< 8> forces. So a single area in the Met might deal with
< 9> 30 murders in a year; even some of the largest forces
<10> outside of London might only deal with 15 to 20. So
<11> there is a huge challenge. The detectives do respond
<12> to that.
<13> But I think the service nationally has
<14> recognised that there are times of enormous change in
<15> investigation, in leadership around these issues
<16> after the Yorkshire Riper case huge developments in
<17> the use of technology and how murders were
<18> investigated.
<19> This tragic case has prompted for the whole
<20> service a review of those issues. There is, as you
<21> are aware, a fundamentally different approach being
<22> taken to the investigation of murders, not just in

<23> London but throughout the service. This tragic case
<24> has been quite properly a shock to the professional
<25> standards and methods of detectives who are anxious

P-306

< 1> to improve and move on.
< 2> THE CHAIRMAN: In all events, Commissioner, you
< 3> accept, as it seems to me, that the repeated
< 4> assurances given to the public that all had gone well
< 5> is something which everyone must be justifiably
< 6> ashamed.
< 7> SIR CONDON: Absolutely. I think there is a great
< 8> sense of regret, Chairman, that in our endeavours to
< 9> support Mr & Mrs Lawrence through their tragic time,
<10> they were not made aware of the failures of the early
<11> stages of that investigation.
<12> THE CHAIRMAN: I want to turn now at once, if I may,
<13> to the question of racism. I am going to ask some
<14> questions and then I am going to hand it over to my
<15> colleagues who advise me.
<16> We have all, of course, looked at Lord Scarman's
<17> report and it has been mentioned more than once in
<18> our debates with ACPO and other bodies. That report
<19> concentrated, did it not, on individual racism; what
<20> is called the bad apple theory?
<21> SIR CONDON: Not exclusively.
<22> THE CHAIRMAN: Not exclusively but that was the theme
<23> that was echoed forward from that report. But do you
<24> accept or do you not accept that unconscious or
<25> covert racism was evident and at large in any area of

P-307

< 1> the Stephen Lawrence Inquiry?
< 2> SIR CONDON: I have been the most vigorous critic of
< 3> the police service on many aspects. If I believed
< 4> with my knowledge now all that I know of this case
< 5> that racism or corruption by any normal use of those

< 6>   terms impacted this case in anyway I would not have

< 7>   hesitated to say so, sir, or to say so today. I

< 8>   honestly sincerely believe that by any ordinary use

< 9>   of those words, those issues did not influence this

<10>   tragic case.

<11>   THE CHAIRMAN: Commissioner, I personally do not want

<12>   to become involved in definitions, you understand,

<13>   because academics have discussed the expression

<14>   "institutional racism" ad nauseam and they will

<15>   continue to do so after this Inquiry.

<16>   Do you accept that in the police force, using

<17>   another expression which I hope is clear, that there

<18>   is apparent, not everywhere, but there is apparent in

<19>   the police force a collective failure through the

<20>   attitudes and approach of police officers,

<21>   particularly at the lower level, and discrimination,

<22>   conscious or unconscious, which amounts to a general

<23>   malaise in certain quarters in the force.

<24>   SIR CONDON: I will answer that specifically, but in

<25>   relation to this case, in relation to this tragic

P-308

< 1>   case I have acknowledged insensitivities, clumsiness,

< 2>   lack of awareness, lack of consideration which should

< 3>   have been dealt with better. My anxiety again with

< 4>   this notion of some mysterious collective will that

< 5>   somehow people don't -- intelligent, well-meaning

< 6>   people don't actually know what they are doing, I

< 7>   think again is a difficult definition to

< 8>   acknowledge.

< 9>   If the peril, if the evil we are trying to deal

<10>   with, sir, if the police service if it is not careful

<11>   can amplify social disadvantage for its use of

<12>   discretion and other issues, then I acknowledge

<13>   totally the challenge. If we are saying that that

<14>   can also lead to insensitivity and clumsiness, I

<15>   acknowledge that.

<16>   Again, I think there is great importance in
<17>   identifying the mischief and finding accurate words
<18>   which describe the mischief and allow us to move on.
<19>   What I am trying to do is not -- I don't have the
<20>   luxury as some of the academics do of merely talking
<21>   about this. I have to live and breath this and give
<22>   clear direction. I have given clear direction around
<23>   the things we are trying to do: Better training to
<24>   make sure we don't treat people just the same and not
<25>   acknowledge them as individuals; monitoring the use

P-309

< 1>   of discretion and so on; but those are some of the
< 2>   challenges.
< 3>   Again if I may invite Mr O'Connor -- as you can
< 4>   imagine we have spent many many days now seeking the
< 5>   right words to assist you and your colleagues.
< 6>   THE CHAIRMAN: Let me if I may give you two examples
< 7>   which may figure in our report. The first really
< 8>   comes from the evidence of Mrs Lawrence herself, who
< 9>   was sensitively asked questions by Ms Weekes during
<10>   the Inquiry, you may remember the passage. She was
<11>   asked how she put the impact of racism. She said
<12>   more than once, and of course I shorten her answers
<13>   -- she said more than once "they were patronising",
<14>   "they patronised me because I was black", and that
<15>   was collective. It wasn't just one officer. It was
<16>   the approach. That was a collective failure.
<17>   The second example is this: Half a dozen
<18>   officers in terms before us refused to accept that
<19>   this was purely a racially motivated or a racist
<20>   crime. One officer said, and reflected on his
<21>   answer, said he thought 50% of his colleagues would
<22>   have had the same view that it might not have been
<23>   racially motivated. Nobody picked them up and nobody
<24>   questioned that plainly wrong approach. So that is a
<25>   collective failure.

P-310

< 1>   You accept that those features may amount to

< 2>   institutional racism?

< 3>   SIR CONDON: Where I think there is a danger in the

< 4>   leap of logic and collection, I am not challenging

< 5>   the areas of the behaviour you have described. To

< 6>   treat anyone patronisingly, for whatever reason, is

< 7>   wrong and offensive. I will say a word in a moment

< 8>   about why I think officers said what they did about

< 9>   motivation. But clearly it is the decision for you

<10>   and your colleagues sir, but by them describing those

<11>   challenges and those issues as institutional racism I

<12>   think you then extrapolate to all police officers at

<13>   all times this notion that they are walking around

<14>   just waiting to do something that is going to be

<15>   labelled "institutional racism" because of some

<16>   collective failure.

<17>   THE CHAIRMAN: I do not think that would be my

<18>   approach, but it would be my approach that it exists.

<19>   SIR CONDON: The mischief exists the challenge is

<20>   what we call it.

<21>   THE CHAIRMAN: What troubles me is this: the

<22>   perception of the Lawrences and the community is that

<23>   racism of that kind, that is to say a collective

<24>   failure, played its part and was apparent in this

<25>   case; other evidence that we have heard echoes that

P-311

< 1>   and suggests that that is a general view.

< 2>   How can that be dealt with if it is not accepted

< 3>   that it exists?

< 4>   SIR CONDON: I think we can -- I am disappointed,

< 5>   Chairman, if you think all I said earlier didn't

< 6>   recognise the existence of these problems and these

< 7>   challenges. I am not going to get hung up on the

< 8>   words. All I am merely saying to you is that those

< 9>   words put together have a common meaning for a lot of

<10>   people in wider society. If you now attribute them
<11>   to a challenge in the way they have not been
<12>   attributed before then I think there is just a
<13>   responsibility to explain that attribution.
<14>   In answering your second point sir, this is not
<15>   an easy environment in which to operate. I can
<16>   cope. I understand the anger. I understand the
<17>   frustration. I am privileged, I feel privileged to
<18>   be in the presence of Mr & Mrs Lawrence again. The
<19>   grief that they have felt I have personally shared,
<20>   but for a group of officers I think who came -- I am
<21>   not defending what they said or how they behaved but
<22>   I think when in such a challenging environment I
<23>   think many of them took comfort in what they thought
<24>   was safe territory. Safe territory is, say: I treat
<25>   everyone the same, I am colour blind. I do not know

P-312

< 1>   what was in the mind, I do not know what was in the
< 2>   mind of the assailants, because we have not got them
< 3>   to the point of prosecution and I think because they
< 4>   have stood time and time again in the witness box and
< 5>   been challenged, how do you know what was in
< 6>   someone's mind, how do you know their motivation. I
< 7>   think they, many of them, erred stupidly in not
< 8>   explaining their actions; and I acknowledge totally
< 9>   why that should give you concern, why it gives me
<10>   concern and why it has led to dramatic changes in
<11>   training to acknowledge these issues.
<12>   THE CHAIRMAN: You see it just strikes me -- I hope
<13>   that this is a golden opportunity for reform -- that
<14>   maybe everybody has to say the reform must be even
<15>   more fundamental than they are planning at the
<16>   moment.
<17>   SIR CONDON: If I could give an example, sir. You
<18>   have listened, you have heard the complexities of the
<19>   ACPO definition for racial incidents. You have heard

<20>　various people say various things and again in the
<21>　chaos, in the fog of war of street encounter and
<22>　street endeavour, police officers quite often fall
<23>　back on what is a safe definition. In relation to
<24>　racial incidents we have been piloting, we have given
<25>　every police officer in a part of London a new form

P-313

< 1>　on racial incidents, the bullet point is in the red
< 2>　box, don't forget if anyone says it is a racial
< 3>　incident, it is. No "ifs", "buts", "maybes"
< 4>　qualifying, if anyone says it is a racial incident,
< 5>　it is. It brings home to police officers, to other
< 6>　professionals and agencies that if there is
< 7>　underreporting of these issues, if people do not face
< 8>　up to the challenges of these issues, we will never
< 9>　reform. So I am not in denial of your analysis, of
<10>　the problems, of the challenges, I merely offer you
<11>　some caution around the use of some of the
<12>　terminology. May I invite Mr O'Connor to speak?
<13>　THE CHAIRMAN: Yes.
<14>　MR O'CONNOR: Chairman, briefly, we acknowledge that
<15>　something was deeply wrong here. We believe that the
<16>　sense of racism is corrosive to a relationship
<17>　between ourselves and the black community. The
<18>　Commissioner's endeavour has been and we hope we have
<19>　taken a step in the direction you were suggesting to
<20>　find common purpose, to find common purpose on the
<21>　way forward, that is the only way great steps are
<22>　taken. We think it will be extremely difficult to
<23>　find common purpose around the definitions that
<24>　academics have used and we think that institutional
<25>　racism in the way it is used, we think it will

P-314

< 1>　challenge the personal honour, the reputation of
< 2>　individuals and the basic moral fitness of our

< 3>   service. We think it has the potential to antagonise
< 4>   and polarise and that is why, sir, the Commissioner
< 5>   in his submission to you and the extrapolation and
< 6>   the action plan that goes with that we have a copy
< 7>   and we hope to offer that to you today, focused on
< 8>   anti-racism. We believe that focusing on that
< 9>   aspiration and that must be the aspiration I would
<10>   hope that we could all share as a common purpose and
<11>   more importantly how to achieve it is a way forward,
<12>   it is a way around which everybody can and should be
<13>   able to mobilise. We have attempted to turn that for
<14>   the first time into real practical endeavour in our
<15>   organisation which can be tested, around which others
<16>   can test us.
<17>   THE CHAIRMAN: Thank you. Just one sideline on this:
<18>   we heard very impressive evidence from the Black
<19>   Police Association on Friday, which I am sure you
<20>   will have read. No doubt their views on this aspect
<21>   of the case will be closely considered.
<22>   SIR CONDON: I had the privilege of encouraging the
<23>   formation of that association and speaking at their
<24>   inaugural meeting and have spent many hours with many
<25>   colleagues within that association. They are a key

P-315

< 1>   resource in all of our endeavour. They are a key
< 2>   resource to John and his new unit. They are a key
< 3>   resource to Denis O'Connor as we take forward our
< 4>   aspirations around policing diversity. I, in
< 5>   speaking to my colleague who joined with me over 30
< 6>   years ago, he talks passionately of his first two
< 7>   years in policing where he went home and cried every
< 8>   night. He went and home and cried every night
< 9>   because of racism in the police service. I have
<10>   spent all of my career and at key moments in it
<11>   seeking to move the service forward and there is an
<12>   endeavour to do so now. No-one has had a more

<13> privileged insight into what it means to be and hear
<14> from black officers in particular in London.
<15> THE CHAIRMAN: I am now going to ask Mr Cook to ask
<16> some questions and we will go on for about another
<17> quarter of an hour and then we will have a break
<18> because the stenographer has a considerable task in
<19> taking everything down: I understand we can continue
<20> so that we may not have to take a break. I will ask
<21> Mr Cook to ask some questions.
<22> MR COOK: Can I come back to the question of
<23> institutional racism. I make no apologies for the
<24> fact that I will eventually come to a question but
<25> there is a long preamble. The person I should

P-316

< 1> apologise to for that is the Chairman.
< 2> Can I first quote from a paper before us from
< 3> the 1990 Trust, which you may not have seen or
< 4> probably have not seen, it refers to the Lambeth
< 5> initiatives which you have spoken about and seem to
< 6> me to be an excellent initiative. It refers to it as
< 7> designed to build confidence:
< 8> "The initiative is predicated on the acceptance
< 9> by the Lambeth Superintendents of the need to tackle
<10> institutionalised racism. This is in contrast to
<11> Metropolitan Police Commanders who refute any
<12> suggestion of the existence of institutional racism.
<13> This is extremely important as it provides the
<14> adequate basis for the development of partnership.
<15> Their acceptance of the existence of institutional
<16> racism is, in our view, a prerequisite to the
<17> restoration of confidence. This view is widely
<18> accepted and understood within black organisations
<19> and the communities that any attempt that resolving
<20> the desperate state of police, black community
<21> relations will ultimately fail if this is not
<22> accepted and understood by the police themselves."

<23> That seems a very clear statement which seems to
<24> have some validity that there is clearly a difficulty
<25> between the Metropolitan Police and its relationship

P-317

< 1> with the black community and there is a need to
< 2> restore and increase confidence in that community.
< 3> I recognise your difficulty with the label of
< 4> institutional racism and your reluctance to accept it
< 5> at any price, at it were, that has been quite evident
< 6> here today. I accept fully that institutional racism
< 7> can mean many things to many people, there are all
< 8> sorts of definitions some of them amount to academic
< 9> treatises and certainly, as the Chairman says, we do
<10> not want to get into that kind of words. But I do
<11> wonder whether the Metropolitan Police Service is
<12> over-defensive on this and related issues. I quote
<13> some of your words this morning, you said:
<14> "The police service can amplify social
<15> disadvantage" a nice sounding phrase, I am not
<16> entirely sure what it means but it seems to be a
<17> substitution for words such as "stereotyping" and
<18> "racism". Another phrase: "The mischief exists the
<19> challenge is what we call it." I would say that the
<20> challenge is to acknowledge it and address it, not
<21> what we call it. In fairness you do speak, all of
<22> you, eloquently and convincingly here this morning
<23> and in the papers that we have received but focusing
<24> on the problem as Mr O'Connor used the phrase
<25> "focusing on anti racism and anti racism policies",

P-318

< 1> but seemed intent on avoiding the words and
< 2> acknowledging there is a problem on which to focus in
< 3> the first instance.
< 4> ACPO, I accept again equally one could
< 5> legitimately deny institutional racism if it is

< 6>   defined solely in terms of deliberate racist
< 7>   policies. No one, as I am aware, makes that
< 8>   suggestion. The Black Police Association certainly
< 9>   did not make that suggestion. ACPO in their
<10>   presentation indicated equally a wish not to get hung
<11>   up on abstract definitions but totally accepted the
<12>   concept of institutional racism, its existence in the
<13>   police service in terms of unconscious prejudice and
<14>   stereotyping and the your own Black Police
<15>   Association made very much the same point. There is
<16>   no doubt equally that unconscious prejudice and
<17>   stereotyping are a major concern of the black
<18>   community and is one, as I said before, that must be
<19>   addressed if confidence is to be restored.
<20>   Paragraph 52 of your Part 2 submission talks
<21>   about "particular care needs to be taken in the use
<22>   of intrusive tactics such as stop and search that
<23>   have the potential" and I stress the word
<24>   "potential", "that have the potential to
<25>   disproportionately impact upon minority ethnic

P-319

< 1>   groups." Every figure I think I have seen published
< 2>   demonstrates not potential but the actuality of that
< 3>   disproportionality. I accept totally and I have been
< 4>   party to it in the past that one could introduce a
< 5>   lot of valid surrounding complexities about
< 6>   demography, school exclusions and employment and
< 7>   everything else but surely there can be little doubt
< 8>   now that these do not explain the degree of
< 9>   disproportionality and that the core problem
<10>   remains. It, therefore, seems from ACPO from the
<11>   Black Police Association from evidence we have heard
<12>   before us and this is the guts of the question, there
<13>   seems to be a developing consensus to the effect that
<14>   unconscious racism by individual officers is
<15>   widespread, it leads to discrimination, it is

\<16\> demonstrated in anomalies in the stop and search
\<17\> figures and it has gone unacknowledged and
\<18\> uncorrected by the police service because of lack of
\<19\> effective training or other measures.
\<20\> Would you accept that proposition? And if
\<21\> institutional racism or even if the word
\<22\> "institutional" were dropped and racism in the
\<23\> police service was described in those terms in that
\<24\> context, would you then accept that the police
\<25\> service is racist and the Metropolitan Police Service

P-320

\< 1\> with it?
\< 2\> SIR CONDON: Thank you very much, Mr Cook, as you say
\< 3\> that is a speech and not a question and I acknowledge
\< 4\> the validity of it.
\< 5\> MR COOK: There is a question at the end of it.
\< 6\> SIR CONDON: I acknowledge the validity of it. Again,
\< 7\> I am disappointed you say those things in the context
\< 8\> of what we have said and done. I, within days of
\< 9\> becoming Commissioner, spoke of the dangers of
\<10\> racism, of the challenge, of the damage that can be
\<11\> done within a police service, by a police service and
\<12\> I have never, I have never denied that challenge.
\<13\> After the tragedy of Joy Gardener, I did things which
\<14\> were profoundly unpopular within the police service
\<15\> because I acknowledge racism in the police service
\<16\> and so on. So I acknowledge and I have said today, I
\<17\> thought I had said today, there is racism in the
\<18\> police service. There can be unconscious racism,
\<19\> there can be deliberate racism, that racism can be
\<20\> played out in discrimination in disproportionality,
\<21\> the unfair use of arbitrary powers, all of those
\<22\> issues I acknowledge, I condemn, I seek to reform, I
\<23\> have never ever challenged and I am disappointed that
\<24\> in your opening remarks you did not give me credit
\<25\> for having acknowledged those things.

P-321

< 1> I feel with great passion, I have tried

< 2> throughout my career to move the service forward on

< 3> of some these big issues. I now believe that this

< 4> Inquiry has mobilised public opinion quite properly

< 5> in looking for new ways forward, we are up to and up

< 6> for the challenge. I am acknowledging now racism in

< 7> the service, all of the things that you have

< 8> described. If, in describing that in ways of

< 9> unconscious or collective, I am not denying any of

<10> that, that does not stop me offering you the

<11> challenges of applying particularly to those issues.

<12> MR COOK: I accept what you say to a degree, but if

<13> we are going to talk about racism in the police

<14> service, whether institutional racism, then it must

<15> be spoken about openly. Some kind of words, some

<16> kind of label must be found.

<17> SIR CONDON: We agree totally.

<18> MR COOK: It would appear to be that it would be more

<19> productive to put efforts into finding an acceptable

<20> definition, an acceptable label rather than resisting

<21> every one that is proffered from everyone else.

<22> The basic question -- forgive me, but it is not

<23> addressed: Would you accept the premise that

<24> "unconscious racism" by individual officers is

<25> widespread and leads to discrimination in the police

P-322

< 1> service?

< 2> SIR CONDON: Not as you put it. If you say

< 3> "widespread".

< 4> THE CHAIRMAN: Ladies and gentlemen, please, I do

< 5> very very genuinely ask you please to allow the

< 6> answers to be given and the questions to be asked,

< 7> otherwise we may have to do it privately and I would

< 8> abhor that. So please, please.

< 9> SIR CONDON: If you say "widespread" -- very easy to

<10> say yes to get a round of applause. I can only say
<11> yes if I honestly sincerely believe it and feel I am
<12> helping you to move forward. If in searching for
<13> that -- be more specific Mr Cook. In terms of your
<14> own experience, do you feel that institutional racism
<15> was widespread in your last force?
<16> MR COOK: I think the stereotyping, and again
<17> stereotyping is certainly widespread in my own force
<18> and would be widespread in all forces.
<19> SIR CONDON: I agree stereotyping is a way that
<20> people go about their daily lives. Stereotyping in
<21> police terms is dangerous, pervasive,
<22> counterproductive and must be stopped in its
<23> pernicious manifestations.
<24> So stereotyping, I acknowledge discrimination, I
<25> acknowledge -- and like you -- the debate, the real

P-323

< 1> challenge is not about scoring points about words.
< 2> The real challenge is how do we move forward in
< 3> policing, in society, to address the evil which I
< 4> think we have accepted and recognised. There is an
< 5> evil around the peril of racism as it affects
< 6> society, policing in particular because police are in
< 7> a privileged position, a powerful position.
< 8> I am not in denial but that doesn't mean to say
< 9> I have to go against my conscious or my intellect and
<10> have to accept every single word you put forward.
<11> MR COOK: I am not seeking my any means to drive you
<12> into a corner, quite the opposite.
<13> SIR CONDON: I haven't been driven into a corner, if
<14> I believe it is the right corner to move the Inquiry
<15> forward.
<16> MR COOK: It goes back to the essential point really
<17> again the 1990 organisation puts it better than I
<18> could, there is a need to demonstrate an acceptance
<19> of some form of racism in the police service in order

<20> to move that forward.

<21> SIR CONDON: I believe we have done that.

<22> Dennis O'Connor is the officer in charge of Lambeth

<23> overall and other places, perhaps he could give a

<24> perspective on what we have said about that training

<25> in the context of racism.

P-324

< 1> MR COOK: I think it is the clarity of the message is

< 2> important. It needs to be a little less equivocal.

< 3> MR O'CONNOR: Chairman, I don't think the message the

< 4> Commissioner is giving is equivocal. The message is

< 5> we accept racism exists and we have chosen to put a

< 6> considerable amount of energy into establishing how

< 7> to stop it existing. How to fight it at every turn.

< 8> How to challenge it where it should be challenged.

< 9> Our proposals here, which I would hope to leave you

<10> with today, I hope will indicate just how far we have

<11> gone with that.

<12> What we have tried to do, and I think this is

<13> important, is we have tried to identify how you do

<14> this; how you actually deal with this problem;

<15> whether you are talking about operationally stop and

<16> search; whether you are talking about not doing

<17> enough about racial investigation; whether you are

<18> looking at the way we recruit people; or whether

<19> managers intervene adequately.

<20> We have tried to put together a package of

<21> interventions based on some of the work at Lambeth

<22> and some of the work elsewhere in London where we

<23> have learned about training. Where we have learned

<24> something about stop and search but we have a long

<25> way to go. Where we have learned about the use of

P-325

< 1> informants. We have tried to build an approach that

< 2> will deal precisely with the problem which we

< 3> acknowledge that you are pointing out to us, Mr Cook,
< 4> and I honestly believe there is nothing between us on
< 5> that. I think the issue that remains is: How do we
< 6> do this? How do we put a package together that will
< 7> work? Because frankly what has been put together in
< 8> the past has not worked. There has been lots of
< 9> words; lots of exultation, but I think the people in
<10> the audience here and we believe we are looking for
<11> action.
<12> SIR CONDON: Mr Cook, your specific challenge: Why
<13> don't I acknowledge? I have stood before a larger
<14> audience than this in Lambeth with Lee Jasper, with
<15> the 1990 Trust in the Hall, in the room, face to face
<16> twice in recent years and stood up and said "as
<17> Commissioner I acknowledge. I hear what you say.
<18> There is racism in the Metropolitan Police Service.
<19> There is use of stop and search which is wholly
<20> inappropriate on many occasions. There is
<21> discrimination. There is stereotyping. Together we
<22> can move those issues forward".
<23> So in the sense of the 1990 Trust or Lee Jasper
<24> suggesting I or we are in denial, there is common
<25> ground. I have stood in their presence with

P-326

< 1> significant audiences in Lambeth and revealed all of
< 2> my fears, aspirations for racism and acknowledged its
< 3> pernicious influence in policing. I am not in
< 4> denial.
< 5> THE CHAIRMAN: The Bishop would like to intervene.
< 6> BISHOP SENTAMU: I still think you are still hung up
< 7> on the bad apple theory still. I want to put to you
< 8> what Mr Paul Wilson said in evidence, a member of the
< 9> Black Police Association. He said: "As I mentioned
<10> in my introductory speech, we consider that
<11> institutional racism plays a significant part in the
<12> way the police perceive the black community and treat

<13> the black community. We consider it to be quite a
<14> central issue" and he went on: "The term
<15> 'institutional racism' should be understood to the
<16> way the institution or the organisation may
<17> systematically or repeatedly treat or tend to treat
<18> people differentially because of their race."
<19> In fact we are not talking about individuals
<20> within the service who may be unconscious as to the
<21> nature of what they are doing, but it is the
<22> (inaudible) of what is being done. In other words,
<23> it isn't about there are people who smoke, but that
<24> because some people smoke there is a lot of smoke in
<25> the room. That is why people actually are describing

P-327
< 1> that there is this differential treating of people
< 2> and it seems to me you seem to acknowledge there is
< 3> racism but actually don't seem to think it has got
< 4> this pervasive effect cumulatively on the black
< 5> community.
< 6> SIR CONDON: No, I would never say that, Bishop. I
< 7> hope you are heard me in your presence many times not
< 8> say that. To use your analogy, just one instance of
< 9> racism by a police officer -- if it is the smoke
<10> analogy -- can contaminate the whole room. The
<11> challenge is not to say that racism does not have an
<12> impact. I acknowledge racism within the service. I
<13> acknowledge stereotyping. I acknowledge much of your
<14> analysis and other people's analysis. I acknowledge
<15> the huge challenge this places the police service in
<16> its relationship with Londoners and minority ethnic
<17> Londoners in particular. So I am not denying that
<18> analysis.
<19> If you feel, as you may, if you feel as an
<20> Inquiry you want to take forward particular words to
<21> describe the problem, clearly that is your
<22> prerogative and we will respond positively to all of

<23> that. I am offering you my views on how I fear that
<24> may polarise views because there won't be a common
<25> understanding of that. There is a common

P-328

< 1> understanding, we have acknowledged it, of racism in
< 2> the police service, of stereotyping, of the
< 3> pernicious influence that can have. You and I
< 4> debated these issues on many occasions and hopefully
< 5> you will give me credit for my acknowledgment of
< 6> racism and how pernicious it can be within the police
< 7> service.
< 8> BISHOP SENTAMU: You have read "Winning The Race",
< 9> the special report. Again there was something there,
<10> in the summary it says: "There was continuing
<11> evidence during the inspection of inappropriate
<12> language and behaviour by police officers, but even
<13> more worrying was the lack of intervention by
<14> sergeants and inspectors". You acknowledge this is
<15> true of the Met as well?
<16> SIR CONDON: Yes I do, absolutely.
<17> BISHOP SENTAMU: That is what probably some people
<18> are referring to as "institutional racism".
<19> SIR CONDON: If that is the term you wish to apply,
<20> fine. I mean, I am not challenging your right to do
<21> it. As I say, nor could I and should I. But for me
<22> the real challenge is how we move forward. I am not
<23> in denial. I have said to you. I have explained to
<24> Mr Cook. You have heard me say----
<25> DR STONE: You have told us ten times. Please don't

P-329

< 1> tell us again you are not in denial.
< 2> SIR CONDON: I do think this is important, Dr Stone,
< 3> because it is about moving forward and making
< 4> process.
< 5> DR STONE: That is exactly why we are here. I think

< 6>   this is the nub of the issue the Bishop is dealing

< 7>   with. I didn't mean to intervene.

< 8>   BISHOP SENTAMU: Sir Paul, I think the question is

< 9>   that if it is the bad apple analogy, you pray to God

<10>   that one day these bad apples may leave the force.

<11>   But the issue really is that the changes need to be

<12>   far more fundamental in the ethos and the culture of

<13>   the police force. That is what it is about. There

<14>   is a culture which rightly or wrongly when it comes

<15>   in contact with the minority communities, it treats

<16>   them differentially, it disadvantages them.

<17>   Therefore, how are you going to change that

<18>   particularly culture?

<19>   Secondly, if you say there is racism in the Met;

<20>   how are you going to change the attitudes and

<21>   practices and what is your strategy? I haven't quite

<22>   yet heard that. May be then I wouldn't be hung up

<23>   about phrases.

<24>   SIR CONDON: I will summarise very briefly, with the

<25>   help of Mr O'Connor, the strategy. But may I say: I

P-330

< 1>   don't rely on the hope that there are a small number

< 2>   of bad apples and they go. I don't subscribe to the

< 3>   bad apples theory. The challenge is far more

< 4>   profound than that. So I don't just rely on the hope

< 5>   that bad apples will come and go. Policing is too

< 6>   important. The exercising of power is too

< 7>   important. But again perhaps out of another voice a

< 8>   quick summary again of the plan that I thought I had

< 9>   set out earlier on, sir.

<10>   MR O'CONNOR: Chairman, Bishop, I would like to

<11>   proffer summary copies of our plan and say a few

<12>   words. (Handed).

<13>   Chairman, unfortunately the rest of the audience

<14>   do not have this in front of them, but what you have

<15>   there are the bonds of the approach that we take, we

<16>   propose to take -- obviously subject to your own
<17>   observations.
<18>   What have we do here? We have looked at Scarman
<19>   in the past. We have looked at exultation and what
<20>   that has done. And yes, Bishop, too we have looked
<21>   at definitions hard.
<22>   What we have tried to do in this package is to
<23>   identify a set of key actions which will change the
<24>   operating context of policing for our police officers
<25>   hopefully to help them do the right things for all of

P-331

< 1>   Londoners.
< 2>   We quite specifically target the operating
< 3>   context, not a training environment; we take account
< 4>   of training, yes, but it is the operating context,
< 5>   all of the leverage and steerage the organisation can
< 6>   bring to bear. Three major headings which we are
< 7>   looking for, tangible products. We want to improve
< 8>   the investigation significantly. We identify a
< 9>   champion to do that. We identify targets for the
<10>   immediate coming months and the next two years. We
<11>   will be testing Mr Grieve around those targets. We
<12>   identify an aspiration around prevention which we
<13>   think has been neglected. Perhaps if it had not been
<14>   we would not be sadly here today talking about
<15>   Stephen's death. We identify targets and a champion
<16>   around that. Anti-racism, around which we believe
<17>   purpose can be built. We identify specific proposals
<18>   on training and more comprehensive approach to
<19>   training which has been contemplated in the past.
<20>   Three levels around roles which you have heard sadly
<21>   too much of where it has not worked, around awareness
<22>   of which you saw some of the evidence where that had
<23>   not been applied, and importantly, around critical
<24>   incidents; recognising those incidents, those
<25>   circumstances when things started to go wrong, early

P-332

< 1>   enough to correct them.

< 2>   We also identify some specific, and we hope

< 3>   imaginative, proposals around recruitment and

< 4>   advancement of minority ethnic officers. And the

< 5>   last, and perhaps toughest task we have set

< 6>   ourselves, is to uncover an address, the exercise and

< 7>   promotion of discretion fairly. That is discretion

< 8>   not just around stop and search, but the use of

< 9>   arrest powers, the use of force, the use of all the

<10>   weighted powers police have.

<11>   You may well say to me "well that sounds like a

<12>   reasonable set of proposals, but they are still a lot

<13>   of things wrong out there" and we would acknowledge

<14>   that and the Commissioner would acknowledge that.

<15>   We believe in addition to those programs over

<16>   the next several years we need to engage now, and I

<17>   mean now, in some immediate activity to address cases

<18>   where difficulties are arising even as we speak. We

<19>   do not claim the world is perfect now and the fast

<20>   track activities we intend to change that culture to

<21>   reinforce that operating context are live

<22>   interventions in cases that officers are involved in

<23>   speaking directly to families, to victims, to find

<24>   out whether we have been sensitive, whether we have

<25>   been professional in discharge of our duties, whether

P-333

< 1>   we have liaised properly. We have not done that in

< 2>   that form before. That will send a powerful signal.

< 3>   Likewise, where communication is failing and it can,

< 4>   we have specific proposals to hopefully draw from the

< 5>   community mediators to help us overcome some of the

< 6>   difficulties that have been experienced and rehearsed

< 7>   to this Inquiry. What we are talking about, Bishop,

< 8>   are a series of serious proposals in the medium term

< 9>   and in now a pincer movement on that operating

<10> context to change it and change it for good.

<11> THE CHAIRMAN: Thank you, Mr O'Connor. Dr Stone has

<12> one more question on this topic and then we are going

<13> to move on to other questions which we have. You

<14> have the drift of our thinkings. Of course these are

<15> not conclusions and everyone must await the report,

<16> but certainly we have been informed by what you told

<17> us and thank you. Dr Stone.

<18> DR STONE: I have had a note from the judge asking if

<19> we could move on to another topic because I feel we

<20> are working and working and working at this topic and

<21> trying to get our minds to meet in ways that are

<22> actually rather difficult. I just cannot quite let

<23> it go and I want to ask one more question, please,

<24> because I think we have to go on with it a bit

<25> further, I am sorry. Like you, I actually feel very

P-334

< 1> deeply, as the judge has said, there is a major

< 2> opportunity opportunity for real reform at the

< 3> moment. I find myself looking upon this Inquiry as

< 4> an opportunity to build a new trust between police

< 5> and their communities and between the communities and

< 6> their police. That is very important. The fact is

< 7> it seems to me, Sir Paul, that a lot of what you are

< 8> doing is already addressing these issues. You have

< 9> addressed a enormous amount of the issues that are at

<10> the heart of institutional racism and actually dealt

<11> with them. One was some years ago, the business of

<12> the height restriction for police officers, which was

<13> discriminatory against Asian people. That has been

<14> dealt with.

<15> As Tom Cook said ACPO officers accepted the

<16> notion of institutional racism and they put it, I

<17> thought, very clearly in terms it is no longer

<18> acceptable to treat people all equally. We have to

<19> treat people, I think you used the word, I have it

<20> down here as "individuals" but I think they said that
<21> little bit more which was important which is we have
<22> to treat people according to their needs and that
<23> seems to be exactly what we are trying to hit at.
<24> You said that the sense of racism is corrosive
<25> of relations with the black communities. I think all

P-335

< 1> of us on this panel have come to recognising
< 2> increasingly during these months that in fact the
< 3> sense of racism is corrosive of the relationships
< 4> with the police with all communities, white and
< 5> black, and I think it is important to recognise that
< 6> this is the heart of good policing, good health
< 7> service deliveries whatever, it is absolutely vital
< 8> that we recognise it is not just an issue of trying
< 9> to win around the black communities.
<10> SIR CONDON: May I respond very briefly, I think it
<11> is important.
<12> THE CHAIRMAN: Just hang on, Dr Stone will come to
<13> the question.
<14> DR STONE: I will come to a very simple question
<15> which is a crucial thing which I think is the last
<16> attempt to try and bridge this gap today, if we can,
<17> or maybe it has to be some other time. It seems to me
<18> that the one really powerful argument you are
<19> presenting to us for not today acknowledging there is
<20> institutional racism in the police, is that you say
<21> the public would not understand and that
<22> relationships with the police would be damaged if you
<23> were to acknowledge there was institutional racism.
<24> I actually felt when I was hearing that I was taking
<25> on board the point that was made earlier about the

P-336

< 1> response of Mrs Lawrence when she was asked by Ms
< 2> Weekes sensitively, as the judge said, what really

< 3> was wrong and she said that "they were patronising to
< 4> us". I actually think, I am sorry, I actually think
< 5> that to say that the public do not understand
< 6> institutional racism is patronising of the public.
< 7> (Disturbance from the public gallery):
< 8> I want to carry on I have a thread, please try
< 9> not to interrupt it is difficult to keep this thread
<10> going, it is one that I picked up this morning, so I
<11> have not got past it completely myself this going.
<12> You see I think that you acknowledged yourself,
<13> Sir Paul, earlier that there has been a change in
<14> public perceptions as a result of the revelations
<15> that have come out during this Inquiry. I don't
<16> think this Inquiry has damaged police public
<17> relations, I think the revelations may well have done
<18> so and I think that you are absolutely right, there
<19> has been a change in public perceptions around the
<20> country and I think one of those perceptions is to
<21> recognise that whether you define it as institutional
<22> racism, that rather sophisticated concept, or whether
<23> you talk about it as being treating people according
<24> to their needs rather than equally, I think people
<25> have grasped that. So I actually do not think it

P-337

< 1> will undermine your endeavours that you are actually
< 2> quite successfully beginning to approach and I think
< 3> what Mr O'Connor has just shown us is a good way
< 4> practical way forward, I do not think it is
< 5> undermining that. I think it is actually undermining
< 6> to go on denying the existence of institutional
< 7> racism.
< 8> What I am, therefore, trying to get towards now
< 9> is that you are nearly there. If you can acknowledge
<10> the list of things that you have touched on,
<11> including the height restrictions, for example, you
<12> are actually in each of those instances you have

<13>   given us accepting that institutional racism exists
<14>   within the police. Sorry I popped about earlier
<15>   before, you keep trying to defend that and I think
<16>   you obviously realised that you are going to be
<17>   pushed on this today and that you must not yield on
<18>   that one, I do not know what reasons there are and
<19>   Tom Cook, I thought, really had a real good go at you
<20>   actually.
<21>   It seems to me, Sir Paul, that the door is
<22>   open. It is like when Winnie Mandela was challenged
<23>   in the Truth Commission in South Africa by
<24>   Desmond Tutu to acknowledge that she had done wrong
<25>   and she just did it and suddenly a whole burden of

P-338
< 1>   weight of sort of challenge and friction melted away
< 2>   as a result. If you and we are to go forward
< 3>   together, as I think we must do, we are never to be
< 4>   wedded in the implementation of recommendations that
< 5>   will come out of this Inquiry to build a new trust
< 6>   which is solidly based rather than a trust that is
< 7>   based on a rather outdated idea of a bobby on the
< 8>   beat, that sort of thing. If we are to go forward I
< 9>   say to you now just say; yes, I acknowledge
<10>   institutional racism in the police and then in a way
<11>   the whole thing is over and we can go forward
<12>   together. That is my question, could you do that
<13>   today? May I say obviously a lot of people here are
<14>   willing you to say "yes" and maybe that actually is
<15>   the nub of it, it is not actually such an awful thing
<16>   to do because the reality of it is you are joining
<17>   all the rest of the institutions in this country, The
<18>   Health Service, The Prison Service, look at the local
<19>   government in Nottingham and in Birmingham and in
<20>   Sandwell, they have not understood this.
<21>   THE CHAIRMAN: You have given the challenge, or the
<22>   question, Sir Paul what is the answer?

<23> SIR CONDON: The answer is that it would be very easy
<24> to please the panel, to please this audience, to walk
<25> out of this room so that very superficial media

P-339

< 1> coverage says, yes, they have said certain things. I
< 2> actually think that would be, in terms of my own
< 3> experience and analysis of the problem, my sincere
< 4> endeavour to move this issue forward I believe it
< 5> would be dishonest for me to say that just to please
< 6> you all, to ease the pain because I think there is a
< 7> danger that it could be as patronising to police
< 8> officers to use the terms in a way that I think is
< 9> not just in the context. If the Inquiry clearly
<10> decides that in using that terms that is the way
<11> forward, we will respond positively to that.
<12> All I am saying, sir, is that on my analysis is
<13> that short-term that term could actually cause more
<14> harm than good. My belief is there is no difference
<15> between the analysis of the problem and a desire --
<16> there is not a police service in the world that can
<17> replicate the intensity and the effort that has gone
<18> into the reform programme in recent years and will
<19> now go forward with more vigour. It is very easy for
<20> people to criticise, not many people want to share
<21> the responsibility for the challenge or for the way
<22> forward.
<23> THE CHAIRMAN: Sir Paul, thank you, we have the
<24> answer and that part of the debate I am going to
<25> close now. Mr Cook has some questions to ask.

APPENDIX D

Recent correspondence

Dr Richard Stone

**Race On The Agenda
Resource for London
356 Holloway Road
London N7 6PA**
tel: **07957 362 129**
stoneashdown@gmail.com
www.hiddenstories.co.uk

Rt Hon Theresa May MP
Home Secretary
Home Office
2 Marsham Street
London SW1P 4DF   3rd June 2014

Dear Mrs May

I write to you because I have been advised by the Civil Service Commission "to refer to the Home Secretary" a serious complaint I made of three counts of suggested misconduct by civil servants during and since the Stephen Lawrence Inquiry. The three counts are:

1. An apparent breach in 1998 by senior Home Office civil servants of their professional independence by attempting to have a planned visit of the Inquiry to Birmingham cancelled.

2. Withholding from the public the transcripts of the hearings, from early 1999 until late in 2005 (ie for 6 years).

3. Withholding the correspondence files from 1999 until late in 2011 (ie for12 years)

I enclose my referral letter to the First Commissioner, Sir David Normington. With it also there is a small bundle of relevant supporting letters and notes, and two replies from the Commission.

I also want to make some positive comments on recent actions you have taken in relation to the Stephen Lawrence case. Since this is something of a personal matter I have put these into a separate letter which I have enclosed with this formal referral.

A fourth count of complaint arose only in April of this year:

4. The need for the Inquiry by Mark Ellison QC into policing of the Stephen Lawrence case was appalling but necessary. I talked with him two weeks before he went public.

As I mention elsewhere, in October 2011 for a second time I had a Parliamentary Question put down by an MP asking when a major part of the archive of the Lawrence

Letter from Richard Stone to Theresa May, Home Secretary (page 1), 3 June 2014

Inquiry would be made available to the public. My first time had been in 2005 to get release of the transcripts. This time it was the correspondence files I was after.

As before the answer to the MP was "in 3 to 4 months, after redaction". Also as before it was only on visiting The National Archive at Kew months later that I found that the files had arrived two weeks or so after the PQ. No announcement. No fanfare. No publicity at all. Just that an archivist said "Yes, 41 boxes are here now."

When I asked Ellison how he had got on at Kew, he looked puzzled. "The Home Office people were very helpful. They gave me access to all their files and I had no difficulty finding any of the information I sought." Did they point him in the direction of the National Archive at Kew? No. They did not. I did not push this revelation any further with Mr Ellison, because I did not want to undermine his valuable report.

Mr Ellison was not even told that 41 boxes of archive material from the Lawrence Inquiry were sent to the National Archives at Kew a year before he started his Inquiry.

This leads me to believe that there are now two archives of our Inquiry: one in the public and one in the private sphere. I had been working on 41 boxes of archived material, and Ellison was working on a totally different set of papers. I know that the chaotic set of papers I saw are all original. He did agree that all the stuff he saw was similarly original - none were copies in either of the two archives.

A year ago I published a book of 'Hidden stories of the Stephen Lawrence Inquiry' (Policy Press of Bristol University - www.hiddenstories.co.uk). It will save time for you and/or your staff to look into it to find details of the first three allegations I make in the letter.

Yours truly

[signature]

Dr Richard Stone OBE, MA(Jurisprudence), BM BCh, MRCGP, FRIPHH

PS. I have written all previous correspondence on my home notepaper. Copies of this formal letter will be sent to MPs and peers who support me, as well as to the wide range of community activists on my mailing list. For correspondence about the formal complaint please note that I am negotiating with Race on the Agenda (ROTA), of which I am a patron, to borrow their address.

Letter from Richard Stone to Theresa May, Home Secretary (page 2), 3 June 2014

Permanent Secretary

2 Marsham Street,
London SW1P 4DF
www.homeoffice.gov.uk

Dr Richard Stone
Race on the Agenda, Resource for London
356 Holloway Road
London
N7 6PA

Reference: T7015/14

01 August 2014

Dear Dr Stone,

Further to Jon Scanlan's letter of 8 July, I am now providing a substantive response to your letter of 3 June 2014 to the Home Secretary about your complaints of misconduct by Home Office officials during and since the Stephen Lawrence Inquiry. I have sought advice from officials in Information Management Services and Policing Directorate in relation to the four specific complaints you raised.

You complained that Mr Wells attempted to cancel the visit of the Inquiry to Birmingham. After careful consideration I have not seen any evidence to suggest that Mr Wells acted with anything other than integrity and impartiality in fulfilling his role as Secretary to the Inquiry. The suggestion that he, senior officials in the Home Office or senior officers in West Midlands Police attempted to prevent the hearing in Birmingham is not supported by the papers at The National Archives or any other material of which I have been made aware.

You also complained that papers were withheld. The papers of the Stephen Lawrence Inquiry were split into four sections:
- Transcripts of Part 1 of the Inquiry (TNA Series NT 2) – 77 files;
- Submissions to Part 2 of the Inquiry (TNA Series NT 1) – 177 files;
- Administrative papers of the Inquiry (TNA Series NT 3) – 41 files; and
- Evidence files – still held by the Home Office – 257 files.

The first three sections are already available to the public at The National Archives (TNA), and were transferred to TNA well in advance of the 30-year statutory requirement for transfer of public records. We recognise the importance of these papers and we have done our best to release them in a timely way within the resources available.

You made a related complaint about the archive now being in two parts. This is unavoidable as the evidence files still held at the Home Office contain information which should not be in the public domain while the investigation into the murder of Stephen Lawrence continues.

1

Reply from Mark Sedwill, Permanent Secretary (page 1), 1 August 2014

This was referenced in the Government's response in July 2009 to the '10 years On' reports produced by you and others. The Metropolitan Police have confirmed to us that this remains a live murder investigation.

We made this material available to Mark Ellison and his barrister, Alison Morgan, during the course of his Review. I have seen no evidence of an attempt to mislead Mr Ellison or Ms Morgan as to the existence of the publicly available material at TNA, and Mr Ellison has confirmed to us that he considered the material as part of his Review.

In summary, I have not been presented with any evidence of conduct by Home Office officials that I consider needs further action or investigation. If you wish to refer this back to the Civil Service Commissioner for review we will, of course, co-operate in full with any investigation the Commission wishes to pursue.

May I take this opportunity to thank you for your comments to the Home Secretary on her decision to call the Ellison Review, and on her commitment to improving policing. The Government has delivered a major reform agenda to make the police more accountable to local communities, to improve the professionalism and integrity of officers, and to ensure fairer and more effective policing of communities, for example, through the comprehensive package of measures the Home Secretary recently announced to improve the use of stop and search. Ministers continue to work with forces and the College of Policing to open up the senior ranks of the police to candidates from different backgrounds, and to ensure that the police workforce is more representative of local communities. This has been a key priority for the Government and will continue to be so.

Yours sincerely,

Mark Sedwill

2

Reply from Mark Sedwill, Permanent Secretary (page 2), 1 August 2014

Index

I

Idrish, Muhammad 53–4, 55–6,
179, 183
Independent 119
Independent Inquiry into the Death
of David Bennett 25, 133
Independent on Sunday 134–5
Independent Police Complaints
Commission (IPCC) 90–1, 92–3,
140
inquiries
convention of silence 5, 133
Secretary 24, 138–9
see also Scarman Inquiry; Stephen
Lawrence Inquiry
institutional racism
addressing 100–2, 134–5
Condon 68–80, 187–233
definition 93–4, 95, 96–100
and double jeopardy 105
Metropolitan Police Service xi–xii,
1, 2–3, 5, 60–2, 66, 68–80, 88,
122, 140–1
Panorama 89
Phillips 80–1
International Covenant on Civil
and Political Rights 103
Islamophobia 125–6

J

Jasper, Lee 12, 86
Jewish Council for Racial Equality
(JCORE) 28, 32–3
Johnson, Boris 141, 152n
Johnston, Assistant Commissioner
Ian 59–64

K

Kelly, David 7, 83
Kendal, Mr 45–6
Kennedy, Baroness Helena 105, 107
Kent Police 139, 140
Khan, Imran 17, 97
Khan, Sadiq 103–4
Knight, Luke 117
at Inquiry 39–40, 46, 48, 49–50,
157n
murder investigation 113
written statement 48–9
Koyair, Abdul 128

L

Law Commission 105–6
Lawrence, Doreen
and Condon 63
Condon's apology 65
Inquiry 19, 21, 23, 38, 44, 48
institutional racism 17–18, 98–9
Johnston's apology 60
and Macpherson 21–3
and Mandela 12–13, 113, 114
and Metropolitan Police Service
4, 97–8
murder investigation 12, 14,
17–18, 71–2, 90, 91, 98–9, 101,
113, 119, 139
private prosecution 4, 17
Stephen's murder 10
and Straw 19, 21–2
Lawrence, Neville
and Condon 63
Condon's apology 65
Inquiry 19, 21, 23, 38, 45, 48
Johnston's apology 59–60
and Macpherson 21–3
and Mandela 12–13, 113, 114
and Metropolitan Police Service
4, 97–8
murder investigation 12, 14, 91, 99,
101, 113, 119, 139
private prosecution 4, 17
Stephen's murder 10
and Straw 19, 21–2
Lawrence, Stephen
murder 5, 9–12
see also Stephen Lawrence Inquiry;
Stephen Lawrence Trust
Lawrence, Stuart xi, 101
Lawson, Ed 38, 45, 60–3, 185
leadership xi, 111–12, 131, 142
addressing racism xii, 33, 135–6
black and minority ethnic officers
137
Condon 81
golden threads 120–1
and Muslim communities 125–8
protests and riots 129–30
Stephen Lawrence case 112–19
stop and search 8, 122–5
Leveson Inquiry 9, 111, 154n
Liberty 31, 103–4, 154n